BUILDING WORLD-CLASS UNIVEI

MW01103954

GLOBAL PERSPECTIVES ON HIGHER EDUCATION

Volume 25

Higher education worldwide is in a period of transition, affected by globalization, the advent of mass access, changing relationships between the university and the state, and the new Technologies, among others. *Global Perspectives on Higher Education* provides cogent analysis and comparative perspectives on these and other central issues affecting postsecondary education worldwide.

Series Editor:
Philip G. Altbach
Center for International Higher Education, Boston College, USA

Editorial Board:
Manuel Gil Antón, *Autonomous Metropolitan University of Mexico, Tlalpan, Mexico*
Molly Lee, *UNESCO Bangkok, Thailand*
Damtew Teferra, *Journal of Higher Education in Africa, Boston College,*

This series is co-published with the Center for International Higher Education at Boston College.

Building World-Class Universities

Different Approaches to a Shared Goal

Edited by

Qi Wang
Shanghai Jiao Tong University, P.R. China

Ying Cheng
Shanghai Jiao Tong University, P.R. China

and

Nian Cai Liu
Shanghai Jiao Tong University, P.R. China

SENSE PUBLISHERS
ROTTERDAM / BOSTON / TAIPEI

A C.I.P. record for this book is available from the Library of Congress.

ISBN 978-94-6209-032-3 (paperback)
ISBN 978-94-6209-033-0 (hardback)
ISBN 978-94-6209-034-7 (e-book)

Published by: Sense Publishers,
P.O. Box 21858, 3001 AW Rotterdam, The Netherlands
https://www.sensepublishers.com/

Printed on acid-free paper

TABLE OF CONTENTS

Section 3: Evaluating World-class Universities from a Ranking/Indicator Perspective

ACKNOWLEDGEMENTS

The editors wish to thank Mr Peter de Liefde, Sense Publishers, for his support in the publication of this volume; Professor Philip G. Altbach, Monan University Professor and Director of the Center for International Higher Education, Boston College; Dr Jan Sadlak, President of IREG – International Observatory on Ranking and Academic Excellence; Mr Derek Maxwell Elli Harris and Mr Peodair Leihy, for the linguistic editing of the manuscript.

QI WANG, YING CHENG AND NIAN CAI LIU

BUILDING WORLD-CLASS UNIVERSITIES

Different Approaches to a Shared Goal

World-class universities, commonly referred to as the most prestigious research universities, are essential in developing a nation's competitiveness in the global knowledge economy. These universities, at the pinnacle of the higher education hierarchy, play key roles in creating and disseminating knowledge, educating a highly skilled workforce for technological and intellectual leadership, and serving the needs of society (Altbach, 2009; Van der Wende, 2009). In the past decade, the development of world-class universities is high on the policy agenda of various stakeholders across the globe (Altbach & Balán, 2007; Huisman, 2008). Various reforms and development strategies at both national and institutional levels have been outlined and observed. This policy concern has also been reinforced and intensified with the proliferation of international league tables (Salmi, 2009; King, 2011). It was in this context that the Graduate School of Education, Shanghai Jiao Tong University, initiated the biennial International Conference on World-Class Universities in 2005. Previous conferences have gathered university administrators, government officials, top scholars and policy researchers from around the world to discuss various issues related to world-class universities.

In the past few years it can be argued that an increasing number of countries, regions and higher education institutions in different parts of the world have joined the same battle for academic excellence. This trend to create or enhance globally competitive universities can be traced not only in developed countries but also in developing ones. While emerging countries and their universities make every effort to enhance their capacity and boost their research performance, the academic superpowers endeavour to maintain – if not further improve – their global positions. However, universities are situated in various higher education systems and are bounded by various cultural, social and historical origins and conditions. How do different countries and regions develop world-class universities? Are they facing the same issues and challenges? Can successful experiences and strategies in one country be copied in other national contexts? The Fourth International Conference on World-Class Universities, held in November 2011 in Shanghai, attempts to further explore and review these questions and issues. Collecting twelve essays originating from the papers presented in the conference, this publication volume intends to provide an in-depth picture of different approaches in pursuit of the shared goal of developing world-class universities, and to reflect the current developmental trends in this field.

Q. Wang, Y. Cheng, & N.C. Liu (eds.), Building World-Class Universities: Different Approaches to a Shared Goal, 1–10.

DEFINING THE SHARED GOAL: WORLD-CLASS UNIVERSITIES

The concept of world-class universities, a term adopted largely interchangeably with global research universities or flagship universities, has been firmly embedded in governmental and institutional policies to promote national competitiveness in the increasingly globalized world. However, the paradox is that the concept has been widely employed without an explicit, clear definition. In 2004, Altbach argued that "everyone wants one, no one knows what it is, and no one knows how to get one". It is commonly agreed that world-class universities are academic institutions committed to creating and disseminating knowledge in a range of disciplines and fields, delivering of elite education at all levels, serving national needs and furthering the international public good (Altbach, 2009; Liu, 2009).

Among scholars, institutional administrators, and policy-makers, one of the common approaches to defining "world-class" is through the creation and ongoing development of league tables, such as the Academic Ranking of World Universities (ARWU) by Shanghai Jiao Tong University, the Times Higher Education World University Ranking and the QS World University Rankings. Despite different methodologies being used in evaluating universities in the international rankings, it is not difficult to observe that these indicators focus heavily on quality of education, internationalization, research output, prestige and impact (Salmi, 2009).

Seeking to define the term, scholars have identified key attributes which world-class universities have and which regular universities do not possess, including highly qualified faculty, talented students, excellence in research, quality teaching with international standards, high levels of government and non-government funding, academic freedom, autonomous governance structures and well-equipped facilities for teaching, research, administration and student life (Altbach, 2004 & 2011). Based on the above elements, Salmi (2009) proposes three complementary sets of factors at play in world-class universities: a high concentration of talent, abundant resources, and favourable and autonomous governance. That is to say, a world-class university will be able to select and attract the best students and the most qualified professors and researchers, to possess abundant and diversified funding sources and offer a rich learning and research environment, and to provide favourable and autonomous governance and encourage strategic vision and innovation, so as to respond effectively to the demands of a fast changing global market.

UNDERSTANDING THE DIFFERENT APPROACHES

Rather than self-declaration, the elite status of world-class university relies on international recognition (Altbach & Salmi, 2011). To help institutions achieve this exclusive stature and enhance their global competitiveness, national governments and the institutions themselves have adopted various strategies and approaches. In spite of many social, cultural and economic differences across the globe, three main and common strategic foci can be recognized, these being competitive funding schemes, internationalization and governance reform at both governmental and institutional levels.

A number of strategic funding programmes have been implemented to promote excellence by different countries and regions. The very first group of special funding schemes included China's 985 Project, Japan's Centres of Excellence and World Premier International Research Centres, Korea's Brain Korea 21 and Germany's Centres of Excellence. As reviewed in this volume, more governments have recently employed special funding schemes, including Taiwan's Five Year – 50 Billion Excellence Initiative (Chapter 3), Russia's National Research University Programme (Chapter 4) and Saudi Arabia's University and Education City projects (Chapter 7). Selected universities and research centres in these countries and regions have been provided extra and concentrated funding to develop excellence of teaching and research. Despite different organizational and management approaches, these initiatives all propose clear aims for excellence, provide adequate funding to "cherry-picked" institutions and research centres, and ensure essential policy support from the governments. Furthermore, these competitive funding schemes are proposed, agreed on and legislated by government and associated organizations. The legislative processes turn these educational initiatives into regulations and laws, which strengthens the authoritative and compulsory nature of the policies. In addition, these funding programmes have further raised awareness of international competition among institutions (Wang, 2011).

Promoting internationalization is another common strategic area in the pursuit of excellence. This can be addressed in various ways, such as curriculum reform, student and faculty mobility, and cooperation and partnership in administration. Different nations and institutions place different emphasis on these aspects to accelerate development. For example, curriculum reform has been encouraged in top universities to extend universities' capacity for international cooperation, to enrich students' learning experiences with a multicultural dimension, and to raise their awareness of global citizenship (Mohrman, 2008), as in Amsterdam University College (Chapter 6). High-quality faculty recruitment has also been encouraged in both national policies and institutional visions. Leading academics are believed to be able to contribute to upgrade the institutions and to establish graduate programmes and research centres in areas of comparative advantage (Altbach & Salmi, 2011). Governments and universities around the world have been making efforts to attract, recruit and keep leading academics, believed to enhance university capacity (Chapter 4, 5 and 7).

To further facilitate the progress of world-class universities, a number of leading universities have formed productive partnership with other prestigious universities, particularly in the industrialized world, by establishing dual-degree programmes, research collaborations, and university consortia (such as Universitas 21, Academic Consortium 21 and the Association of Pacific Rim Universities). This form of international collaboration has also served as a platform for students and faculty exchange, and the sharing of resources and ideas.

Appropriate governance is another key element that determines the performance of higher education systems and research universities. Governance issues embrace a range of features: autonomy, leadership, regulatory frameworks, strategic visions, competitive environments and organizational cultures (Salmi, 2009 & 2011). Many countries and regions have focused on benchmarking exercises and emphasized notions of "international standards" and "quality enhancement". Several chapters in this volume explore examples of governance's importance in building world-class universities.

Despite common strategic foci observed across the globe, it is not difficult to identify different emphases, procedures and mechanisms adopted within these approaches. Altbach and Salmi's research (2011) reminds us that education reform and changes do not happen in a vacuum, and a complete analysis of operating a world-class university needs to take into consideration the ecosystem within which institutions evolve. The ecosystem includes the elements of the macro environment, leadership at the national level, governance and regulatory frameworks, quality assurance frameworks, financial resources and incentives, articulation mechanisms, access to information, location and digital and telecommunications infrastructure (Salmi, 2011:336-337). Some of these factors might be absolute requisites and others might not be entirely indispensable, due to each country's cultural, socio-economic and political context. However, all these factors are certainly significant (Altbach & Salmi, 2011). Countries and those overseeing their higher education systems need to carefully assess their needs, resources and long-term interests and design their strategies based on their national and institutional models. There is no universal model or recipe for making academic excellence (Altbach, 2004; Salmi, 2009). International experience might be helpful to provide experience and lessons; however, a simple policy copying exercise may not transpose effectively from one country or university to another.

CONTRIBUTIONS TO THIS VOLUME

Reflecting the above points, the present volume provides insights into recent and ongoing experiences of building world-class universities, both at a national level and at an institutional level. The book is structured into three sections: "Building World-Class Universities from a National/Regional Perspective", "Managing World-Class Universities from an Institutional Perspective" and "Evaluating World-Class Universities from a Ranking/Indicator Perspective".

Building World-Class Universities from a National/Regional Perspective

This section discusses the role of world-class universities in national education and research systems, addressing issues and concerns that governments need to take into account in making education policies. Illustrating policy contexts, it particularly focuses on and updates world-class university development in developing countries and countries in transition.

Simon Marginson begins with his chapter by reiterating the importance of cultural-historical differences and situated national and local contexts in understanding different models for making world-class universities. Appreciating

Salmi's argument regarding "different pathways" to making strong institutions within the "tertiary education ecosystem", Marginson argues that there is more than one method for modernizing a higher education system, more than one kind of state project in higher education and more than one possible framing of the same goal of achieving the "world-class university". He argues that a complete and sophisticated comparison of these different approaches should focus on the roles of nation-state, political culture, educational practices in the family and in society, modes of governance in higher education, relationships between the state and higher education institutions, financial resources for higher education and the nation's engagement in global higher education. Based on the above analysis, Marginson proposes possible models or roads to world-class university status being an American system, a Westminster system, Post-Confucian systems, Nordic systems, Central European systems, and Francophone systems.

Based on the above argument, the chapter proceeds to focus on the rise of higher education and research in East Asia and Singapore, following what Marginson terms the Post-Confucian Model. In contrast to the English-speaking nations and Western Europe, the Post-Confucian systems feature strong state steering and control over higher education's development, and individual commitment to self-cultivation through learning. These two level features interact with each other, forming unique conditions for financing higher education, with both state and household investments. With individual learners' share of costs, states manage to provide concentrated investments to develop elite universities effectively. One of the achievements of this Post-Confucian Model is characterized by rapid development in both educational participation and research quantity, while improving the quality of leading institutions and research. Marginson concludes that this Post-Confucian Model will be "increasingly influential in future years".

To follow Marginson's argument, Yung-Chi Hou, Martin Ince and Cung-Lin Chiang review the case of Taiwan, specifically to assess the effectiveness of its special funding scheme, the "Five Year – 50 Billion Excellence Initiative". Higher education in Taiwan has witnessed great changes in the last twenty years, entering the stage of universal participation in higher education and generally having reduced education inequality. To further address the competitiveness issue, the government launched its excellence initiative in 2006, aiming to build at least one university as the world's top 100 in five years and at least 15 key departments or cross-campus research centres as the top research institutes in Asia in ten years. Through statistical analysis using certain indicators, progress has been recorded in research performance, internationalization, and university and industry collaboration. Hou argues that the pursuit of comprehensive excellence at universities will constructively promote its standing in rankings; however, a barren auditing exercise simply aiming at acquiring "world-class" status might potentially widen the inequality gap between leading and following universities.

Nikolay Skvortsov, Olga Moskaleva and Julia Dmitrieva's contribution demonstrates Russia's approaches to promoting academic excellence. Realizing its universities' relatively poor performance in global higher education, the Russian government has initiated a series of reform since the 1990s. One of the core challenges facing the nation is the past separation of research and the university education, a feature of the Soviet system. To strengthen its research capacity and to ultimately improve Russian universities' competitiveness in the world, the government has consistently invested in higher education sector through various funding programmes; the development of the Innovative University programme, the establishment of several "federal universities", and support for the National Research University programme along with a number of Targeted Federal programmes. A critical analysis on the Russian context shows both progress and challenges. Rather than mere funding schemes, Russian universities need to strengthen internationalization strategies (in particular international research collaboration), reform the university curriculum, integrate the Russian higher education format into the European system, and tackle issues of information policy. The authors emphasize that effective governance and strategic planning is of great importance for Russia's bid to create world-class universities by setting realistic goals, ensuring sustainable financial support, and creating a transparent evaluation system.

Managing World-Class Universities from an Institutional Perspective

The second section analyses different strategies and approaches adopted by institutions around the world. Three cases are included in this section, each of which presents unique approaches in terms of promoting an institution's competitiveness. In addition to well-known approaches, such as attracting talent, fostering strong governance and cultivating high quality of teaching and research, this section attempts to shed light on how to speed up the steps in building world-class universities, how to maintain elite positions, how to balance research and teaching in the endeavour for excellence, and how to encourage different higher education stakeholders to collaborate. Again, to fully understand the three cases in this section, both national contexts and institutional conditions need to be included.

As mentioned in the above section, governance and strategic leadership are crucial in developing excellence in teaching and research. Lauritz B. Holm-Nielsen provides an interesting chapter on Aarhus University in Denmark, reflecting the importance of strategic governance at institutional level to sustain elite university development and to reinforce its global competitiveness. Aarhus University is ranked in the top 100 universities in some evaluations of world universities. Rather than being complacent of its current status, university leaders are highly aware of the fast-changing context of the global economy, and actively engaged in extensive reform to create a modern university that is flexible enough to manoeuvre effectively in a world of change. Since 2006, Aarhus University has undergone the most comprehensive academic reorganization in its history. This transformation is guided by clear principles: interdisciplinarity, flexibility and interaction with the world based on profound research quality. Organizational restructuring enables the university to have fewer and stronger departments, lean management structures, as well as to develop increasingly interdisciplinary research meeting the demands of society. One point standing out from Aarhus University's experience is the leadership's active involvement with staff, students and researchers in its transformational design.

Adopting the case of Amsterdam University College (AUC), Marijk Van der Wende argues that developing liberal arts and science education can be one possible approach in responding to increasing criticisms of low-performing undergraduate education and in meeting the demand for a differentiated higher education system in the 21st century. The quality of undergraduate education has been questioned in almost all countries in the context of higher education massification, with over-specialization, over-size classrooms, student disengagement and limited international dimensions. Concerns have also been raised in relation to the popular movement for building research universities and global university rankings; that is, that undergraduate education has been compromised by research dominance. Under these circumstances, AUC adopts a liberal arts and science approach in designing its undergraduate curriculum. The curriculum focuses on interdisciplinarity, scientific reasoning, global knowledge, civic knowledge and research-based learning, to prepare students with knowledge and skills for the global knowledge economy. Van der Wende again argues that, despite the global trend of adopting this liberal arts and science education model in developing undergraduate educational excellence, it should not be considered as a panacea for all problems.

In addition, the case of AUC presents an example of local institutional collaboration for global competition. The college was a new institution established in 2009, as a joint effort undertaken by two elite universities, the University of Amsterdam and VU University Amsterdam. The collaboration between the two universities not only has covered undergraduate level programmes, but also has been extended to graduate education, research, technology transfer and regional outreach.

Higher education development in Saudi Arabia, in particular the building of world-class universities, has led to heated international debate. Sadiq M. Sait's chapter on King Fahd University of Petroleum & Minerals (KFUPM) reviews current developments and strategies for higher education reform in the Kingdom, and illustrates how the national strategies and policies are being interpreted and implemented at the institutional level. In the context of the global knowledge economy, the Kingdom's wealth will not be sustainable if it solely relies on its oil reserves. To achieve a key position both in the Middle East region and in the world, the Kingdom needs to develop its human capital and research excellence. Strategies adopted in KFUPM may also be observed in other countries, such as concentrating research resources, attracting talented personnel, stressing research and innovation, developing quality assurance and accreditation. The KFUPM case shows that, in addition to abundant financial resources, universities need both strong government support and strategic institutional management to build teaching and research excellence.

7

Evaluating World-Class Universities from a Ranking/Indicator Perspective

The third section of this manuscript occupies a context of increasing development of global university rankings and indicator research in the field of higher education. This section intends to review the role of such rankings in higher education management, and to discuss how rankings and their results are adopted and applied in promoting excellence at both a national and institutional level. It also provides an in-depth analysis and updates regarding the latest research development on indicators for measuring and evaluating excellence.

Since the emergence of global university rankings in 2003, the interrelated connection between world-class universities and university rankings has been a heated topic around world. In his contribution, Seeram Ramakrishna provides a general and critical discussion on global university ranking developments and its impact on various higher education stakeholders at different levels, such as students, academics, university leaders, and governments. Due to technological and methodological limitations, current global university rankings can only rank certain aspects of university activities and performances. This has led to criticisms and complaints towards rankings. In spite of their limitations and restrictions, global university rankings will continue to impact different stakeholders' decision-making and policy implementation, such as national funding initiatives observed across the world. In this sense, Ramakrishna concludes that the global order of universities may change and the influence gap between universities in academic superpower nations and emerging academic nations may be narrowed.

To follow Ramakrishna's arguments, the next two chapters examine the impact of rankings on institutional behaviour and the rational use of rankings in institutional management. Freya Mearns and Tony Sheil's chapter focuses on the experience of Griffith University in Australia and demonstrates that constructive analysis of world university rankings and classifications may enhance benchmarking exercises at a university and further extend an institution's understanding of itself and its counterparts. Rather than simply checking the rank a university enjoys, the university leadership can identify internationally successful universities for future benchmarking exercise. The chapter suggests that going beyond merely reading the ranking numbers, universities shall analyse features and histories of similar universities, and review in detail the "breakthrough" strategies undertaken to solve critical concerns. Of equal importance, the university needs to assess its strengths and weakness in different aspects of performance, so as to set achievable targets and deliver strategic outcomes. The authors also argue that such benchmarking exercises would not be possible before the emergence of global university rankings and classifications, as they provide increased transparency, accountability and accessibility of data.

Danie Visser and Marilet Sienaert's contribution echoes Mearns and Sheil's arguments that university rankings can become a catalyst in university strategic reform, especially in the developing world. The authors emphasize that, in a developing country, global excellence is important, but so too are social justice and equity. Rather than setting advancement in the international league table as a goal in itself, the University of Cape Town has taken a rather "soft" approach. Aware of the university community's varied reactions and opinions to university rankings, the university helped its faculty to understand the emerging global university rankings, including goals and philosophies behind the rankings, biases, strengths and weaknesses, as well as rankings' impact on funders and policy makers. The university actively engaged the faculty in identifying relevant issues and indicators in their specific departments, and prompted them to understand that rational analysis of rankings provides the means of evaluating their own performance in relation to the university's goals. Through this practice, the university decided upon four strategies and principles that will specifically enable it as a university in the global south to achieve excellence in an increasingly globalized and competitive world, these being an increasing focus on its specific location in Africa, increasing international collaboration, increasing research visibility and increasing support to researchers at all levels. Both the Griffith University and the University of Cape Town cases show that an appropriate analysis focused on the institution itself and the ecosystem within which the university is located is a solid premise upon which to develop a strategy that plays to its strengths and resources.

Gerard A. Postiglione and Jisun Jung extend analysis on ranking impact with a focus on individual academics and their research productivity. Using data from two international surveys, this chapter analyses commonalities shared by the most highly productive researchers in four Asian countries and regions: South Korea, Japan, mainland China and Hong Kong SAR. The initial findings suggest that, in addition to demographics and academic background, institutional characteristics and environment are perceived to influence academics' research productivity. Related to world-class universities, academic freedom and competitive performance-based management both matter to top tier academics' performance.

The last two chapters in this publication present updates on the development of university rankings, particularly in response to some criticism broached in the volume. Simon Pratt reviews the Global Institutional Profiles Project initiated by Thomson Reuters. This project aims at creating informative profiles of universities covering multiple aspects of a university mission. It allows different users and stakeholders to select relevant data and provide analytical tools to help them understand performance indicators. The profile data are collected from multiple sources, including results of the Thomson Reuters Annual Academic Reputation Survey, data provided by universities, and bibliometric data from the Web of Science. Ultimately, the Profile project will allow the higher education community to gain better understanding and capture a fuller picture of institutional performance. Isidro F. Aguillo and Enrique Orduña-Malea argue that fast-changing academia needs new indicators for evaluation. Rather than emphasizing research performance, the Webometrics ranking provides a different perspective on world-class universities by assessing universities' web visibility and impact, aiming to offer far larger coverage, including universities in emerging and developing countries, and an evaluation model that takes into account academic missions as a whole.

This book not only represents a contribution to ongoing discussion on the topic of building world-class universities, but also a continuation of the previous three volumes on this topic – "World-Class Universities and Ranking: Aiming beyond Status" (Sadlak & Liu, 2007), "The World-Class University as Part of a New Higher Education Paradigm: From Institutional Qualities to Systemic Excellence" (Sadlak & Liu, 2009) and "Paths to a World-Class University" (Liu, Wang & Cheng, 2011).

REFERENCES

Altbach, P. G. (2004). The costs of benefits of world-class universities. *Academe, 90*(1), 20–23.

Altbach, P. G. (2009). Peripheries and centers: Research universities in developing countries. *Asia Pacific Education Review, 10*, 15–27.

Altbach. P. G. (Ed.). (2011). *Leadership for World-Class Universities: Challenges for Developing Countries.* London: Routledge.

Altbach, P. G. & Balán, J. (Eds.). (2007). *World Class Worldwide: Transforming Research Universities in Asia and Latin America.* Baltimore: Johns Hopkins University Press.

Altbach, P. G. & Salmi, J. (Eds.). (2011). *The Road to Academic Excellence: Emerging Research Universities in Developing and Transition Countries.* Washington, DC: The World Bank.

Huisman, J. (2008). World-class universities. *Higher Education Policy, 21*(1), 1–4.

King, R. (2011). *Universities Globally: Organizations, Regulation and Rankings.* Cheltenham: Edward Elgar.

Liu, N. C. (2009, February). *Building Up World-class Universities: A Comparison.* Presentation at 2008-2009, Research Institute for Higher Education, Hiroshima University.

Liu, N. C., Wang, Q., & Cheng, Y. (Eds.). (2011). *Paths to a World-Class University.* Global Perspectives in Higher Education, 43. Rotterdam: Sense Publishers.

Mohrman, K. (2008). The emerging global model with Chinese characteristics. *Higher Education Policy, 21*(1), 29–48.

Sadlak, J. & Liu, N. C. (Eds.). (2007). *The World-Class University and Ranking: Aiming Beyond Status.* Bucharest: UNESCO-CEPES.

Sadlak, J. & Liu, N. C. (Eds.). (2009). *The World-Class University as Part of a New Higher Education Paradigm: From Institutional Qualities to Systemic Excellence.* Bucharest: UNESCO-CEPES.

Salmi, J. (2009). *The Challenge of Establishing World-Class Universities.* Washington, DC: The World Bank.

Salmi, J. (2011). The road to academic excellence: Lessons of experience. In P. G. Altbach & J. Salmi (Eds.), *The Road to Academic Excellence: Emerging Research Universities in Developing and Transition Countries.* Washington, DC: The World Bank.

Wang, Q. (2011). A discussion on the 985 Project from a comparative perspective. *Chinese Education and Society, 44*(5), 41–56.

Wende, M. C. van der. (2009). *European Responses to Global Competitiveness in Higher Education.* Research and Occasional Paper Series, No.7, 2009. Berkeley: Center for Studies in higher Education, University of California.

AFFILIATIONS

Qi Wang, Ying Cheng, & Nian Cai Liu
Graduate School of Education,
Shanghai Jiao Tong University, China

SECTION 1

BUILDING WORLD-CLASS UNIVERSITIES FROM A NATIONAL/REGIONAL PERSPECTIVE

SIMON MARGINSON

DIFFERENT ROADS TO A SHARED GOAL

Political and Cultural Variation in World-Class Universities

INTRODUCTION

In *The Challenge of Establishing World-Class Universities*, Jamil Salmi (2009) explores what nations and institutions need to do to create "globally competitive universities". He finds that these universities are characterized by a concentration of talent, abundant resources and favourable governance arrangements. In *The Road to Academic Excellence: The Making of World-Class Research Universities*, Phillip Altbach and Jamil Salmi (2011) provide a set of individual cases. In his concluding chapter Salmi expands on the necessary characteristics. He points to internationallization strategies as a means of accelerating development, and the importance of the broader "tertiary education ecosystem", in which would-be world-class universities are located. This includes the "macro-environment", covering the legal, political and economic setting; national leadership; the governance and regulatory framework, including institutional autonomy and accountability; financial resources and incentives; articulation and information mechanisms; geographic location; and digital and communications infrastructures (Salmi, 2011, pp. 336-337).

The argument and its supporting evidence are convincing, but there is one limitation, this being that the factors that condition the development of world-class universities are defined solely in generic terms. Moreover, the generic attributes and conditions of the world-class university that have been identified by Altbach and Salmi vary from country to country, and university to university. That is, practices of governance, resources, leadership and autonomy take many forms depending on national and local influences. In addition, as will be discussed, these many forms seem to clump together in regional groupings that share common cultural elements and these regional groupings are the "different roads to a shared goal" in the chapter title.

In sum, in the chapter there is reflection on the different roads that universities in different parts of the world are taking towards the common goal of the world-class university. It begins with discussion of the nature of a world-class university and of its operating conditions, with it being argued that it is better to understand the goal not in terms of ranking position (a norm-referenced definition), but rather in terms of objective features (a criterion-referenced definition). This is followed by exploration of the different roads to the world-class university. The term

Q. Wang, Y. Cheng, & N.C. Liu (eds.), Building World-Class Universities: Different Approaches to a Shared Goal, 13-33.

"different roads" is not used in the sense of Salmi's (2009, p. 39) "different pathways", meaning differing organizational strategies for making stronger institutions within a national system, such as upgrading, merger or the creation of new institutions. Rather, "different roads" refers to cultural-historical differences manifest in development strategy, especially variations in the role and character of government, in relations between nation-state and higher education institutions, and in the social practices of education. The chapter contends that there can be and are different roads to the world-class university governed by the cultural-historical traditions. This means that it is not essential to imitate all details of American or Western European evolution. This is encouraging and possibly liberating for emerging systems, although some national traditions can be obstacles to the goal. In the final part of the chapter there is illustration of the contention about different roads with reference to higher education and research in East Asia and Singapore. In this region the melding of Western influenced modernization with the distinctive East Asian state tradition and Post-Confucian educational practices, has led to a specific dynamic in relation to the development of higher education.

The research underlying this chapter is in two parts. First, since 2004 the author has carried out 21 individual case studies of national research universities, in 19 separate systems. This includes 16 research universities in East and South East Asia and the Western Pacific, plus three comparator universities in North America and two in Netherlands.[1] The research for these studies has included interviews with university presidents/vice-chancellors/rectors, deputy presidents, leading administrators with responsibilities for international activities, the deans in engineering and social science, and a group of professors from the latter two disciplines. The case studies have been focused on the global perspectives, strategies, links and activities of these universities, most of which are the leading research institutions in their nations. Particular attention has been given to synergies and also tensions between government and the universities in relation to global activities. The studies have unearthed much information on how the universities concerned, and the various governments are approaching the issues of global competition, rankings so as to build world-class universities. Second, the chapter also draws on the author's various contributions to theorization of the global higher education setting, including some conceptually-oriented studies with empirical mapping (Marginson & Rhoades, 2002; Marginson, 2006; Marginson, 2007; Marginson, 2008a; Marginson & Van der Wende, 2009a, 2009b; Marginson, Murphy & Peters, 2010; Murphy, Peters & Marginson, 2010; King, Marginson & Naidoo, 2011; Marginson, Kaur & Sawir, 2011).

WORLD-CLASS UNIVERSITIES

What is a World-Class University?

Case study research (e.g. Marginson, 2011a) and the relevant literature (Hazelkorn, 2008 & 2011) confirm that the drive towards world-class university status is widespread, with only a few emerging nations being untouched by this movement.

That is, the leading universities in most countries want to be world-class universities or take it for granted they have reached that level already, and governments almost everywhere want their leading institutions to be recognized on the global scale. Many emerging nations have set targets related to the achievement of world-class universities that are based on position in the global rankings. Such aspirations were not as widespread prior to the birth of global rankings at Shanghai Jiao Tong University in 2003. Nevertheless, rankings did not cause the world-class university movement, for this has been underpinned by growing global convergence and partial integration in world higher education; the economics of innovation and knowledge-intensive production; and the practices of "competition states" (Cerny, 1997) focused on building global capacity. Moreover, the need for information, mobility and effective action at the global level drives continuous observation and comparison on the basis of common global systems (Marginson, 2011c, 2011d) and this deepens the desire to match the stronger institutions.

All nations now need a developed higher education system with research capability; just as they need clean water, stable governance and a standardized financial system. They need universities that can "participate effectively in the global knowledge network on an equal basis with the top academic institutions in the world" (Altbach & Salmi, 2011, p. 1). Nations unable to interpret and understand research, a capacity that must rest on personnel themselves capable of creating research, find themselves in a position of continuing dependence. The fact that the achievement of one or more world-class universities depends on achieving a certain level of economic development (there are few world-class universities in countries with per capita incomes of less than US$15,000 per year, with China being the major exception) does not obviate the national need for such institutions in low-income countries. That is, even if the goal is not within reach in the next generation, a nation can progress towards it. For their part, all national universities want to connect globally and to cut a larger figure in the world, on the basis of self-determining strategies, while sustaining both institutional autonomy and government financial support.

But what is a "World-Class University"? Universities well placed in the rankings rarely use the term, for it is an aspirational term mainly used by emerging systems. Mostly, "world-class" is simply aligned with presence in the ranking, though there are varying opinions about where the boundary falls (top 50? top 100? top 500?). However, whilst rankings map global competition and help to drive improved performance, they do not provide an empirically verifiable material basis for identifying "world-class" institutions. This is because ranking systems are norm-referenced not criterion referenced. That is, a university's rank tells us where it stands in relation to other universities, but not where it stands in relation to objective measures of capacity or output. It is true that from the point of view of the university itself, rank is vitally important. That is, all research universities strive for prestige, because status (Podolny, 1993) matters more to them than money (Bourdieu, 1988; Frank & Cook, 1995; Hansmann, 1999; Brint, 2002; Geiger, 2004; Veder, 2007; Brown, 2011). However, from the point of view of government, what matters is the contribution that higher education makes to the economy and society and that contribution is determined by objective capacity and performance. In other words, viewed from outside higher education competition, what matters is not the position in the university hierarchy as an end in itself, but the fundamental activities that sustain an institution's positions in the hierarchy. Under this perspective, what creates an institution's value to graduates, employers, nations and the world is not the level of its rank but the quality of its work.

While every nation needs research universities operating at global standard, it would be meaningless to say that every nation needs top 50 or top 100 universities, because by definition, this is impossible. There is not room for all nations to have a top 100 university and if capacity is sufficient, rank does not matter. If a quality ought to be universally distributed it makes no sense to define it solely in terms of zero-sum competition. In relation to this, an alternative to the norm-referenced world-class universities is the criterion-referenced notion of the "Global Research University" (Ma, 2008; Marginson, 2008b), which allows for the material elements underpinning the performance of institutions to be observed and measured. Moreover, there is no limit to the number of universities (and systems) that can acquire these qualities, for the tag "global research university" is not confined to the top 50 or 100 institutions.

What then is a global research university? Its qualities have been identified by Altbach and Salmi (2011; Salmi, 2009). It is a university embedded effectively in its local and national contexts on an ongoing basis, and one that also has an established a global role and presence. In addition, it is adequately resourced in revenues and human skills, and its systems of governance foster openness, initiative and the freedoms necessary to make strategic executive decisions in relation to developing new knowledge and interpretations across the range of disciplines. Moreover, it is partly internationalized and so aware of what is happening in other institutions. Further, it exhibits strong global connectivity in communications, collaboration, two-way flows of knowledge and ideas, and continuing flows of faculty and students moving in and out of the institution. Above all it has research capacity sufficient to generate globally significant output in the sciences and social sciences, thus enabling it to position itself in worldwide knowledge circuits and claim the reputation of a bona fide modern university.

The Role of Research

Research is the most important element, for several reasons. First, knowledge is the common currency, the medium of exchange through which universities deal and collaborate. That is, knowledge is a global public good in the economic sense (Stiglitz, 1999), which flows freely across borders and is used everywhere without losing value. Further, globalization has enhanced its universal character and intrinsic importance. Second, the creation, interpretation and codification of knowledge, as research, are the functions that distinguish universities from other educational institutions, and most other social organizations. Third, since the emergence of the Humboldt model of the teaching and research university in nineteenth century Germany, followed by its adaptation to the US, which began at Johns Hopkins University, research has been increasingly central to the modern idea of a university (Kerr, 2001).

Fourth, research has become one of the indexes of global competition between nations, and many national governments pursue nation-building investments in research as a principal aspect of economic competitiveness. Zones of accelerated research include: mainland China (Li et al., 2008), Korea, Taiwan China and Singapore; parts of Europe including Germany and France; and the US, where the Obama administration doubled funding for the National Science Foundation and National Health Institute research programs in 2009. The centrality of research in nation building is grounded in the role of science and technology in military and economic competitiveness, which long predates the birth of the Internet. It goes back at least to the application of industrial innovations to military developments in the nineteenth century (Bayly, 2004). Perhaps the key moment in the positioning of research in global competition was the American use of nuclear weapons at the end of world war two. This technology rested on developments in the science of nuclear physics. Therefore, perhaps appropriately, the pattern of competitive investments in research and development is sometimes called the "arms race in innovation". Competition between nations in research is also described as a "war on talent" where national systems that are expanding their research capacity are better positioned to attract global doctoral students, post-doctoral and senior researchers as well as industry project monies. Further, as the competition between nations tends towards becoming a universal competition, global patterns are entrenched. This illustrates Bayly's point that in the modern era, nation building and globalization go hand in hand (Bayly, 2004). Hence, the university functions of knowledge creation, dissemination, storage and transmission, and research training, have spread from some nations to most nations, as indicated by the common global character of the world-class university movement.

Finally, research is the index of value in global competition between individual universities that is fostered and expressed in the rankings. As noted, competition between research-intensive universities is a status competition, i.e. status, ultimately, is derived from research performance (e.g. of many see Dill, 1997; Horta, 2009). In other words, research determines the value of each university "brand", even regulating the market in undergraduate education. Advanced research performance does not necessarily generate high quality teaching, but has an impact because students are focused on the "brand" value of degrees. That is, most students enrol in the university that has the highest status they can achieve, and this is determined by objective research performance, which cannot be fudged. Regarding this, if a university is not strong in research, marketing cannot make it look strong and thus it must have real, demonstrable capacity and output in terms of recognized indicators of research.

Conditions of a Global Research University

Salmi (2009) and research by the author (Marginson, 2011a) concur on the conditions necessary to establish and maintain a long-term global research

17

university. First, there are the enabling conditions external to such a university. Within a nation-state there must be a strong desire for the prestige and capacity that it can bring. In addition, the nation must have the economic capacity to finance such universities on a sustainable basis from a combination of public and private sources. Further, policies, regulatory frameworks and funding programs must be favourable to, and not unfavourable to, the evolution of a global research university. In relation to these matters, "Research universities must have adequate and sustained budgets; they cannot succeed on the basis of inadequate funding or severe budgetary fluctuations over time" (Altbach, 2011:25).

Second, there are the conditions internal to the global research university. Again, as with external conditions, there must be a strong desire to create and maintain such an institution. Moreover, there must be human resources and physical capacity adequate to support research, teaching, communications and institutional leadership and organization; including professionalized service delivery and executive leadership. There should be institutional autonomy sufficient to enable strategic decisions and initiatives, including global initiatives. Internal governance and organizational culture should sustain openness and continually improving performance. There must be global connective capacity, especially in communicating knowledge and managing two-way people flows. Further, resources for research should be allocated on a merit basis. Finally, there must be academic freedom sufficient to enable creative initiative and global connectedness across all disciplines.

The third condition is time, for it is impossible to become a sustainable global research university overnight. Perhaps the minimum time needed is 12 to 15 years, even if resources are excellent, initial leadership outstanding and good decisions are made without many errors. Regarding this, the Hong Kong University of Science and Technology (HKUST), founded in 1991, medium in size but already one of the strongest research universities in East Asia, fulfilled all of these conditions and took just over a decade to become established at the global level (Postiglione, 2011). In contrast, in spite of the last decade of stellar investments in Saudi Arabia, especially in the newly established King Abdullah University of Science and Technology, that nation has yet to achieve a substantial lift in the nation's publications performance, as measured by the National Science Foundation (National Science Foundation [NSF], 2012). Saudi Arabia will take longer than Hong Kong.

DIFFERENT ROADS TO THE WORLD-CLASS UNIVERSITY

The research science system is a global one, articulated as a single set of English-language publications that provide the most authoritative, though not the only, knowledge in those disciplines. Knowledge in the humanities, the professional disciplines and parts of the social sciences are more nationally bound than the science-based fields, which set the norms of the global research university. This implies that the world-class university to which all aspire has a sizeable element of universality that permits it to be considered in generic terms at the global level, as has been the case so far in this chapter.

However, to follow this line of thought exclusively would be to suggest there is only one kind of modernity, and only one method for modernizing a higher education system. That is, it would suggest there is only one kind of state project in higher education and only one possible framing of the world-class university. However, as noted in the introduction, the world-class university is situated in national and local contexts that vary considerably. This variation includes differences in the non-sciences and in organizational systems and cultures; and in the larger setting, in social approaches to higher education and knowledge, in the nature and role of government, in practices of freedom, and in relations between society, state and higher education. In other words, the generic conditions for building the global research university can vary quite markedly in content. For example, as Altbach and Salmi (2011, p. 3) note, the world-class university needs a high concentration of talented academics and students, significant budgets, and strategic vision and leadership, yet some world-class budgets are largely state financed, whereas in other cases tuition fees for the student are high. This is because the political economy of cost sharing is highly variant, reflecting differences in political cultures, including differing conceptions of the balance of responsibility between state, institutions and families. In some cases the necessary strategic vision and leadership is expressed at institutional level, and universities are much more global in outlook than their governments, whereas in other cases government is key or even decisive. However, sometimes both state and university think globally in the same way, as in Singapore.

In short, there are different roads to the same goal, which is the world-class university. Up to now American approaches to system-building and institution-building have dominated much of the thinking about world-class universities. This is not surprising given that the US houses half of the top 100 research universities and produces half of the top 1% most cited research papers (Shanghai Jiao Tong University [SJTU], 2012; NSF, 2012), and the fact that forms typical of Anglo-American higher education have been absorbed into the design of ranking systems. However, future thinking about world-class universities will be more plural, given that other models are emerging, especially in East Asia. Already, in reality, regardless of the norms of policy thinking and ranking systems, the different world-class universities are by no means the same as each other. That is, no one should perpetuate the illusion that all nations and institutions are operating on the same basis, any more than it should be assumed that they are operating on an equal basis. As Wang Hui puts it in *The End of the Revolution: China and the Limits of Modernity*:

> For 300 years, all of humanity has certainly become more closely linked to one another through colonialism, unequal trade and technological development. Yet a common path hardly exists between the colonizer and the colonized, between Africa and the US, or between China and the European powers. (2009, p. 85)

Neo-institutional theory suggests that key to understanding the variations between higher education systems, is variation in nation-state forms and strategies. That is, different state forms and political cultures shape the distinctive roads to the world-class university. Arguably these roads are also shaped by different educational cultures (Marginson, in preparation). Moreover, it is noticeable that the different roads (and systems) of higher education tend to be not so much national, as regional or sub-regional, reflecting historical overlaps and clustered cultures. As Tu We-Ming remarks in *Confucian traditions in East Asian modernity* (1996): "Culture matters ... economic facts and political institutions are laden with cultural values" (pp. 4–5).

It is hypothesized that these different roads to the world-class university can be found to be distinctive to the higher education systems in the US; the Westminster systems (UK, Australia, New Zealand); the Post-Confucian forms of East Asia and Singapore (Marginson, 2011b); the Nordic systems (Valimaa, 2011); the Central European or Germanic systems; the Francophone systems and in Saudi Arabia and the Gulf States. There might also be other roads: for example a Latin American variant (a "Bolivarian Model"?) partly shaped by the Bonapartist model in France and Italy; emerging approaches in higher education systems in South Asia and Central Asia, etc.

Comparison of the Different Roads to the World-Class University

If so each of these differing roads to the world-class university needs closer definition, research observation and analysis, so they can be more effectively compared with each other. Regarding the latter point, some roads may be shown to be more effective than others in reaching the common goal of the world-class university. That is, different paths may have varying strengths and weaknesses.

Space does not allow a full investigation and discussion of the different roads in this chapter. This is a project for a future time, but comparison could focus on:
- the character and role of the nation-state;
- the prevailing political culture;
- educational practices in the family and in society;
- modes of governance, leadership, management and organization in higher education;
- relations between the state, higher education institution and society;
- financing and cost sharing in higher education;
- the degree and type of global openness, engagement and initiative, including the contribution to the global architecture in higher education.

The remainder of this chapter focuses on one road to the world-class university that is of considerable interest at present, and is clearly different to that of the Anglo-American universities that dominate in the literature, namely, the trajectory of Post-Confucian higher education. Table 3 at the end of the chapter compares the Post-Confucian higher education systems to the US and Westminster systems.

THE POST-CONFUCIAN MODEL

The Post-Confucian systems are those of mainland China, Hong Kong SAR, Macau SAR, Taiwan China, South Korea, Japan, Vietnam and Singapore. These systems are quite different in many ways, in particular, with regards to language and political cultures, and there are political tensions between these countries. Nevertheless, they share common traditions in relation to the state and education, elements that are determining of the distinctive features of Post-Confucian higher education. [2] For the most part their systems also share a common economic position, with all except mainland China and Vietnam having achieved Western European levels of wealth. However, mainland China has doubled its average income in the last five years, and education-strong Shanghai, Beijing and Eastern China are much wealthier than most of the country. Table 1 provides data on gross national income (GNI) per capita for the focal countries.

Table 1. Gross national income per head in the Post-Confucian nations/systems (2010)

Nation/system	GNI PPP* per capita（US$）
Singapore	55,790
Hong Kong SAR	47,480
Macau SAR (2009)	45,220
Taiwan	35,700
Japan	34,460
South Korea	29,010
Mainland China	7640
Vietnam	3070
India**	3550

* PPP: Purchasing Power Parity.
** India, not a Post-Confucian nation, is included for comparison purposes.

Source: The World Bank (2012b); CIA, (2012)

On the basis of this economic platform, participation is expanding towards universal levels, institutional quality is rising, the number of research papers is growing very rapidly, and world-class universities have emerged. However, within the group there are two exceptions to this pattern of dynamic growth. One is Japan, which developed a high quality system of higher education and university research thirty years earlier and now seems to be marking time. The other is Vietnam, which is growing in terms of student numbers from a low base, but as yet is too under-developed in terms of economic capacity to achieve the Post-Confucian take-off in research and establish world-class universities or global research universities.

Features of the Model

The Post-Confucian systems have developed within the framework of the comprehensive East Asian nation-state that originated under the Qin and Han dynasties in China. In this tradition there is none of the anti-government political culture typical of the US, for in the Post-Confucian world, politics and government are in command, not the markets (Gernet, 1996). There is some variation within the group. The state domination of the economy and society is open in the one-party states of Singapore and mainland China, whereas, it is expressed more indirectly via the bureaucracy where there are contestable polities, in places such as: Korea, Japan and Taiwan. Nevertheless, although in the latter systems political leadership may change, there is continuity in government itself and, what is more, work in government enjoys high social prestige. For example, in Post-Confucian systems many bright graduates opt for careers in the senior levels of government rather than in business or the medical or legal professions that attract most elite graduates in the English-speaking countries.

The Post-Confucian systems also rest on the Confucian tradition in education, which first flowered on a broad basis in the Song dynasty in China. The core of this tradition is family-based commitment to self-cultivation via learning, together with the use of universal systems of examinations as a method of social selection, first developed for the meritocratic selection of state officials under the Han dynasty. In the home, education is automatically understood as part of the duty of the child to the parent and the duty of the parent to the child. At the societal level, the high stakes character of the examination, which mediates status competition, underpins the value placed on education. Further, in Post-Confucian countries and regions the respect for education is long-standing and more deeply rooted than in Europe and North America. At the same time, the evolution of East Asian higher education has also been powerfully influenced by Western education, especially the US research university. Regarding this, "catch-up" with the West has been a major driver of East Asian policy since the Meiji period in Japan and templates grounded in new public management that originated in the UK have shaped reform in East Asia as they have everywhere else. Moreover, the original Confucian focus on moral self-cultivation has been economized, with the main focus now appearing to be on the utility of higher education for individuals and for the economy. Consequently, there are concerns in mainland China (as in the West) that the university is losing its soul. Often this is seen as a function of Westernization, but the problem is more complex than that, as explained next.

It is a mistake to see Western modernization as displacing educational tradition in East Asia, for the relation between tradition and modernity is one of exchange, not of displacement. That is, Post-Confucian universities, like their societies, are hybrids of East and West and as such they are creating something new: a distinctive modernization in education and research. What are the distinctive conditions and attributes of the Post-Confucian model of higher education? Four have been identified so far in this discussion: the comprehensive Sinic nation-state; the practices in the family associated with Confucian self-cultivation via education; the neo-Confucian institutional forms, such as the examination; and economic growth as a platform for educational evolution. There are four other elements. First, the roll-out of tertiary education participation rates to near universal levels, partly financed by households. Second, sustained, deep and distinctive practices of internationalization, which take bi-cultural forms and third, the spectacular growth of research and development activity. The second and third elements provide the principal condition for the fourth aspect, an advancing role on the global scale. Each of these elements is now examined in turn.

Participation and Student Achievement

Typically, the Post-Confucian systems have been making progress rapidly in both the quantity and quality of schooling and higher education and they seem to have avoided the trade-off between advances in quality and quantity that are endemic to Anglo-American systems. They also seem to have avoided a trade-off between public and private financing. Typically both government and households are sharing the cost of expanding participation. As the tertiary system matures, the proportion of tuition paid for by the household rises and the state focuses an increasing part of its funding on the academically elite national research universities and their students as well as on social equity objectives.

Tertiary participation exceeds 85% in both South Korea and Taiwan. In mainland China, participation was less than 5% in 1990, whereas it is now approaching 30% and the target for 2020 is 40%, which would bring China close to the Organization for Economic Cooperation and Development (OECD) countries' average. The standard of institutions varies, with some arguing that graduates are inadequately prepared for a fast developing manufacturing sector. A recent World Bank report refers to a combination of "low-skill glut and high-skill shortage" in graduate labour markets (The World Bank, 2012a, 194). However, the government's 211 and 985 programs have singled out the leading universities for evolution at a higher level of quality and global competitiveness and the bulk of globally significant research is concentrated in those institutions. In only six years, the number of mainland Chinese institutions in the Academic Ranking for World Universities (ARWU) top 500 has almost tripled, from eight to 23 (SJTU, 2012). Currently, the main challenge is to improve the standards of the rest of the institutions and to spread participation into more families in the countryside.

As pointed out above, tertiary participation in all Post-Confucian nations is partly funded by households. Moreover, even very poor families often invest heavily in the costs of schooling and extra tutoring and classes outside formal school. Many families spend as much on education as American families spend on housing. In Korea, where the trend towards household funding has gone furthest, 77.7% of all costs of tertiary education institutions are paid by the private sector, including 52.1% by households, and just 22.3% by the government. In Japan the private sector share is 66.7% (OECD, 2011:244). In addition, the drive to invest privately in children's education is manifest also in the remarkable level of investment in extra schooling in its different forms, with Levin (2011) estimating that in Korea this probably exceeds 3% of gross domestic product (GDP).

No doubt the investment in extra learning is integral to the levels of student achievement, for the results of the 2009 OECD Programme for International Student Assessment (PISA) survey suggest that East Asia and Singapore constitute the world's strongest zone for student learning (OECD, 2010). For example, in mean student scores in mathematics, the top five systems in the world are all Post-Confucian: Shanghai (600), Singapore (562), Hong Kong SAR (555), South Korea (546) and Taiwan (543). Japan is in ninth place with 529. East Asia and Singapore's systems perform almost as well in science, having five of the top six systems, including Japan (in fifth place) and for reading, with four of the top five systems. This constitutes a strong starting point for tertiary education and graduate literacy.

Internationalization

Salmi (2011) notes that internationalization is central to those Post-Confucian universities that aspire to world-class university status.

> Both Shanghai Jiao Tong University (China) and Pohang University of Science and Technology (the Republic of Korea) made a strategic decision to rely principally on Chinese or Korean academics trained in the best universities in North America or Europe and, to a large extent, to recruit highly qualified foreign faculty. Significantly increasing the percentage of courses taught in English is an integral part of this strategy, as well. (Salmi, 2011:326)

Other internationalization strategies include a strong emphasis on global publishing and the widespread use of cross-national benchmarking. Universities in Korea, Japan, Taiwan and China have especially focused on American examples, but all Post-Confucian systems also follow what is happening in Western Europe, thus demonstrating their embracing the notion of there being a plurality of good practice. Moreover, all Post-Confucian systems send some personnel abroad for doctoral training. In addition, there is growing openness to foreign faculty and students, although Japan and Korea have been slower to accept this than the other systems. At the forefront of these developments, Singapore has brought branches of leading foreign universities onto the island.

Research and Global Role

East Asia and Singapore are emerging as the world's third great zone of research, development and innovation, after the US and Canada, and North Western Europe and the UK. Japan, long having been a world leader in science, has now been joined by Korea, Taiwan, Singapore, the Hong Kong SAR and of course, mainland China. Moreover, East, Southeast and South Asia, together spend almost as much on research and development (R&D) as the US and most of East Asia and Singapore sustain rates of investment in R&D, especially business R&D, at European levels. Regarding this, in 2009, Korea spent 3.4% of GDP on R&D, Japan, 3.3%, Taiwan, 2.9% and Singapore, a slightly lower level of 2.4%. Mainland China, where R&D investment was at 1.7% of GDP, now spends about 40% of the American budget on R&D and is increasing spending at the extraordinary rate of 20% a year (NSF, 2012). The national target is 2.5% of GDP by 2020, which would bring China to the level of investment in the US, if China's GDP exceeds the American GDP as expected. As in Korea, a relatively low proportion of mainland China's research budget goes to universities, about one-tenth, but university resources for research are expanding along with all other R&D. In fact, policy in these two countries places strong emphasis on R&D for industry. This strategy appears to be working: between 1995 and 2008, the US share of worldwide high technology exports dropped from 21 to 14%, whilst China's share rose from 6 to 20% (NSF, 2010).

Increased investment leads to greater output. In 2009, China, Japan, South Korea, Taiwan and Singapore, between them, produced a total number of science papers equal to 80% of the US output. In fact, mainland China, which was only the 12th largest producer of science papers in 1995, is now the second largest in the world, having passed Japan in 2007. There has also been an exceptionally rapid growth of outputs in each of: Korea, Taiwan and Singapore, but there has been little recent change in Japan (NSF, 2012). However, the growth in research funding and output has yet fully to show itself in citation performance and in the ARWU ranking. That is, apart from the first five universities from Japan (Tokyo, Kyoto, Osaka, Nagoya and Tohoku), there are no East Asian or Singaporean institutions in the top 100 and only five non-Japanese universities in the top 200, these being: the National University of Singapore, Seoul National in Korea, the National Taiwan University, Tsinghua, and the Chinese University of Hong Kong (SJTU, 2012). However, there is a lag before publications show up in citations numbers and a further lag before cites reach the Shanghai Jiao Tong index and so these figures may be out of date. Moreover, the weight given to Nobel Prizes (30%) also disadvantages East Asia.

The comparative performance of East Asian systems can also be monitored using the Leiden Ranking (Centre for Science and Technology Studies Leiden University [CWTS], 2012) which works with Thomson Web of Science (2012) data3. The Leiden data set can be used to identify the number of universities that published over 5000 papers in the years 2005-2009 that also had more than 10% of their papers in the top 10% in the field, thereby combining a quantity measure with a quality measure. Under this approach the performance of East Asian universities is more impressive in relation to volume than in relation to citation levels.

As Table 2 shows, in terms of paper volume there were 19 Post-Confucian universities in the world top 100 universities, led by Tokyo. Citation is dominated by US universities, with 64 of them having published both 5000 papers and having at least 10% of their publications in the top 10%. Moreover, there were 47 such universities in Europe, concentrated in the northwest, but just 12 from East Asia and Singapore, these being: Tokyo University in Japan, National University and Nanyang in Singapore, Korea Advanced Institute of Science and Technology in Korea, Hong Kong University and the Chinese University in Hong Kong, and six in mainland China: Tsinghua, Peking, Fudan, the Science and Technology, Nanjing and Jilin universities. However, another 20 Asia Pacific universities had published more than 5000 papers but had less than 10% in the top group (CWTS, 2012). As quality lifts citation rates in East Asia will surely follow and the region will start to look more like Europe.

Table 2. World top 100 universities in East Asia and Singapore by volume of scientific papers (2005-2009)

Institution	Volume of science papers 2005-2009	World rank on paper volume	Proportion of papers in top 10% most cited in field (%)
The University of Tokyo (Japan)	18,382	4	10.2
Kyoto University (Japan)	14,941	11	9.5
Seoul National University (South Korea)	13,052	19	8.9
Zhejiang University (mainland China)	13,037	20	9.1
Osaka University (Japan)	12,266	25	8.1
National University of Singapore (Singapore)	11,838	29	13.8
Tohoku University (Japan)	11,736	30	7.9
Tsinghua University (mainland China)	11,478	34	10.8
National Taiwan University (Taiwan)	11,302	35	8.9
Shanghai Jiao Tong University (mainland China)	10,683	40	8.2
Peking University (mainland China)	9153	53	10.4
Kyushu University (Japan)	8462	62	6.8
Hokkaido University (Japan)	8043	71	6.1
Yonsei University (South Korea)	7399	79	7.8
Nagoya University (Japan)	7203	87	8.1
Nanyang Technological University (Singapore)	7136	90	11.9
National Cheng Kung University (Taiwan)	7126	92	8.5
Fudan University (mainland China)	7061	94	11.1
Tokyo Institute Technology University (Japan)	6932	99	8.3

Source: CWTS (2012)

The National University of Singapore stands out. It is sixth in Asia on the number of papers and regarding the proportion of papers in the top 10% in the field, it is first in Asia among institutions with more than 4000 papers and 82nd in the world. Japan's universities perform much better on the size criterion than the quality criterion. Moreover, flagship system leaders, such as the National Taiwan University and Seoul National University, fall below the 10% mark for high quality papers. However, most East Asian systems have developed medium sized specialist science and technology universities with good citation rates, such as Pohang and KAIST in Korea, the Hong Kong University of Science and Technology, which at 14.9% it is ranked 58th in the world on the Leiden top

10% citations measure, and several universities in China, including Nankai and the University of Science and Technology (CWTS, 2012).

Mainland China's performance on comparative research quality is uneven. For example, in 2010 China's researchers wrote just 3.6% of the top 1% most cited papers in all fields, as compared with a figure of 48.9% in the US. However, paper volume and quality vary greatly by discipline, with there being some fields in which China is already a world leader in terms of quality. For example, in engineering, chemistry, computer science and mathematics, China's share of world papers is close to double its overall share of all science papers and its share of the world's top 1% of papers in these disciplines is high. In engineering China has 12.3% of the world's most highly cited work, already one third the level of the US and more than twice that of Japan. Further comparisons with the US reveal chemistry citations stand at 30% of the American level and these figures are 25% for computer science and 20% for mathematics (NSF, 2012), which shows a strong base for future development. On the other hand, in medicine and the biological sciences the picture is completely different, with China having less than 1% of the world's top 1% of papers. By comparison, the US has more than half of the world's top 1% of papers in each of these fields (NSF, 2012). However, the most striking feature is the rate of change in China, for in 2000 it had 0.6% of the top 1% most cited papers in Chemistry and yet ten years later its share had jumped to 10.6%. Moreover, the proportion of its papers that are at the top 1% level is moving towards the average level for all countries (NSF, 2012). In fact, despite the language barrier, much of the science in China is improving at a very rapid rate.

The jury is still out on whether the freewheeling liberal American culture in both universities and civil society provides the US with a decisive advantage in producing research of the highest quality. This freedom is perhaps more apparent in American civil society than the universities, which are weighed down by performance regimes and the mimetic effects of competition for the middle position in disciplinary fields. In China there is open and feisty discussion within the party, government and universities, about many policy issues. In addition, with some exceptions, the atmosphere in the leading universities seems to be as liberal as in most parts of the world, and there is more engagement in policy issues than in many national systems. On the other hand, discussion in civil society and on the Internet is more restricted than in the US and most of Western Europe, which could slow the progress of improvement in higher education, and progress in the application of discoveries in higher education to society and industry.

The question of dual leadership in the universities, where the party secretary sits alongside the president, is ambiguous. On the one hand it can be seen as continuous interference in academic judgment. On the other hand it can be seen as a form of distributed leadership that buffers the direct role of the party-state, and therefore assists universities to secure partial university autonomy, as for example in Min Weifang's tenure as Party Secretary at Peking University (Hayhoe et al.,

2011, pp. 111–114). Again, the jury is out. The larger concern is government control of senior appointments.

> The president is usually appointed by the government or is elected by the academic community and subsequently approved by authorities. The appointment system might prevent the university from selecting the most suitable leaders for its development. (Wang, Wang & Liu, 2011, pp. 42–43)

What is clear is that mainland China's government wants research universities that are creative and globally effective. In that respect government and university leaders agree, and they both agree that creativity can be partly engineered from above, although they may disagree about who should do this, and both might be at variance with practicing researchers and scholars. These tensions are common to all higher education systems. What is distinctive about the East Asian systems is the state is a larger factor than in the English-speaking countries and much of Europe. The strong East Asian state provides advantages in world-class university development, especially its marvellous capacity to focus resources, to drive performance on the basis of planned targets that are real targets, and to move continually forward. On the other hand the state may limit what can be achieved, in that it often inhibits peer judgments in research, or retards the flow of knowledge through society and the innovation spaces in the economy.

At the same time, in this discussion it is important to recognize that in East Asia meanings of "public", "private" and "autonomy" are not the same as in the US or Europe. That is, human freedoms have both a universal component and a nationally and culturally specific one and this reality pertains to the research university itself.

> Once one can excel in terms of productivity and meet the State's criteria for producing valuable and useful knowledge, one may enjoy a high level of intellectual authority. This type of intellectual authority is not identical with academic freedom in the Western context, but in some ways it provides even more flexibility and greater power than does academic freedom. There is certainly some overlap between these two concepts, yet clearly a different emphasis. Westerners focus on restrictions to freedom of choice, whereas Chinese scholars looking at the same situation focus on the responsibility of the person in authority to use their power wisely in the collective interest. (Zha, 2011, p. 464)

The term "academic freedom", which is used to denote a kind of freedom particularly appropriate to the university in the Western context … is not a good fit for China. On the one hand, Chinese scholars enjoy a greater degree of "intellectual authority" than is common in the West, due to the history of the civil service examinations and the close links contemporary universities have with major state projects. On the other hand, there is a strong tradition of "intellectual freedom" in China, which is rooted in an epistemology quite different from that of European rationalism. It requires

Table 3. Comparison of Post-Confucian and English language country systems

	Post-Confucian systems (East Asia & Singapore)	United States' system	Westminster systems (UK, Australia, NZ)
Character of nation-state	Comprehensive, central, delegates to provinces. Politics in command of economy and civil society. State draws best graduates	Limited, division of powers, separate from civil society and economy. Anti-statism common. Federal	Limited, division of powers, separate from civil society and economy. Some anti-statism. Unitary
Educational culture	Confucian commitment to self-cultivation via learning. Education as filial duty and producer of status via exam competition (and producer of global competitiveness)	Twentieth century meritocratic and competitive ideology. Education common road to wealth/status, within advancing prosperity	Post 1945 ideology of state guaranteed equal opportunity through education as path to wealth and status, open to all in society
State role in higher education	Big, state supervises, shapes, drives and selectively funds institutions. Over time increased delegation to part-controlled presidents	Smaller, from distance. Fosters market ranking via research, student loans then steps back. Autonomous presidents	From a distance. Shape system through policy, regulation, funding and supervising the market. Autonomous vice-chancellors
Financing of higher education	State financed infrastructure, part of tuition (especially early in model), scholarships, merit aid. Household funds much tuition and private tutoring, even poor families	State funds some infrastructure, tuition subsidies, student loans. Households vary from high tuition to low, poor families state dependent	Less state financed infrastructure now. Tuition loans, some aid. Growing household investment, but less than East Asia. Austerity
Dynamics of research	Part household funding of tuition, ideology of world-class universities, university hierarchy: together enable rapid state investment in research at scale. Applied research has dominant. state intervention.	Research heavily funded by federal government unburdened by tuition. Some industry and civic/philanthropic money. Basic science plus commercial IP	Research funded (more in UK) by government, also finances tuition. Less philanthropy and civic money than US. Basic science, applied growth, dreams of IP
Hierarchy and social selection	Steep university hierarchy. "One-chance" universal competition with selection into prestige institutions. World-class universities are fast track for life	Steep institutional hierarchy mediated by SAAT scores. Some part second chances, mainly public sector. Top world-class universities are fast track for life	Competition for place in university hierarchy mediated by school results with some part second chances. World-class universities provide strong start
Fostering of World-Class Universities	Part of tradition, universal target of family aspirations. Support for building of world-class universities by funding and regulation. Emerging global agenda	Entrenched hierarchy of Ivy League and flagship state universities, via research grants, tuition hikes, philanthropy. Source of global pride	Ambivalence in national temperament and government policy on status of top institutions. Private and public funding has hit ceilings

that knowledge be demonstrated first and foremost through action for the public good, also that knowledge be seen as holistic and inter-connected, rather than organized into narrowly defined separate disciplines. (Hayhoe, 2011, p. 17)

This is another fruitful area for future comparative research.

CONCLUSION

The East Asian dynamism underlines the importance of states and educational cultures in explaining world-class university formation. Table 3 compares the differing approaches to system organization and educational and political culture in the US, the Westminster countries (the UK, Australia and New Zealand) and the Post-Confucian systems.

In the English-speaking countries the state is John Locke's limited liberal state, demarcated between state, judiciary, market and civil society, and subject to continual questioning of the legitimacy of government. For example, in the US many believe the state should be neutral in relation to differing conceptions of the good life. In East Asia the state is different. It is seen as proper for the state to focus on particular notions of the good life, even in Hong Kong where the political culture comes closest to those of the English-speaking world. In the Post-Confucian systems it is taken for granted that the state is central to society and its ordering. In fact, it is impossible to imagine Post-Confucian higher education and research (or society) in the absence of the state, for without its driving intervention there would have been no take-offs in higher education.

At the same time, without Confucian learning at home, as passed from generation to generation, state policies would have had less purchase. In contrast, in this respect – ironically given their adherence to the Adam Smith limited state – the English-speaking nations and Western Europe are more state dependant. This is because the family motivation for education is not as universal as in East Asia and Singapore. Post-Confucian higher education can only be understood by recognizing the *interrelationship* between state political culture and family educational culture. This relationship is very positive for educational development. Because Post-Confucian households are willing to fund a significant part of tertiary costs, and the family and social competition together drive increasing participation in tertiary education, this frees up state resources to concentrate investments on infrastructures, globally-focused research universities, the research budget and the most talented students and researchers. On the basis of this social division of labour, unique in the higher education world, Post-Confucian countries and regions have been able to move forward at one and the same time, and at a rapid rate, on the quantity of participation, the quality of institutions, and the volume and quality of research, establishing a layer of world-class universities with varied missions.

So far, there has been no other road to the world-class university as time-effective as this and it is contended that the Post-Confucian model will be increasingly influential in future years. For example, it is possible that although non-Confucian nations do not possess the same cultural and political conditions, they may pursue a new road to obtaining world-class universities by combining features of the Post-Confucian and US models.

NOTES

[1] The universities concerned are Universitas Indonesia, the Australian National University, University of Tokyo in Japan, Universidad Nacional Autonoma de Mexico, University of Toronto in Canada, University of Auckland in New Zealand, Chulalongkorn University in Thailand, the University of Twente in the Netherlands, Leiden University in the Netherlands, University of Malaya in Malaysia, the National University of Singapore, University of Illinois (Urbana-Champaign) in the US, Vietnam National University in Hanoi, Peking University in China, Shanghai Jiao Tong University in China, Royal University of Phnom Penh in Cambodia, National University of Laos; the University of the Philippines, Diliman; the University of Hong Kong, SAR China; Seoul National University in South Korea; and the National Taiwan University.

[2] In this group of countries there is a closer convergence in education than in society as a whole.

[3] Leiden provides separate indicators of each of paper quantity, and the proportion of papers in the top 10% most highly cited in their field, a quality indicator. The world gold standard on quality is Massachusetts Institute of Technology, which has 25.2% of its papers in the top 10% by cite rate.

REFERENCES

Altbach, P. (2011). The past, present and future of the research university. In P. Altbach & J. Salmi (Eds.), *The Road to Academic Excellence: The Making of World-Class Research Universities* (pp. 11–32). Washington: The World Bank.

Altbach, P. & Salmi, J. (Eds.). (2011). *The Road to Academic Excellence: The Making of World-Class Research Universities*. Washington: The World Bank.

Bayly, C. (2004). *The Birth of the Modern World 1780–1914: Global Connections and Comparisons*. Oxford: Blackwell.

Bourdieu, P. (1988). *Homo Academicus*. Cambridge: Polity.

Brint, S. (2002, June). *Higher Education in "The Age of Money"*. Paper to a Ford Foundation Meeting on markets in higher education, Tampa. Riverside: University of California.

Brown, R. (Ed.) (2011). *Higher Education and the Market*. New York: Routledge.

Centre for Science and Technology Studies Leiden University. (2012). *The Leiden Ranking 2011*. Retrieved April 12, 2012, from http://www.leidenranking.com/default.aspx

Cerny, P. (1997). Paradoxes of the competition state: The dynamics of political globalization. *Government and Opposition, 32*(2), 251–274.

Dill, D. (1997). Higher education markets and public policy. *Higher Education Policy, 10*(3/4), 167–185.

Frank, R., & Cook, P. (1995). *The Winner-Take-All Society*. New York: The Free Press.

Gernet, J. (1996). *A History of Chinese Civilization* (2nd ed.). Cambridge: Cambridge University Press.

Geiger, R. (2004). Market coordination of higher education: The United States. In P. Teixeira, B. Jongbloed, D. Dill, & A. Amaral (Eds.), *Markets in Higher Education: Rhetoric or Reality?* (pp. 161–183). Dordrecht: Springer.

Hansmann, H. (1999). *Higher Education as an Associative Good*. Yale Centre for International Finance, Working Paper No. 99-13. New Haven: Yale Law School, Yale University.

Hayhoe, R. (2011). Introduction and acknowledgements? In R. Hayhoe, J. Li, J. Lin, & Q. Zha (Eds.), *Portraits of 21st Century Chinese Universities: In the Move to Mass Higher Education* (pp. 1–18). Hong Kong: Springer/Comparative Education Research Centre, The University of Hong Kong.

Hazelkorn, E. (2008). Learning to live with league tables and ranking: The experience of institutional leaders. *Higher Education Policy, 21*(2), 193–215.

Hazelkorn, E. (2011). *Rankings and the Reshaping of Higher Education: The Battle for World-Class Excellence.* London: Palgrave Macmillan.

Horta, H. (2009). Global and national prominent universities: Internationalisation, competitiveness and the role of the state. *Higher Education, 58*(3), 387–405.

International Monetary Fund. (2012). *World Economic Database.* Retrieved from http://www.imf.org/external/pubs/ft/weo/2011/02/weodata/index.aspx

Kerr, C. (2001). *The Uses of the University* (5th ed.). Cambridge: Harvard University Press.

King, R., Marginson, S., & Naidoo, R. (Eds.). (2011). *Handbook on Globalization and Higher Education.* Cheltenham: Edward Elgar.

Levin, H. (2011, September 26). Teachers College, Columbia University. Conversation with the author. Melbourne.

Li, Y., Whalley, J., Zhang, S., & Zhao, X. (2008). *The Higher Educational Transformation of China and its Global Implications.* NBER Working Paper No. 13849. Cambridge: National Bureau of Economic Research.

Ma, W. (2008). The University of California at Berkeley: An emerging global research university. *Higher Education Policy, 21*(1), 65–81.

Marginson, S. (2006). Dynamics of national and global competition in higher education. *Higher Education, 52*(1), 1–39.

Marginson, S. (2007). The public/private division in higher education: A global revision. *Higher Education, 53*(3), 307–333.

Marginson, S. (2008a). Global field and global imagining: Bourdieu and relations of power in worldwide higher education. *British Journal of Sociology of Education, 29*(3), 303–316.

Marginson, S. (2008b). "Ideas of a University" for the global era. Paper for seminar on *Positioning University in the Globalized World: Changing Governance and Coping Strategies in Asia.* Centre of Asian Studies, The University of Hong Kong; Central Policy Unit, HKSAR Government; and The Hong Kong Institute of Education, 10-11 December, The University of Hong Kong.

Marginson, S. (2011a). Global perspectives and strategies of Asia-Pacific universities. In N. Liu, Q. Wang, & Y. Cheng (Eds.), *Paths to a World-Class University: Lessons from Practices and Experiences* (pp. 3–27). Rotterdam: Sense Publishers.

Marginson, S. (2011b). Higher Education in East Asia and Singapore: Rise of the confucian model. *Higher Education, 61*(5), 587–611.

Marginson, S. (2011c). Imagining the global. In R. King, S. Marginson, & R. Naidoo (Eds.), *Handbook of Higher Education and Globalization* (pp. 10–39). Cheltenham: Edward Elgar.

Marginson, S. (2011d). Strategising and ordering the global. In R. King, S. Marginson, & R. Naidoo (Eds.), *Handbook of Higher Education and Globalization* (pp. 394–414). Cheltenham: Edward Elgar.

Marginson, S. (in preparation). *Higher Education, the Nation-State and Post-Confucian Culture.*

Marginson, S., Kaur, S., & Sawir, E. (Eds.). (2011). *Higher Education in the Asia-Pacific: Strategic Responses to Globalization.* Dordrecht: Springer.

Marginson, S., Murphy, P., & Peters, M. (2010). *Global Creation: Space, Mobility and Synchrony in the Age of the Knowledge Economy.* New York: Peter Lang.

Marginson, S., & Rhoades, G. (2002). Beyond national states, markets, and systems of higher education: A glonacal agency heuristic. *Higher Education, 43*(3), 281–309.

Marginson, S., & Wende, M. C. van der. (2009a). The new global landscape of nations and institutions. In OECD *Higher Education to 2030, Vol. 2: Globalization* (pp. 17–62). Paris: OECD.

Marginson, S., & Wende, M. C. van der. (2009b). Europeanisation, university rankings and faculty mobility: Three cases in higher education globalisation. In OECD *Higher Education to 2020, Vol. 2: Globalization* (pp. 109–172). Paris: OECD.

Murphy, P., Peters, M., & Marginson, S. (2010). *Imagination: Three Models of the Imagination in the Age of the Knowledge Economy*. New York: Peter Lang.

National Science Foundation. (2010). *US National Science Board: Globalization of Science and Engineering Research*. Retrieved from http://www.nsf.gov/statistics/nsb1003/

National Science Foundation. (2012). *Science and Technology Indicators 2012*. National Science Board. Retrieved from http://www.nsf.gov/statistics/seind12/.

Organization for Economic Cooperation and Development. (2010). PISA 2009 Results: What students know and can do. In *Student Performance in Reading, Mathematics and Science* (Vol. 1). Paris: OECD.

Organization for Economic Cooperation and Development. (2011). *Education at a Glance 2011: OECD Indicators*. Paris: OECD.

Podolny, J. (1993). A status-based model of market competition. *American Journal of Sociology, 98*(4), 829–872.

Postiglione, G. (2011). The rise of research universities: The Hong Kong University of Science and Technology. In P. Altbach & J. Salmi (Eds.), *The Road to Academic Excellence: The Making of World-Class Research Universities* (pp. 63–100). Washington: The World Bank.

Salmi, J. (2009). *The Challenge of Establishing World-Class Universities*. Washington: The World Bank.

Shanghai Jiao Tong University. (2012). *Academic Ranking of World Universities*. Retrieved from http://www.shanghairanking.com/ARWU2011.html

Stiglitz, J. (1999). Knowledge as a global public good. In I. Kaul, I. Grunberg, & M. Stern (Eds.), *Global Public Goods: International Cooperation in the 21st Century* (pp. 308–325). New York: Oxford University Press.

The World Bank. (2012a). *China 2030: Building a Modern, Harmonious and Creative High-Income Society*. In conjunction with the Development Research Centre of the State Council, the People's Republic of China. Washington: The World Bank.

The World Bank. (2012b). *Data and Statistics*. Retrieved from http://data.worldbank.org/indicator

Thomson Reuters. (2012). *Web of Science*. Retrieved April 12, 2012, from http://thomsonreuters.com/products_services /science/science _products/a-z/web_of_science/

Valimaa, J. (2011). The corporatisation of national universities in Finland. In B. Pusser, K. Kempner, S. Marginson, & I. Ordorika (Eds.), *Universities and the Public Sphere: Knowledge Creation and State Building in the Era of Globalisation* (pp. 101–119). New York: Routledge.

Vedder, R. (2007). *Over Invested and Over Priced: American Higher Education Today*. Washington: Center for College Affordability and Productivity.

Wang Hui. (2009). *The End of the Revolution: China and the Limits of Modernity*. London: Verso.

Wang, Q. H., Wang, Q., & Liu, N. (2011). Building world-class universities in China: Shanghai Jiao Tong University. In P. Altbach & J. Salmi (Eds.), *The Road to Academic Excellence: The Making of World-Class Research Universities* (pp. 33–62). Washington: The World Bank.

Wei-Ming, T. (Ed.). (1996). *Confucian Traditions in East Asian Modernity: Moral Education and Economic Culture in Japan and the Four Mini-Dragons*. Cambridge: Harvard University Press.

Zha, Q. (2011). Is there an emerging Chinese model of the university? In R. Hayhoe, J. Li, J. Lin, & Q. Zha (Eds.), *Portraits of 21st Century Chinese Universities: In the Move to Mass Higher Education* (pp. 451–471). Hong Kong: Springer/Comparative Education Research Centre, The University of Hong Kong.

AFFILIATIONS

Simon Marginson
Centre for the Study of Higher Education,
University of Melbourne, Australia

YUNG-CHI HOU, MARTIN INCE AND CHUNG-LIN CHIANG

THE IMPACT OF EXCELLENCE INITIATIVES IN TAIWAN HIGHER EDUCATION

INTRODUCTION

Over the past decade, the term "world-class" has been used widely to describe how a university develops its capacity to compete in the global higher education marketplace. With the growth of competition between nations in our knowledge-based economy, the creation of world-class universities is becoming a national agenda item in developing as well as developed countries in Asia. Consequently, "policymakers in many countries have prioritized building research universities that would help their countries obtain a superior position in the global competition", particularly in the East Asian region (Shin, 2009:669). Marginson (2010, please also see the previous chapter) has indicated that accelerated public investment in research and world-class universities has forged a unique culture, which he called the "Post-Confucian Model" in the East Asian region.

What does a world-class university look like? In his book *The Challenge of Establishing World-Class Universities*, Jamil Salmi (2009) defines a world-class university as having three major indispensable components, that is: a high concentration of talent, including excellent faculty and brilliant students, abundant resources to offer a rich learning environment and conduct advanced research, and favourable governance features that encourage strategic vision, innovation and flexibility, and which enable institutions to make decisions and manage resources without being encumbered by bureaucracy. Salmi also synthesized that, generally, most nations adopt three major types of strategy for establishing world-class universities: upgrading a small number of existing universities, merging existing institutions into a new university, or creating a new one (*ibid*).

In response to the problem of building a world-class university efficiently, several Asian countries and regions have chosen to invest in research universities and centres to lift their volume of research output in order to move up the global rankings quickly (Shin, 2009; Marginson, 2010). Several excellence programmes have been created in East Asia: in 1998 mainland China approved a special funding programme to build research universities as part of its 985 project; the South Korean government supported the 1999 Brain Korea 21 (BK21) programme; and in 2001, the Japanese government established a plan to foster around 30 universities to become "world-class" institutions (Oba, 2008; Shin, 2009; Yonezawa, 2010). Similarly, the "Five Year – 50 Billion Excellence Initiative" was launched in Taiwan China, to build at least one university as one of the world's top 100

Q. Wang, Y. Cheng, & N.C. Liu (eds.), Building World-Class Universities: Different Approaches to a Shared Goal, 35–53.

universities in five years and at least 15 key departments or cross-campus research centres as the top research institutes in Asia in ten years (Hou, 2012).

These excellence programmes are clearly aimed at building at least one world-class university within a period of time through the policy of funding concentration, which significantly enhances a chosen university's volume of research papers, international collaborations and exchanges. On the other hand, the effectiveness of this approach and its impact on Asian higher education have becoming a challenging issue inside individual countries, because it raises matters such as overemphasizing meritocratic culture and disseminating research output internationally (Shin, 2009).

The main purpose of the paper is to compare the goals, funding policy and selection criteria of the excellence programmes in Asian nations. Within wider Asian ambitions, from the political, economic and cultural perspectives, the effectiveness of Taiwan's "Five Year – 50 Billion Excellence Initiative" will be assessed as a case study and the challenges being faced, subsequently, will be discussed.

EXCELLENCE PROGRAMMES IN CHINA, JAPAN, SOUTH KOREA, AND TAIWAN

From the early 1950s onwards, most research funding in the US and the UK was allocated to a small number of elite universities, which has led to them both having a larger number of world-class universities than Asian nations. Learning from the Western experience, mainland China, Taiwan China, Japan and South Korea, started in the 1990s to develop so-called "excellence" programmes which involve allocating resources to a small number of universities to enhance their research power and their attractiveness to top students at the global level. Examples, as mentioned above, include the 985 Project in mainland China, the Brain Korea 21 programme in South Korea, the "Five year – 50 Billion Excellence Initiative" in Taiwan, and the Global 30 Project in Japan. Regarding these initiatives, many East Asian countries are demonstrating the belief that a funding concentration policy will have the same result for them as it has had for the US and the UK. However, there has been continuous debate over the effect of these policies and on the performance of the recipients of this type of funding within each nation. Yale University President Richard C. Levin observed the "excellence" trend among East Asian nations and came up with two main reasons for it. First, many of these nations understand the importance of university-based scientific research in driving economic growth. Second, they expect to "educate graduates for careers in science, industry, government, and civil society who have the intellectual breadth and critical-thinking skills to solve problems, to innovate, and to lead" (Levin, 2010).

Next, four excellence programmes in mainland China, South Korea, Japan and Taiwan are reviewed in relation to their origins and goals.

The 985 Project in Mainland China

Prompted by a concern for higher education quality and competitiveness, the Chinese government launched two major initiatives, named the 211 Project, in 1995 and the 985 Project, in 1998. Whereas 100 universities were selected to receive special funding to improve their overall performance in the 211 Project, the 985 Project was mainly aimed at establishing 10 Chinese universities in top global ranking positions in the 21st century. Regarding this, on the 100th anniversary of Peking University's establishment, the then-President Jiang stated that China needed to develop some world-class universities to assist in the modernization of Chinese society (Halachmi & Ngok, 2009; Wang, 2010). In 1998, the first nine recipients officially recognized by the Ministry of Education formed a "C9 Group" to achieve the 985 Project's global target. This programme was subsequently expanded, and in all, 39 universities were selected to receive special financial support, but no new university has been added to this list since 2007.

The second phase of the programme from 2004 to 2007 focused more on quality improvement of scientific research output. Regarding the outcomes, Wang has contended that both the 985 Project and the university ranking system "have made a significant impact on the quality of China's rapidly proliferating institutions of higher education" (Wang, 2010).

The Brain Korea 21 Programme in South Korea

To respond to concern over the low quality of Korean higher education, the Ministry of Education and Human Resources Development launched the Brain Korea 21 programme in 1999. It was aimed at producing "next generation leaders with creativity", by providing fellowship funding to graduate students, postdoctoral researchers and contracted based professors, on an institutional level (Korea Research Foundation, 2010). In the first phase, from 1999 to 2005, the Ministry of Education and Human Resources Development awarded US$1.4 billion to 67 universities with doctoral programmes, with 87.1% being allocated to science and engineering studies. During the second phase, which started in 2006, the programme will award US$2.1 billion on the basis of departmental-level excellence and university-industry links (RAND, 2010).

The Global Centre of Excellence Project in Japan

Japan's "Global Centre of Excellence" started in 2001 and was intended to foster around 30 universities to become "world-class" institutions to stimulate the national economy (Yonezawa, 2010; Oba, 2008), which is often referred to as the Global 30 Project. The selection criteria and process used mean that the government selects research units as centres of excellence, instead of institutions (and from 2006, "Global Centre of Excellence"). In 2008, the Ministry of Education, Culture, Sports, Science and Technology (MEXT) launched a further project named "Global 30" and stressed "the importance of securing a leading position for Japanese higher education in Asia through promoting internationalization of higher education and maintaining Japan's share in the international student market" (Yonezawa, 2007:3). To this end, the ministry set the goal of recruiting 300,000 international students to study in Japan by 2020. In the 2009 first round selection, the government only selected 13 universities, based on the setting of specific institutional goals and their accomplishment by a predetermined date (Yonezawa, 2010), with each being granted between US$22 million and US$44 million.

Table 1. Comparison of excellence initiative projects among mainland China, South Korea, Japan and Taiwan

	Mainland China: the 985 Project	South Korea: Brain Korea 21	Japan: the Global Centre of Excellence	Taiwan: the "Five Year – 50 Billion Excellence Initiative"
Starting year	Phase one: 1998~ 2003 Phase two: 2004~2007	Phase one: 1999~2005 Phase two: 2006~2012 (7 years)	Phase one (COE): 2002~2007 Phase two: 2008~	Phase one (Five-year 50 Billion Programme): 2006~20010 Phase two (Moving into Top Universities Programme): 2011~ 2015
Goal and Mission	To provide 39 Chinese universities with extra funding so some gain top global rankings	To cultivate global leaders	To recruit 300,000 international students	To develop at least one university as one of the world's top 100 universities in five years and 10 fields or research centres as "world-class"
Focus	Research, international reputation	PhD programmes, future leaders	Internationalization, economy	Research/ international reputation
Number of recipients	39 universities	67 universities	19 to 30 universities	11~12 universities
Total funding	US$10 billion	US$3.5 billion	US$2.5 billion	US$1.67 billion

The "Five Year – 50 Billion Excellence Initiative" in Taiwan

In response to the quest for a world-class university, the government launched the project called "Five Year – 50 Billion Programme for Developing a First-Class University and Top Research Centres", in 2006. The programme had the aim of having at least one university as one of the world's top 100 universities in five years and at least fifteen key departments or cross-campus research centres as the top in Asia in ten years (Hou, 2012; Hou et al., 2012). From 2006 to 2010, 11 universities were selected and funded through the project. The second round, from 2011 to 2015 which involved, changing the programme's name to "Moving into the Top Universities Programme", is focused more on developing 10 fields or research centres as "world-class" by 2015 (Department of Higher Education, 2011).

TAIWAN'S RESEARCH EXCELLENCE INITIATIVES

Global Competition and the Excellence Initiative in Taiwanese Higher Education

Since the 1990s, Taiwan's higher education has expanded dramatically, with respect to both the number of institutions and the number of enrolled students. As of 2011, the number of higher education institutions had increased to 165, with a total student enrolment of 1.3 million (Department of Higher Education, 2011), representing a gross enrolment ratio of 78.6%. It is evident that these quantitative increases have lifted Taiwan from the stage of mass higher education to that of universal access to higher education and generally reduced education inequality. However, the expansion has also caused several concerns, particularly how to enhance Taiwan's global competitiveness.

In response to competitiveness issue in higher education, the Taiwanese government started to reform its higher education system in the late 1990s, with a particular focus on: provision, regulation and financing (Mok, 2002). In 2002, Taiwan's Higher Education Macro Planning Commission (HEMPC) was founded by the government, with the aim of promoting Taiwan's higher education excellence. In 2003, it proposed a national plan to the government to assist a number of selected universities and research centres through concentrated investment. Subsequently, the Ministry of Education launched various types of excellence initiatives with different intended objectives, including three big projects the "Development Plan for World-Class Universities and Research Centres of Excellence", the "Teaching Excellence Initiative" and the "Academia-Industry Collaboration" (Ministry of Education, 2011a).

The foremost, was the first excellence initiative launched by the Ministry of Education, in 2005, whilst the second phase started in 2011and its title was changed to "Moving into the Top Universities" (Department of Higher Education, 2011). With a yearly total funding of US$330 million for 10 years, the recipient universities were expected to reach the rank of the top institutions around the world through infrastructure upgrading, the employment of outstanding faculty from overseas and participation in international academic collaboration. Moreover, the selected universities were encouraged to integrate various research resources, build teaching and research capacity and develop substantial collaborations with foreign prestigious universities (Ministry of Education, 2011b).

The first phase was mainly aimed at enhancing the international visibility of Taiwanese higher education by having at least one university in the world's top 100 universities within 10 years and 10 outstanding research centres or fields in the Asian top 50 within five years. In order to accelerate talent cultivation and foreign recruitment, strengthen research advantage, and foster innovation, the second phase has five specific goals: internationalizing top universities and expanding students' global perspectives, promoting research and innovation quality, building international capacity of faculty and students, strengthening collaborations between universities and industry, and enhancing graduates' competence to respond to social and market demands (Department of Higher Education, 2011).

In order to manage and execute the excellence programme effectively, the Ministry of Education developed a well-structured model in terms of policy making and implementation. Regarding this, the Advisory Committee, the University Strategic Alliance, and the University Advisory Committees are responsible for policy making at the: national, cross campus and institutional levels, respectively. Moreover, at the implementation stage, the review committee is mainly in charge of setting up review standards and criteria, reviewing proposals, and determining funding amounts and the assessment panel helps to assess the performance of institutions as well as supporting the on-site visit teams. The professional external review committee assists the assessment panel in evaluating research performance by individual field and provides the assessment panel with review outcomes as references. To increase the efficiency of individual institutions, the Ministry of Education also set up a main management office and a working group, which are responsible for quality control of implementation at the governmental and institutional levels, respectively. The working group, which consists of all institutional representatives, assists the management office in coordinating with institutions, discussing standards of quality control, and in reporting implementation progress by institutions to the Ministry of Education (see Figure 1).

Funding Allocation and Ranking Outcomes

According to the Ministry of Education, from 2006 to 2010, the National Taiwan University received US$500 million, up to 30% of the total funds available, compared to National Cheng Kung University with 17%, National Tsing Hua University, with 11.2% and National Chiao Tung University, with 8.6%. In addition, there were five recipients with less than 5% of the total. Further, only two private universities were funded initially, but one was not funded after 2008 (see Table 2).

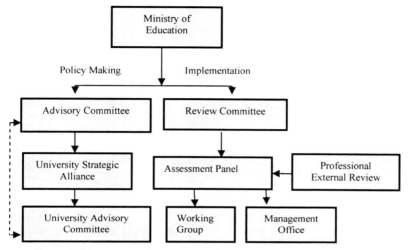

Figure 1. Management Organization of Development Plan for World-Class Universities and Research Centres of Excellence

Table 2. The Ministry of Education grants to universities (2006 to 2011)
(US$ in million)

Institutions	2006	2007	2008	2009	2010	Total five-year funding		2011
National Taiwan University	100.0	100.0	100.0	100.0	100.0	500	30%	103.3
National Cheng Kung University	56.7	56.7	56.7	56.7	56.7	283.5	17%	53.3
National Tsing Hua University	33.3	33.3	40.0	40.0	40.0	186.6	11.2%	40.0
National Chiao Tung University	26.7	26.7	30.0	30.0	30.0	143.4	8.6%	33.3
National Central University	20.0	20.0	23.3	23.3	23.3	109.9	6.6%	23.3
National Sun Yat-sen University	20.0	20.0	20.0	20.0	20.0	100	6%	13.3
National Yang Ming University	16.7	16.7	16.7	16.7	16.7	83.5	5%	16.7
National Chung Hsing University	13.3	13.3	15.0	15.0	15.0	71.6	4.3%	10.0
National Taiwan University of Technology and Science	10.0	10.0	6.7	6.7	7.3	40.7	2.4%	6.7
National Cheng Chi University	6.8	10.0	6.7	6.7	6.7	36.9	2.2%	6.7
Chang Gung University	10.0	10.0	6.7	6.7	6.7	40.1	2.4%	6.7
Yuan Ze University	7.7	10.0	–	–	–	17.7	1.1%	–
National Taiwan Normal University	–	–	–	–	–	0		6.7

Source: Department of Higher Education (2011)

According to some global rankings, such as the Academic Ranking of World Universities (ARWU), Quacquarelli Symonds (QS) World University Rankings and the Higher Education Evaluation and Accreditation Council of Taiwan (HEEACT), there are around seven to eight Taiwan institutions in the top 500, including: the National Taiwan University, the National Cheng Kung University, the National Tsing Hua University, the National Chiao Tung University, Chang Gung University, the National Central University and the National Yang Ming University, and the National Sun Yat Sen University. Only Chang Gung University is a private institution.

It emerges that the institutions in the top 500 have all been recipients of the "Five Year – 50 Billion Excellence Initiative" by the Ministry of Education (see Table 3). They shared 90% of the total funding in the QS ranking, compared with 88.2% in the ARWU ranking, and 83.9% in the HEEACT ranking. Moreover, the top three recipients in the top 500 in the three rankings are all national universities and to the public's surprise, Chang Gung University, with amongst the lowest extra funding at US$40.1 million, performed better than many of the other recipients. However, generally speaking, there is a high level of correlation between the three global ranking outcomes and Ministry of Education funding, i.e. the greater the additional funding the institution gains, the higher it ranks.

Assessment of Academic Output

To assess their actual performance, Taiwanese institutions will be reviewed first on three key indicators, including research, internationalization, and university and industry collaboration.

Research outputs   According to the Department of Education, the number of Science Citation Index (SCI) papers produced each year by the 11 selected universities grew by 49% and Social Science Citation Index (SSCI) papers by 172% between 2005 and 2010. The number of highly cited (HiCi) papers increased by 129% within five years (see Table 4), but the number of papers published in Nature and Science was declining slightly.

Internationalization   In addition to the volume of research papers, the recipients were expected to upgrade their infrastructure and facilities, to hire outstanding international faculty, and to collaborate with foreign universities in international academic programmes. As Table 5 shows, the number of international degree-seeking students has increased by 79% from 2005 to 2010, and that of exchange students by 193%. In addition, the number of international conferences held and academic collaborations in research has grown approximately two and a half times. When it comes to the recruitment of international scholars, there is a tremendous progress in the growth rate of up to 700 % (see Table 6).

Table 3. Ranks of Taiwan universities in the ARWU, QS and HEEACT global rankings (2006–2010)

Global rankings	Institutions	2006	2007	2008	2009	2010	% of Total fund
QS	National Taiwan University	108	102	124	95	94	90%
	National Tsing Hua University	343	334	281	223	196	
	National Cheng Kung University	386	336	354	281	283	
	National Chiao Tung University	401–500	401–500	401–500	389	327	
	National Yang Ming University	392	401–500	341	306	290	
	National Taiwan University of Technology and Science	401–500	401–500	401–500	351	–	
	National Central University	401–500	398	401–500	401–500	398	
	National Sun Yat-sen University	–	401–500	401–500	401–500	–	
ARWU	National Taiwan University	181	172	164	150	127	88.2%
	National Tsing Hua University	346	317	308	297	314	
	National Chiao Tung University	440	327	322	327	313	
	National Cheng Kung University	384	367	350	262	256	
	Chang Gung University	–	–	426	408	406	
	National Central University	–	501	493	441	443	
	National Yang Ming University	479	471	498	449	447	
HEEACT	National Taiwan University	Starting 2007	185	141	102	114	83.9%
	National Cheng Kung University		360	328	307	302	
	National Tsing Hua University		429	366	347	346	
	National Chiao Tung University		471	463	456	479	
	Chang Gung University		–	–	479	493	
	National Central University		–	–	483	–	
	National Yang Ming University		–	475	493	–	

Source: ARWU (http://www.arwu.org/); QS (http://www.topuniversities.com/university-rankings); HEEACT (http://ranking.heeact.edu.tw/en-us/2011/homepage/)

Table 4. Publications of the 11 selected universities

Research performance	2005 (Prior to the programme)	2010 (The 5th year of the programme)	Increase rate
Number of SCI papers	11320	16906	49%
Number of SSCI papers	589	1589	170%
Number of A&HCI	29	79	172%
Nature & Science	15	14	–7%
Number of HiCi papers in the last 10 years	294	673	129%

Source: Department of Higher Education (2011)

Table 5. Number of international students of the 11 selected universities

Internationalization of international students	2005	2010	Increase rate
Number of international students	4033	6973	79%
Number of exchange students	629	1843	193%
Number of international conferences	180	405	125%
Number of international collaborations	171	331	94%

Source: Department of Higher Education (2011)

Table 6. Number of international scholars at the 11 selected universities

Internationalization of faculty	2005	2009	Increase rate
Number of top researchers serving as project leaders in research centres	220	431	1.95%
Number of international scholars	182	1,276	700%

Source: Department of Higher Education (2011)

University and industry collaboration   One of the assessment indicators of the programme is what percentage of research outcomes were transferred into industry and benefited society through university-industry links. In 2010, the total funding generating from collaboration between universities and industry at the 11 selected universities was close to US$679 million and the income generated from intellectual property more than tripled (see Table 7).

Table 7. Volume of university – industry collaborations by the
11 selected universities

Results of industry-university cooperation projects	2005	2010	Increase rate
Funding generating from industry-university collaborations (including commissioned training programmes)	US$528.8 millions	US$679.4 millions	28%
Funds from enterprise sectors for industry-university collaborations (excluding the commissioned training programmes)	US$44.7 millions	US$55.7 millions	25%
Amount derived from intellectual property rights	US$4.2 millions	US$15.8 millions	276%
Numbers of patents and new products	320	736	137%
Numbers of patent licences and the licensed number of models	86	304	253%

Source: Department of Higher Education (2011)

Meta Assessment

In order to measure its actual effectiveness and impact on Taiwanese higher education, the Research, Development and Evaluation Commission conducted a reassessment of the Ministry of Education's Excellence Programme in terms of mission and goals, review criteria and process, and impact at the end of 2010. The study adopted both qualitative and quantitative approaches to collect opinions from eight of the 11 recipient universities and from four international scholars of higher education. A survey targeting 138 top administrators from 11 universities and 30 reviewers was also conducted. All respondents were asked to fill out the five-scale questionnaires and present their opinions regarding four categories, including the goals, criteria, outcomes and impacts. The response rates were 42.8% and 36.7%, respectively (RDEC, 2010).

Mission and goal Over 80% of the respondents agreed that some of the missions and goals for enhancing the internationalization and excellence of Taiwan's higher education were appropriate, namely: improving the infrastructure of universities, cultivating top talent and increasing the volume and quality of publications. However, there is a lower level of agreement on the goal of setting up incubators on campus, with an average score of 3.9 from the institutions and 3.5 from the review panel. Compared with the other expected goals, both types of respondents disagreed on using global rankings as one of the measures (see Table 8).

Table 8. Respondents' attitude towards the mission of the programme

	Items	Institutions		Review panel	
		Mean	SD	Mean	SD
Qualitative	Internationalization and excellence in higher education	4.4746	0.6527	4.4545	0.5222
	Quality improvement of organizational governance and management	4.2712	0.7151	4.1818	0.6030
	Average	4.3729	0.6893	4.3182	0.5679
Quantitative	Number of top academic talents and professional	4.4310	0.6783	4.2727	0.6467
	Number of academic outcomes and research outputs	4.3276	0.9250	4.3636	0.5045
	Recruitment of top international scholars and researchers	4.3509	0.7674	4.1818	0.6030
	Academic exchanges and collaboration with domestic and foreign universities and research centres	4.2281	0.7324	*3.9091*	*0.7006*
	Number of university incumbent centres	*3.9123*	*0.9118*	*3.5455*	*0.8202*
	Average	4.2509	0.8235	4.0545	0.7050
	Overall	4.2867	0.7879	4.1299	0.6757

Source: The Research, Development and Evaluation Commission (RDEC) (2010)

According to Table 10, the institutional respondents tended to agree strongly on the statements of the need "to enhance the quality of university research and innovation and international visibility" and "to enhance the academic environment and quality of provision" positively. In fact, institutional respondents agreed more on items such as "to enhance the quality of university research and innovation and international visibility" and "to enhance academic environment and quality of provision" more than the other type. Moreover, the average scores on three statements regarding "outcomes of global rankings" were the lowest. In other words, both types of respondent didn't consider "having top ranked universities" as one of the expected outcomes (see Table 9).

Review criteria and process Most respondents agreed that recipients should be reviewed in terms of teaching as well as research. Regarding the review criteria, the institutional respondents tended to be more negative than the review panel (see Table 10). As to the review team, procedures, and control model, many institutional contributors questioned the professionalism and qualifications of the review panel and criticized aspects of the audit system, such as "submission of mid

Table 9. Respondents' attitudes toward expected outcomes

Items	Institutions		Review panel	
	Mean	SD	Mean	SD
At least one university ranked top 100 in the ARWU, QS and HEEACT global rankings within 10 years	3.5424	1.0879	3.8182	0.9816
At least one university ranked top 50 in the ARWU, QS and HEEACT global rankings within 15-20 years	3.3390	1.0766	3.5455	0.9342
At least ten fields or research centres ranked top in Asia in the ARWU, QS and HEEACT global rankings within five years	3.7119	1.1604	4.0909	0.5394
To enhance the quality of university research and innovation and international visibility	4.5424	0.5966	4.2727	0.6467
To attract top academic researchers and professionals from industry	4.2712	0.7388	4.0909	0.7006
To form substantial collaboration with foreign research academies and centres	4.2881	0.6708	3.9091	0.8312
To develop an objective assessment framework and granting model for institutions applying excellence projects	4.3051	0.7011	4.1818	0.9816
To enhance the academic environment and quality of provision	4.5593	0.5341	4.4545	0.5222
To integrate interdisciplinary research resources	4.2203	0.7208	3.8182	0.7508
To enhance overall national competitiveness	4.3898	0.6700	4.0000	0.7746

Source: RDEC (2010)

Table 10. Respondents' attitudes toward review criteria

Items		Institutions		Review panel	
		Mean	SD	Mean	SD
Governance and management		4.0207	0.9663	4.1455	0.8259
Infrastructure (equipment, facilities, internet, student dorms, international student house, library, etc.)	E-classroom and IT infrastructure	4.3621	0.6407	3.9091	0.7006
	Average	4.5115	0.5764	4.3333	0.7773
	(1) Internationalization	4.1186	0.7675	3.8182	0.6030
	(2) Financial resources	4.0169	0.8406	3.6364	0.5045
Research and teaching	(3) Alumni performance	4.1186	0.767	3.5455	0.6876
	Average	4.1849	0.7703	4.0918	0.7192

Source: RDEC (2010)

reports every three months", "number of on-site visits by external reviewers", and "no flexibility for funding allocation and accounting system" (see Tables 11 and 12).

Table 11. Respondents' attitude towards the review panel

Items	Institutions		Review panel	
	Mean	*SD*	*Mean*	*SD*
Composition of the review panel (academia, government, and industry)	4.0545	0.5242	*3.8182*	*0.6030*
Professionalism of the review panel	*3.8182*	*0.6963*	4.0000	0.6325
Schedule and timing for on-site visits	*3.8364*	*0.7395*	*3.9000*	*0.5676*

Source: RDEC (2010)

Table 12. Respondents' attitudes towards the review and control model

Items	Institutions		Review panel	
	Mean	*SD*	*Mean*	*SD*
Number of on-site visits by external reviewers	3.4068	0.7904	3.9091	0.5394
Submission of mid reports every three months	2.8983	1.0119	3.1818	0.8739

Source: RDEC (2010)

Impact on higher education Most respondents agreed with "the programme assisted recipients to enhance international visibility", "developing academic features" and "improving their ranks in global ranking". However, there was a slight divergence between universities and reviewers' attitudes towards "carrying out social responsibility and sharing the pubic with academic output", with 86% of institutional respondents expressing the belief they did as compared to 72% of reviewers. Both types of respondents also agreed that the programme led to several problems, such as "research is [esteemed] over teaching on campus", and that "the gap in educational resources between recipients and non-recipients" is widening faster than ever (see Table 13). Generally speaking, the respondents from the review panel were more pessimistic than those from institutions about the impact of the programme on Taiwanese higher education.

DISCUSSION

Public Concerns over Goal Achievement and Teaching Quality

The global competitiveness of universities has turned into a complicated issue of balancing the teaching and research missions of an institution. Moreover, there has been widespread discussion of the appropriateness of various assessment instruments, including rankings, overall higher education quality and an individual

Table 13. Respondents' attitudes towards the impact on higher education

Items	Institutions		Review panel	
	Mean	SD	Mean	SD
Emphasis on research over teaching	2.9310	1.1373	3.2727	0.7862
Emphasis graduate education over undergraduate education	2.7458	1.1976	2.9091	0.8312
Emphasis sciences over social sciences and humanities	2.6607	1.2399	2.9091	0.9439
Widening the gap in resources among institutions	3.1864	1.2659	3.2727	1.1909
Reduction of general education budget	2.4407	1.1028	2.5455	1.1282
Average	2.7584	1.20155	2.9091	1.02355
Enhancement of excellence campuses	4.1864	0.8803	4.0000	0.4472
Strengthening of institutional features and academic performance	4.3559	0.8461	4.0909	0.5394
Enhancing international visibility	4.4576	0.8371	4.2727	0.4671
Improving their ranks in the global rankings	4.4915	0.8978	4.1818	0.6030
Carrying on more social accountability and academic duties	4.3051	0.8760	3.6364	0.6742
Average	4.40253	0.86425	4.04545	0.570925

Source: RDEC (2010)

university's performance. Although the number of Taiwanese higher education institutions moving into the top 500 has been steadily growing and the number of publications has increased significantly, the excellence programme has provoked severe criticism over its indicators and purposes from Taiwan college presidents. Similarly, the Taiwanese general public has expressed concern about the concentration on the performance of a few selective institutions in both research output and teaching quality through targeted investment, for the targeted institutions are expected to improve upon the latter as well (Hou, 2012).

Moreover, many non-recipients are worried that research-oriented indicators might be adopted as the only criteria in the selection process for the second stage of the Excellence Programme in 2011. Some have contended that, the definitions used for "world-class university" and "top research centres" are variously interpreted. Furthermore, the Ministry of Education has not identified clearly which global ranking should be used as evidence for goal-achieving. Most important of all, the general public has voiced its alarm that teaching quality will be sacrificed owing to the new reward systems. According to HEEACT programme accreditation outcomes in the first cycle, the percentage of accredited programmes in two recipients was lower than 90% (Hou, 2012).

Rankings or not Rankings

It is evident that the rankings have their methodological limitations and in particular, they have led to what Neubauer has termed "reductionism". That is, they can lead to an unbalanced campus culture of research over teaching, whereby the emphasis shifts to the accumulated publication indexes and the use of reputational surveys (Neubauer, 2010) and hence the multi-functioning nature of a healthy university is lost. The QS ranking minimizes this problem with the use of a survey of employers, as well as university faculty/student ratios. However, no list of the strongest universities can capture all the intangible, life-changing and paradigm-shifting work that universities undertake. A global ranking cannot even fully capture some of the basics of university activity – learning and teaching quality. Besides, "using citation counts as a way of measuring excellence also presents serious problems", because these data "emphasize material in English and journals that are readily available in the larger academic systems", like in US, UK. Many studies also show that those with medical schools and departments in the hard sciences generally have a significant advantage, because these fields generate more external funding and researchers in them publish more articles (Altbach, 2006).

In the survey reported on above it was found that most respondents disagreed with rankings, but nevertheless, they are still having a considerable impact on higher education institutions in Taiwan. First, the fact that an increasing number of Taiwanese universities have been moving into the top 500 in the global rankings demonstrates that the efficacy and success of the Ministry of Education's Excellence Initiative programme. More and more Taiwanese institutions, including teaching-oriented universities, are encouraged to use the performance indicators of the global rankings as a benchmark to set their institutional long-term goals, such as "Moving into the Top 500". In fact, many have changed their institutional policies in some respect, such as Tam Kang University whose board of directors requested university administrators make a self-improvement plan based on each indicator of the HEEACT's global ranking outcomes (Hou, 2012).

Second, there is indeed a high positive correlation between the global ranking of institutions and their level of government funding. This suggests that the global rankings will marginalize teaching focused institutions, leaving them on the "knowledge periphery" of Taiwan's higher education system. In addition, the global ranking inevitably causes fiercer competition between universities, resulting in contestation over the allocation of government resources between research-oriented and teaching-type institutions. Moreover as higher education becomes more globalized the pressure from international competition and public accountability will accelerate the importance of accreditation and ranking in Taiwan.

Hawkins has advised that the excellence initiatives in Taiwan and other Asian nations should be re-examined to see what they have achieved thus far and whether: the continuous investment was worth it, whether they can be restructured to better achieve the goals and whether there should be a "mini" excellence initiative to help the smaller higher education institutions or private institutions (2010, personal communication). At the same time, there should be money to encourage innovation and excellence in teaching independently from the excellence initiative (Salmi, 2010, personal communication). In fact, Taiwan government has provided other resources for other institutions to permit teaching quality enhancement.

A world-class university is a university with world-class people, especially in research. Asian excellence initiatives are already hunting for talent globally and their ability to deliver supportive work environments and good infrastructure (as well as agreeable salaries) makes them a formidable competitor with Western institutions for obtaining the best people. All in all, if Asian nations still aim to develop one or more world-class universities, they still have to fund only a few targeted schools with extra money to help reach that goal. That is, it will be impossible for all institutions to have this status (Morse, 2010, personal communication) and in fact, it will be available only to a privileged few.

CONCLUSION

"Competitiveness" and "concentrated investment" are two principles for higher education policy making in East Asia and it is inevitable that universities will continue to monitor closely their position in university rankings. However, there is little that most universities can do to improve its position in rankings in the short term. The way to climb the rankings is to become attractive to top staff and students, develop key research areas, engage internationally, and have enough resources to do things properly. These, we believe, are all things that well-run universities should be doing anyway.

Understandably, this study's findings concur with the view that the more nations invest in targeted institutions, the more they achieve. For example, mainland China's increased funding has led to more output in papers, internationalization and excellence. However, the financial sustainability of these investments is a big challenge for Asian nations, because "striving to achieve excellence should be an on-going goal regardless of the world-class university idea" (Hawkins, 2010, personal communication). For those who worry about the gap in quality and size, there will always be gaps in complex systems. The case of Taiwan has demonstrated that these worries regarding inequality are turning into a reality. However, although the gap between leading and following universities may grow, we agree that these nations need world-class universities and research centres.

Asian universities that act in this way will, over the medium term, become significant players on the world stage and hence, feature strongly in the world rankings. However, they are urged to approach the problems in that order, not the other way around, that is, a high ranking should come as a result of the pursuit of comprehensive excellence and not as a barren auditing exercise aimed simply at acquiring the badge of being a world-class university.

REFERENCES

Altbach, P. G. (2006). The dilemmas of ranking. *International Higher Education, 42*. Retrieved February 22, 2006, from http://www.bc.edu/bc_org/avp/soe/cihe/newsletter/Number42/p2_Altbach.htm

Department of Higher Education. (2011). *Five Year – 50 Billion Programme for Developing First-Class University and Top Research Centers*. Retrieved April 1, 2011, from http://www.edu.tw/high/itemize.aspx?itemize_sn=3520&pages=1&site_content_sn=1234

Halachmi, A., & Ngok, K. (2009). Of sustainability and excellence: Chinese academia at a crossroads. *Public Administration Review, 69*(December), 13–20. Retrieved April 10, 2012, from http://gms.sysu.edu.cn/kyglxt/lunwen/uploads/keyan/2304.pdf

Hawkins, J. (2010, June). Personal communication.

Higher Education Evaluation and Accreditation Council of Taiwan. (2011). *Performance Ranking of Scientific Papers for World Universities*. Retrieved from http://ranking.heeact.edu.tw/en-us/2011/homepage

Hou, Y. C. (2012). Impact of excellence programmes on Taiwan higher education in terms of quality assurance and academic excellence -examining the conflicting role of Taiwan's accrediting agencies. *Asian Pacific Education Review, 13*(1), 77–88.

Hou, Y. C., Morse, R., & Chiang, C. L. (2012). An analysis of positions mobility in global rankings: Making institutional strategic plans and positioning for building world-class universities. *Higher Education Research & Development*. (In press).

Korea Research Foundation. (2010). Official website. Retrieved January, 2011, from http://www.krf.or.kr/KHPapp/eng/mainc.jsp

Levin, R. C. (2010). *The Rise of Asia's Universities. President Levin's Speeches and Statements*. Retrieved January 1, 2011, from http://opac.yale.edu/president/message.aspx?id=91

Marginson, S. (2010). Higher education in the Asia-pacific: Rise of the Confucian model. *Evaluation in Higher Education, 4*(2), 21–53.

Ministry of Education. (2011a). *Education in Taiwan 2010–2011*. Retrieved April 1, 2011, from http://120.96.85.10/news055/2011070702.asp?c=0200

Ministry of Education. (2011b). Developing world-class universities and valuing higher education. *Higher Education, Technological and Vocational Newsletter*. Retrieved April 1, 2011, from http://120.96.85.10/news055/2011070702.asp?c=0200

Mok, K. H. (2002). Reflecting globalization effects on local policy: Higher education reform in Taiwan. *Journal of Education Policy, 15*(6), 637–660.

Morse, R. (2010, November 23). Personal communication.

Neubauer, D. (2010). Ten globalization challenges to higher education quality and quality assurance. *Evaluation in Higher Education, 4*(1), 13–38.

Oba, J. (2008). Creating world-class universities in Japan: Policy and initiatives. *Policy Futures in Education, 6*(5), 629–640. Retrieved April 10, 2012, from http://dx.doi.org/10.2304/pfie.2008.6.5.629

Quacquarelli Symonds. (2011). *World University Rankings*. http://www.topuniversities.com/university-rankings.

RAND. (2010). *Evaluating the BK 21 Programme*. Retrieved April 1, 2011, from http://www.rand.org/content/dam/rand/pubs/research_briefs/2008/RAND_RB9332.pdf

Salmi, J. (2009). *The Challenges of Establishing World-Class Universities*. Washington, DC: The World Bank.

Salmi, J. (2010). Personal communication.

Shanghai Jiao Tong University. (2011). *Academic Ranking of World Universities (ARWU)*. http://www.arwu.org/

Shin, J. C. (2009). Building world-class research university: The Brain Korea 21 project. *Higher Education, 58*(5), 669–688.

The Research, Development and Evaluation Commission. (2010). *Meta Evaluation on Development of a World-class University and Top Research Centre Programme*. (RDEC-CON-099-001). Unpublished.

Wang, G. H. (2010). *China's Higher Education Reform*. Retrieved February 16, 2011, from http://www.chinacurrents.com/spring_2010/cc_wang.htm

Yonezawa, A. (2007). Japanese flagship universities at a crossroads. *Higher Education, 54*(4), 483–499.
Yonezawa, A. (2010, June). Personal communication. Japan: JIHEE.

AFFILIATIONS

Yung-Chi Hou (Angela)
Graduate School of Educational Leadership and Development,
Fu Jen Catholic University, Taiwan
Dean of the Office of Research and Development
Higher Education Evaluation and Accreditation Council of Taiwan, Taiwan

Martin Ince
Martin Ince Communications Limited
London, UK

Chung-Lin Chiang
Fu Jen Catholic University, Taiwan

NIKOLAY SKVORTSOV, OLGA MOSKALEVA AND
JULIA DMITRIEVA

WORLD-CLASS UNIVERSITIES

Experience and Practices of Russian Universities

INTRODUCTION

Russia is undergoing a socio-economic transition to a new innovative economy, which requires new systematic reform. Throughout this transformation process, Russian higher education institutions are expected to expand their research activities. Research has, however, seldom been a competitive tradition or priority in Russian universities, which has impacted upon the quality of education (Dezhina, 2011). Given the less impressive performance of Russian universities in global higher education, the Russian government has initiated a series of policies to integrate research and education, ultimately to develop world-class education and research in Russia. This paper provides an account of these national policies and approaches, and analyses issues and challenges facing Russia and its higher education sector.

RESEARCH IN RUSSIAN HIGHER EDUCATION

There are more than 1100 higher education institutions in Russia. Among them, 33.5% are granted the status of university, 18.5% are academies and 48% are institutes.[1] In total, more than seven million students are studying at Russian higher education institutions, with more than 5.8 million students in state public universities and more than 2.6 million students under budget financing.

During the Soviet period, there were only public institutions in the higher education sector. Since the breakdown of the Soviet Union, the higher education system has undergone reform. At the beginning of the 1990s, the higher education system in Russia included both public and private institutions. In the Soviet period, the number and size of universities was strictly limited. The other institutions were named "institutes". This did not necessarily mean that the level and quality of education in those institutes was insufficient. But there were only a limited number of higher education institutions with university status in the country with strong domestic and international reputations. Those of these universities within today's Russia were mainly in Moscow, Saint Petersburg, Kazan, and Novosibirsk. At the beginning of 1990s, the number of higher education institutions increased and former institutes were upgraded and granted with university status. This has

Q. Wang, Y. Cheng, & N.C. Liu (eds.), Building World-Class Universities: Different Approaches to a Shared Goal, 55–69.

brought serious challenges, as some of the institutes did not correspond to the norms of the university as it is widely understood. The main reason for such public reforms was to make all the institutions putatively equal for state purposes.

It has been argued that research has never been a competitive advantage of Russian universities (Schiermeier, 2010). Higher education institutions and the Academy of Sciences (a research powerhouse for most of the Soviet period) have not been closely integrated. Rather, there has been a clear-cut division of responsibilities: universities are traditionally confined to teaching and learning, while fundamental research is mainly conducted by the Academy of Sciences, the prestigious scientific and research institution in the country, and in industrial sectors. According to the Centre for Science Research and Statistics (2011), while progress has been observed, higher education institutions' involvement in research production is still low: there were 603 higher education institutions engaged in research and development (R&D) activities, only 17.05% of all R&D performing institutions in Russia in 2009. Only 6.53% of all the personnel participating in R&D are university researchers. Higher education institutions counts for 7.35% of Russia's total domestic R&D expenditure. In other words, university research has not played a primary role or been considered a core activity in both the Soviet and the post-Soviet systems.

It is in this context that the government of the Russian Federation has initiated and implemented a series of policies to develop research and higher education institutions and to integrate science and education over the past ten years.

NEW NATIONAL APPROACHES TO BUILDING WORLD-CLASS UNIVERSITIES

The first attempt to integrate higher education and basic research can be traced back to the late 1990s when the government adopted the programmes titled "State support for the integration of higher education and basic research 1997–2000" and "Basic Research and Higher Education". Universities managed to train qualified researchers, and to establish research and education centres. However, in addition to limited funding received, these programmes focused on building partnerships between the Academy of Sciences and universities, thus universities' research performance was only strengthened to certain extent (Dezhina, 2011).

In the mid 2000s, the government of the Russian Federation reiterated that the configuration of R&D needed to be changed, and science and education should be integrated and balanced. The government has consistently and actively invested in higher education sector. The budget financing has doubled from US$2.8 billion in 2006 to US$5.5 billion in 2009. Between 2010 and 2012, the budget for the innovation and infrastructure development in higher education institutions amounts US$310 million. In addition, a series of reforms has been initiated, including developing the Innovative University programme, establishing several "federal universities", supporting the National Research University programme along with a number of Targeted Federal Programmes. A group leading universities has also actively engaged in forming strategic plans and integrating into international networks. It is believed that such reforms will lead to more effective results than that of the old education system, will enhance higher education quality and ultimately improve Russian universities' competitiveness in the world economy.

Developing Innovative University Programme

Between 2006 and 2008, the Innovative University programme was implemented in the framework of the National Priority Project[2] by the Ministry of Education and Science of the Russian Federation (MESRF) to promote innovation in the higher education sector. Two years' funding was granted to selected universities to develop new educational techniques and materials, to provide research and professional training to faculty members, and to improve infrastructure and equipment. Through a competitive application process, 57 universities were selected as innovative universities. Altogether, the government financial support amounts to more than US$1 billion (MESRF, 2012a).

Creating Federal Universities and Business Schools

Within the National Priority Project, other programmes include organizing federal universities and creating high-class business schools.

The Federal University Programme was introduced in 2005 to optimize regional educational structure and strengthening national university network (MESRF, 2012b). Receiving special status and funds from the federal government, the strategic mission of a federal university is to develop competitive human capital in the fields of education, science, culture and management, to promote both domestic and international academic exchange, to integrate research and education, to address strategic problems of innovative development, and to improve the competitiveness of leading industries within the regions (Dezhina, 2011). The selected federal universities are expected to upgrade education and research performance and to reach a position within the top 100 universities worldwide by 2020 (Spiesberg, 2011). Two pilot universities, the Siberian Federal University and the Southern Federal University were formed in 2006, through merging several regional universities with different profiles in the federal districts, thus becoming the largest institution in the country. So far, there are eight federal universities in Russia. The total budget for top universities is US$2.3 billion between 2010 and 2012. For Federal Universities it amounts for US$0.6 billion (MESRF, 2011).

In addition, two elite business schools were established in 2006, to address the country's critical demand for experienced personnel with executive-level training. The two schools are the Skolkovo School of Management, located in Moscow and built from scratch, and the Graduate School of Management at Saint Petersburg State University (MESRF, 2012c).

Implementing the National Research University Programme

In August 2009, the Ministry of Education and Science launched the Programme National Research University. As part of the governmental effort to modernize Russia's education and research system, this programme is intended to develop national research universities across the country. Specifically, the programme aims to enhance the quality of Russia's higher education and research, to create opportunities for technological advancements and to boost Russia's economic growth (Schiermeier, 2010).

National research universities, selected from among Russian higher education institutions, are expected to play a leadership role in strengthening university research. The main features of these selected universities are to generate innovative knowledge, to develop knowledge and technology transfer, to conduct both fundamental and applied research, to build an effective system of postgraduate education and to develop advanced training programmes. In other words, the mission of the selected national research universities is to contribute to national science and technology development, to train qualified workforce, and thus to improve Russia's competitiveness in the global arena.

A nationwide competition was organized to select the universities both in 2009 and 2010. 12 out of 110 participating universities were granted the status of "national research universities" in 2009, and 15 out of 151 universities were granted the status in 2010. Each selected university will receive federal funding (up to US$60 million) for the first five years, to support the innovative development programmes in priority fields selected by the universities (MESRF, 2009; Smolentseva, 2010).

In November 2009, the Russian Parliament passed legislation on the special and unique status for the two leading universities, that is, Lomonosov Moscow State University and Saint Petersburg State University. Under federal government budgeting, these two universities are entitled to employ additional admission criteria and examinations and issue their own degree certificates.

Training and Attracting Young Scientists

Another important programme, which aims to develop research and education in the higher education sector and to tackle the ageing of scientific personnel in particular, has been introduced within the framework of the Federal Targeted Programmes[3] and is called "Scientists and Science Educators for an Innovative Russia". A total of US$3 billion will have been invested between 2009 and 2013, of which 90% is granted by the federal government. More than 50% of the financial support is expected to support research projects, which involves a significant number of young scientists and students. The rest of the funding will be spent on upgrading infrastructure and research equipment for students and scientists (MESRF, 2012d). Despite arguments regarding difficulties in implementing the project and insufficient coordination, this programme has assisted the development of young scientists and increased their participation in research and education. Statistics show that 14,500 young scientists involved in the program in 2009, 34,400 in 2010 and 35,600 in 2011. In addition, more than 9,000 research contracts have been awarded annually.

Furthermore, this programme also aims at attracting young Russian scientists working abroad to direct research projects in Russia, through a programme called "Grant Opportunities for Russian Scientists Living Abroad". Through sustainable cooperation with Russian scientists who work and live abroad, the programme intends to promote the exchange of skills and experience for national scientific development, as well as to build scientific networks. For example, in 2011, 84 research projects are selected and financed with up to US$69,000 for each project per year.[4]

Developing Networks of University Leadership

The above-mentioned universities have formed a network and become a basic platform to discuss issues and provide solutions in the field of higher education in Russia. The network activity leads to the creation of the Association of Leading Universities in Russia, initiated by several university rectors. The member universities include Saint Petersburg State University, Ural Federal University, Higher School of Economics, Lomonosov Moscow State University, and other federal universities and national research universities. Its current president is the rector of Saint Petersburg State University, Nikolay Kropachev.

The main task of the association is to address problems and issues facing top universities, and to provide governments with briefings and proposals to tackle urgent challenges. One of the challenges the association has been working on concerns transparency issues in the higher education sector and the state examinations system.

Meanwhile, another important organization for universities is the Russian Rectors' Union. It is an all-Russia public organization founded in 1992. It currently brings together upwards of 1000 rectors and presidents of public higher education institutions and 100 rectors and presidents from the most prestigious non-government higher education institutions.

The Union intends to coordinate Russian higher education development and connections in the fields of economics, law, humanities, and sciences. Among the key tasks of the union are the discussion of higher education development, in particular education and research, to provide policy recommendations to relevant government organizations, to maintain higher education quality, to strengthen the authority of the national education system in Russia and beyond its borders (the Russian Rectors' Union, 2012).

The union's core members meet with the Prime Minister and members of the Russian Government every year. These meetings end with the adoption of new government protocols, which to a great extent frame the work of the government authorities supervising the sphere of education, as well as the Russian Rector's Union, for the next year.

The Union takes an active part in developing legislation, by interacting directly with the State Duma and the Federation Council of the Federal Assembly. All drafts of laws regulating legal relations in the sphere of education and higher education undergo scrutiny from the Russian Rectors' Union and mandatory discussion at the regional councils of rectors.

Integrating Higher Education with Business Sector

It is also worth pointing out that the Russian government has adopted strategies to develop education and science through integrating the business sector and through collaborating in international science and educational activities.

According to Federal Law, higher education institutions and research organizations have special rights in terms of establishing commercial entities. The main aim is to convert intellectual property into economic development. It is estimated that about 1000 such entities will have been built by the end of 2012, most of which will be established within higher education institutions. These entities are small commercial organizations with, typically, ten or more qualified staff, and provide the opportunity to earn mid-level salaries for faculty members. For example, Saint Petersburg State University has been strongly involved in this project, as the university believes that commercial entities or companies offer opportunities both students and researchers and provide proper equipment and space to conduct research studies. Up to 2011, three companies were created within the university, that is, Saint Petersburg State University Centre for Geology Limited Liability Company, Saint Petersburg State University R&D Centre of Information Technologies Limited Liability Company, and the Innovative Centre of Transport Researches Limited Liability Company. The production of these entities caters to market demands. To support further innovation reforms, the university plans to establish business incubators within the university, so as to open new possibilities and create additional facilities for researchers. Such reform aims at encouraging young scientists to engage in research, to build up their competitiveness in the modern market economy and to seek possible investors for further development.

In addition, several government regulations are targeted to enhance higher education institutions' research capacity and integrate R&D within the wider Russian economy. These regulations include the following:
- to develop modern competitive high technology and productions through collaboration between higher education institutions and economic organizations in the field of R&D;
- to provide state support to develop higher education institutions' innovative infrastructure and innovative entrepreneurships;
- to create world-class research laboratories by inviting and attracting world leading scientists.

To realize such developments and support R&D in universities, solid financial support for research is required. A total of 82 higher education institutions have become winners of competitive funding under these government regulations and laws. 12 universities in particular have benefited from the three above-mentioned regulations. There have been several other programmes of innovation development sponsored by state owned companies. The total budget of these projects increased from US$0.7 billion in 2010 to US$2.8 billion in 2011 alone.

A Summary of Russian National Reforms

Global competition in the educational services market has brought about new challenges in knowledge creation. It has been argued worldwide that, in a knowledge-based economy, research and innovation determines a nation's competitiveness and its position in the global market. Meanwhile, universities are leaders in education and research processes and play a role in the transfer of ideas into operational innovation. In particular, elite higher education institutions in any education system take a leading role in participating in international competition. In other words, one of the priorities that education policy needs to observe in order best to serve the nation is to build world-class universities with strong competitiveness. A world-class university typically exhibits a range of features, e.g. a concentration of talent, an abundance of resources, and appropriate governance (Salmi, 2009).

It is important that national policy address emerging challenges in the era of globalization. The development of any higher education institution is impossible without strategic planning from with the university itself. It is also true that appropriate measures need to be taken by the state. Policy governing the national educational system plays a key role in the process of building a world-class university. The state should inspire and develop awareness of the importance of building world-class universities. The state conducts educational policy and decides whether to aim for all education being of even or variegated quality and how many institutions the country can afford to support to pursue becoming world-class universities, and what national strategies are appropriate to the chosen course. As Salmi (2009) suggests, three basic strategies can be adopted to establish world-class universities: to select and upgrade existing universities, to merge a number of existing institutions and/or to create new universities from scratch.

In Russia, the higher education system combines these approaches, which is covered in the previous section. The federal government has chosen and granted two independently budgeted federal educational institutions, Lomonosov Moscow State University and Saint Petersburg State University. These two universities enjoy special features and are affiliated directly to the Russian Government. Such reform makes it possible for these two universities to set their own education standards, to extend research and education opportunities and to develop infrastructure and facilities. The other approach adopted by the Russian government is to establish a few federal universities by merging regional universities. This aims to extend cooperation in cultural and business activities within a region and ultimately to build world-class universities.

To summarise, all of the governmental measures reviewed in this section have created a solid basis for constructing world-class universities. These approaches and the new management system allow both the government and institutions to adopt policies in accordance with the political, cultural and social development in different regions in the Russian Federation. It also pushes higher education development to a new level.

CHALLENGES FOR FURTHER INTEGRATION INTO THE
GLOBAL HIGHER EDUCATION ARENA

In relation to the Russian context, this section will analyse the challenges and possible approaches to integrating education more fully with research, so as to develop a few Russian higher education institutions as world-class universities recognized worldwide. These challenges might also apply to other nations and their higher education systems.

The first challenge concerns public relations. Each relevant university's information policy needs to be directed at both the national and international levels. The information policy should include a full English version website, where practical information on study and research can be found. Universities should use a single institutional name to be employed in any database, education portals and websites. Most of Russian universities provide insufficient information in English on their official websites as well as at the disposal of different international rankings and databases such as Scopus and Web of Science. Russia does not need to create its own ranking tool specifically for its universities. The only aim of such a national ranking should be to assess the effectiveness of budgetary funding of universities. Universities must not shy away from global rankings, as these league tables can provide insightful information and inform future educational reform, which institutions will need to bolster their reputations. It is necessary for universities to be engaged fully in international processes in this modern networked society. In addition, at the governmental level, there has been awareness of the inadequate web visibility of national universities. Official recommendations of the Russian government have been formulated to tackle this issue.

The second challenge facing Russian universities is to strengthen internationalization strategies. To encourage collaboration with researchers and academics from other parts of the world, to continue promoting R&D activities within the higher education sector, and to expand collaboration at the governmental level are all strands for the possible enhancement of Russian universities in engaging in the global research community.

To develop international research collaboration, international researchers and academics should be invited not only as visiting scholars but also to participate and develop joint research projects. Between 2010 and 2011, the Government of the Russian Federation held an open grant competition, which is called "Megagrants" to support scientific research projects implemented under the supervision of leading scientists in Russian higher education institutions. [5] According to the competition criteria, there were no citizenship limitations or national priorities. This grant programme allowed researchers to create joint laboratories and develop new research products. The programme has enabled and encouraged Russian scientists to collaborate with their international peers with the assistance of practical funding opportunities.

In addition, the increasing use of federal targeted programmes is also a significant development encouraging of international collaboration, as these programmes allow for targeted actions that transcend traditional administrative boundaries and their fixed duration provides a certain degree of adaptability. There is usually a trade-off between adaptability and stability, however, and this applies to the federal target programmes given the limited duration of their funding.

There have been recent increases in the number of higher education institutions and university personnel conducting R&D activities. The number of higher education institutions performing R&D increased from only 390 in 2000 to 603 in 2009, and the number of R&D personnel increased from around 40,000 in 2000 to about 50,000 in 2009 (Centre for Science Research and Statistics, 2011). Despite its being a relatively small proportion of the total R&D institutions and personnel in the country, the higher education sector was the only sector of significant R&D growth over the last decade. This is the result of deliberate government policy as outlined in the previous section, to integrate education and research activities better. The reasoning behind these moves is that academics who are regularly engaged in scientific research can pass on contemporary knowledge to students, especially graduate students, more effectively. Despite these obstacles, a group of leading universities has actively developed research in recent years. They have strategic plans for developing their research and for their integration into international networks.

This is a healthy development, as it brings education and research activities closer together and offers a measure of research competitiveness with the academies of science. This should help to boost research quality and efficiency in Russia. Increased policy emphasis on R&D in higher education institutions is, however, leading to greater stratification of the Russian higher education system. This is no bad thing in itself, but should be based on a set of criteria broader than research performance and include indicators of teaching quality.

Special international projects, initiated by the Ministry of Education and Science of the Russian Federation and supported by relevant international governmental organizations are great ways to implement policies to develop internationalization. One of the best examples would be the collaboration between the Ministry of Education and Science and the German Academic Exchange Service. Two Russo-German programmes named in honour of Immanuel Kant and Mikhail Lomonosov are designed to support young researchers and postgraduate students in the field of social sciences and humanities, and natural and technical science respectively. At the university level, for example, Saint Petersburg State University has signed special agreements to collaborate with the German Academic Exchange Service, named after Dmitry Mendeleev. This programme is intended to assist researchers to pursue joint research and to find colleagues with whom to collaborate.

A third challenge facing Russian universities is how to combine the study process and learning outcomes. Education policy and its outputs should meet the market demand for both employers and society, in this global knowledge economy. These are features of the post-Soviet transitional period and its consequences in Russia; previously, the university was focused on one and only one employer: the state. This feature is reflected in the curricula. Internship programmes are combined with study programmes. Careers centres and student unions have been established in all Russian universities, to facilitate graduates' employment seeking. One of the main problems facing Russian universities is how to build a stronger link between studies and learning outcomes.

A fourth challenge concerns integrating Russian higher education into the European system. The transformation of the country's educational system to conform to the bachelor-master's degree model has been a laboured process.[6] Notwithstanding that the old system had its advantages, we recognize that the two-degree system of bachelor and master's degrees allow Russian higher education institutions to be involved more deeply into international education activities. The transformation period has not been easy, especially for regional universities. But this does not mean that the quality of education changed for the worse.

A fifth challenge relates to university rankings and evaluation. Rankings are considered as part of broader features of evaluation and quality assurance. There have been both international and national rankings. In Russia, rankings have included Scientific and Publication Activity of Russian Universities, the Ranking of Russian Higher Education Institutions, the National Ranking of Russian Educational Institutions and the Scale of Scientific Visibility of Russian Higher Educational Institutions.

These rankings focus on scientific and publication activities, as it is believed that research activity and its productivity is evidenced by publications. The methodology and indicators include, for example, the average annual number of grants by Russian Foundation for Humanities per staff member, the average annual number of grants by Russian Foundation for Basic Research, the number of articles in the Russian Citation Index database and their impact, the number of journals recognised by the Higher Attestation Commission.

One can find out the dynamics of publication activities for each university by using the following indicators:

– the number of publications of Russian universities in Scopus and Russian National Citation Index;
– publications and grants by Russian Foundation for Humanities and Russian Foundation for Basic Research;
– the distribution of publication activities by the financing sources in Russian leading universities;
– the distribution of publication activity by joint collaborators;
– publication activity in joint federal programmes.

So, it is necessary to note the following factors:

Firstly, the data on the number of publications and citations are relevant if observed within a definite period of time.

Secondly, the number of joint projects with Russian organizations is exactly checkable and there practically could not be any misunderstandings in how and what to count, as opposed to the share of those articles produced with the international cooperation.

Thirdly, as for the Hirsch index – only applying to the last five years – a similar approach to timeframes should be adopted.

Russian universities are far behind many foreign universities in terms of research publication and its related indicators. Possible ways to improve the quality of Russian journals include inviting prestigious foreign scientists as editors, and translating abstracts from Russian into English. Russian scientists should also indicate their affiliation with their home university, when they sign work contracts with foreign partners. We need stricter administrative measures and reforms. Today a university cannot be highly evaluated in any international ranking if it has no or almost no publications by its researchers and academics in highly cited journals. Furthermore, if scientists would like to be known in world academic society, they should publish their research results in international scientific journals, books or proceedings.

Unfortunately, the number of publications in international science journals by Russian scientists is lower compared with that in domestic journals. Russian scientists, especially in the fields of social science and humanities, are used to publish their results mostly in domestic journals and papers. Partially it can be explained by historical isolation of soviet science, which has led to results and innovations traditionally being presented at the level of the national academic society. The second issue is language. In Russia, most journals are published only in Russian and are not translated in English. It does not necessarily mean that the quality of these journals or publications is insufficient and research outputs are not significant. Comparing the impact factor in Russian Citation Index, which is the national database of research papers and journals, with that of Journal Citation Reports for Russian journals translated into English, a similar value can be found. This language issue is very urgent not only for Russia but also for other countries with traditional publications in national languages, for example Italy. Conversely, in Germany, scientific journals are mostly published in English. Such a key feature increases both its competitiveness in the academic community and in the world academic rankings. The issue of language should be solved not only at the university level but also at the level of publishing houses and at governmental level. It should conduct reforms to create appropriate frameworks to make national journals visible among the international academic community.

The main feature of Russian scientists' presentations in international journals is the prevalence of publications in Physics and Chemistry, as compared with most other countries. The publications in others research field, especially medicine, social sciences and humanities, are almost unknown to foreign scientists, because more than 90% of them are only in Russian. Figures 1, 2 and 3[7] demonstrate the distribution of publications in terms of research areas in Russia, mainland China and Canada, based on the data from Scopus (2006–2010), and easily reflect disproportion.

A third issue concerns an academic division between the humanities, natural sciences and information technology. Russian humanities have also a strong research heritage. Mostly they publish their results in monographs or papers in multi-authored monographs. The existing ranking methodologies do not always include statistics on monographs, despite the very latest modifications of Web of Science to introduce a Book Citation Index.

Another problem concerns the affiliation of the author, an issue subject to bureaucratic and political wrangling. Saint Petersburg State University has enhanced the rewards for publications in highly cited journals displaying the author's university affiliation.

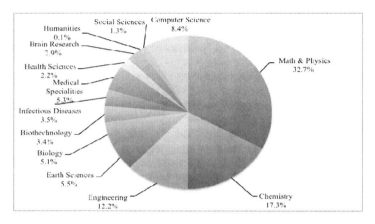

Figure 1. The distribution of publications in terms of research areas:
Russia (2006–2010)

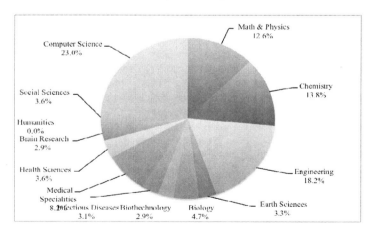

Figure 2. The distribution of publications in terms of research areas:
China Mainland (2006–2010)

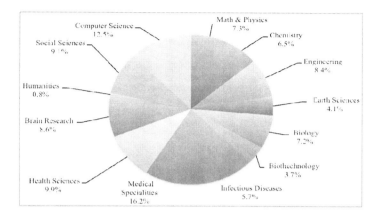

Figure 3. The distribution of publications in terms of research areas:
Canada (2006–2010)

CONCLUSIONS

The progress reviewed in this chapter is not enough yet for Russia to create world-class universities. Lessons need to be learned from the country's unsuccessful experience. Despite the necessary national reforms to R&D and the integration of education and science in higher education institutions, the practical implementation of policies is not always achieved. The reasons include: gaps in national legislation, misunderstandings within university management, insufficient experience of the academic society in research grant management.

Universities should set achievable goals. It might be naïve to forecast a concrete date by which to expect that world-class universities have developed. Sustainable financial support to universities and funding for international research projects developed by faculties is not enough. It is necessary to organize expert oversight, free from administrative pressure and conflicts. Concerns have also been raised in regard to grant evaluation, especially those programmes supported by the state government. Transparent selection and evaluation procedures need to be assured, as well as expert commissions. Government and universities should be open-minded when choosing fields for research investments. Financial support and concentration should not only be oriented to market demands, but also be highly correlated to national research strengths and the facilities available.

To conclude, the Russian experience shows that a promising strategy for building world-class universities is to inspire system transformation at both the university and national government levels.

NOTES

[1] According to the Federal law *About Higher and Postgraduate Education*, the "university" is the institution of higher education that implements educational programs of higher and postgraduate

education on a wide range of training courses (majors). It provides training, retraining, and (or) the training of highly qualified personnel, scientific and pedagogical workers. It performs basic and applied scientific research across a broad spectrum of sciences, and is the leading scientific and methodical centre in its areas of activity. The "academic" is the institution of higher education that implements educational programs of higher and postgraduate education. It provides training, retraining, and (or) the training of highly qualified workers for a specific area of scientific and educational activities. It performs basic and applied research mainly in one area of science or culture, and is the leading scientific and methodical centre in their area of expertise. An "institute" is the institution of higher education that implements educational programs of higher education, as well as a rule, postgraduate educational programs of vocational education. It provides training, retraining, and (or) training of workers for a specific area of professional activity. It conducts basic and (or) applied research.

[2] In September 2005, President Putin initiated the Russian Federation's National Priority Projects to ensure political stability, to sustain economic and technological growth, and to improve the quality of life for Russian citizens. This programme aims at developing the country's welfare by investing the state's growing financial resources in four developmental aspects, that is, the public health, education, housing and agriculture sectors.

[3] Several reforms within the framework of Federal Targeted Programmes have been implemented since 2009. Such reforms include "Research and Development in the Priority Fields of Science and Technology Complex of Russia in 2007-2013", "Scientists and Science Educator of an Innovative Russia for the period 2009-2013", and "Development of Infrastructure of the Nano-Industry in the Russian Federation for the years 2008-2011". The total value of these financial support programmes has increased three times and adds up to US$1 billion. Federal Targeted Programmes have been recognized as effective tools to realize the state economic and social policies.

[4] Please see the official site of Federal Target program "Scientists and Science Educators for an Innovative Russia", http://fcpk.ru/catalog.aspx?CatalogId=1946.

[5] The competition was held according to the Governmental Resolution No.220 "On measures designed to attract leading scientists to Russian institutions of higher learning" (April 9, 2010).

[6] Under the Soviet system, specialist degrees were awarded after five years of study.

[7] Data on publication structure are obtained from SciVal Spotlight, analytical instrument by Elsevier, based on Scopus.

REFERENCES

Centre for Science Research and Statistics. (2011). *Russian Science and Technology at a Glance: 2010*. Moscow: CSRS. Retrieved April 2, 2012, from http://www.csrs.ru/english/statis/sc/sc2010.htm

Dezhina, I. (2011). Developing Research in Russian Universities. *Russie.Nei.Visions*, 57. Retrieved April 2, 2012, from http://www.ifri.org/?page=contribution-detail&id=6457&id_provenance=97

Ministry of Education and Science of the Russian Federation. (2009). Twelve Russian universities will receive a status of national research universities. (Press room news) Retrieved April 2, 2012, from http://eng.mon.gov.ru/press/news/4183/

Ministry of Education and Science of the Russian Federation. (2011). *Vladimir Putin: Good Quality, Modern Education – Key to Sustainable Development of our Country*. Retrieved April 2, 2012, from http://eng.mon.gov.ru/press/news/

Ministry of Education and Science of the Russian Federation. (2012a). *Innovative Programs in Institutions of Higher Education*. Retrieved April 2, 2012, from http://eng.mon.gov.ru/pro/pnpo/vuz/

Ministry of Education and Science of the Russian Federation. (2012b). *Creation of New Universities in Federal Districts*. Retrieved April 2, 2012, from http://eng.mon.gov.ru/pro/pnpo/fed/

Ministry of Education and Science of the Russian Federation. (2012c). *Creating Business-schools of the World Level*. Retrieved April 2, 2012, from http://eng.mon.gov.ru/pro/pnpo/bsh/

Ministry of Education and Science of the Russian Federation. (2012d). *On Measures for Training the Scientific and Scientific-pedagogical Personnel of the Innovative Russia.* Retrieved April 2, 2012, from http://eng.mon.gov.ru/ruk/ministr/dok/4131/

Muravyev, M. (2011, November 8). Russian universities financial support. *Science and Technology in Russian Federation.* Retrieved April 12, 2012, from http://www.strf.ru/material.aspx?CatalogId=221&d_no =41577

The Russian Rectors' Union. (2012). *About the Russian Rectors' Union.* Retrieved April 2, 2012, from http://rsr-online.ru/english/about.htm

Salmi, J. (2009). *The Challenge of Establishing World-Class Universities.* Washington, DC: World Bank.

Schiermeier, Q. (2010). Russia to boost university science. *Nature, 464,* 1257. Retrieved April 2, 2012, from http://www.nature.com/news/2010/100427/full/4641257a.html

Smolentseva, A. (2010). In search of world-class universities. *International Higher Education, 58,* 20–21.

Spiesberger, M. (2011). *Erawatch Country Reports 2010: Russian Federation.* European Commission: Erawatch. Retrieved April 2, 2012, from http://erawatch.jrc.ec.europa.eu/ erawatch.

AFFILIATIONS

Nikolay Skvortsov, Olga Moskaleva, & Julia Dmitrieva
Saint-Petersburg State University, Russia

SECTION 2

MANAGING WORLD-CLASS UNIVERSITIES FROM AN INSTITUTIONAL PERSPECTIVE

LAURITZ B. HOLM-NIELSEN

MAKING A STRONG UNIVERSITY STRONGER

Change without a Burning Platform

INTRODUCTION

On an October day in 2010, a professor of economics was lecturing students at the Aarhus School of Business at Aarhus University on labour market dynamics. The professor was Dale T. Mortensen, a Niels Bohr Professor at Aarhus University, who for a number of years had divided his time between Aarhus University and Northwestern University in Chicago, US. Immediately before his lecture, Professor Mortensen received a call with the news that he was to receive the Nobel Prize in Economic Sciences for his ground-breaking research on labour market dynamics. After the lecture, national and international media rushed in, and for a few hours, Aarhus University was turned completely upside down. Once again, the quality of the research performed at Aarhus University had received international acclaim, and the university could now boast of a second contemporary Nobel laureate; the first one being Professor Jens Christian Skou, who in 1997 received the Nobel Prize in Chemistry for his research on the sodium-potassium pump.

In those very same days and weeks, the senior university management team was finalizing a reorganization of the university. Staff, students and researchers had been involved in the design of a new and improved organization and now the process of assessing existing structures and developing a strategy was coming to an end. The result was to become the most comprehensive transformation in the history of Aarhus University. The planned transformation was clearly not designed with a view from a burning platform, for research was successful, Aarhus University was financially strong and ranked among the top 100 in all recognised evaluations of the quality and reputation of the world's universities. Aarhus University was clearly not in a crisis. So why reorganize it completely and risk rocking a very steady and successful boat?

The overarching question that preoccupied Aarhus University's leaders at the time was this: "How do we prepare Aarhus University for the challenges of the future?"

CHANGE IN TIMES OF STRENGTH

The world of higher education is changing, and the role of universities is changing with it. Students and researchers are increasingly mobile and communication and travel across the world have increased significantly over the last two decades. The

Q. Wang, Y. Cheng, & N.C. Liu (eds.), Building World-Class Universities: Different Approaches to a Shared Goal, 73–87.

balance of power and influence in the world is shifting and many universities feel the pressure of increased competition as other regions move up the value chain. As a consequence, universities are being forced to adopt a perspective that transcends regional and national borders; society demands that they take on new roles and open up to the surrounding world; and Aarhus University must focus on how to maintain its position among the elite universities of the world.

Increasingly, research funding is subject to national and international competition as well as being applied to major strategic research programmes that cut across disciplines and research areas. To be able to perform proactively, flexibly and professionally in order to attract research funding in a situation of global competition, the individual university must enjoy increased strategic freedom to design structures that invite interdisciplinary research and international collaboration (Holm-Nielsen, 2010). In a nutshell, much more autonomy and much higher accountability are needed. Additionally, for a world-class university to ensure the necessary academic continuity and development to be able to attract research funding, it needs to attract the most talented students and researchers. Competition for the best minds is increasingly global and it is therefore crucial for universities to offer attractive and flexible conditions for performing research.

In times of crisis, governments may look towards higher education for easy cutbacks. This is a very short-sighted strategy, for on the contrary, there is a need to improve the framework conditions for universities and to make substantial investments in education and research in order to remain competitive in a globalised world and meet the challenges of tomorrow. However, the solution is not just a matter of allocating more resources to universities. New and improved structures need to be implemented for universities to achieve excellence, and at least four major issues must be addressed: acquiring research funding, attracting talent, meeting the demands of society for knowledge, and improving the quality of education. Moreover, the world is faced with unprecedented challenges of a global nature. Issues such as climate change, limited energy resources, epidemic diseases and food security, cut across borders and scientific and scholarly disciplines. Just as these challenges transcend existing paradigms, so do the solutions and under the right circumstances, universities can contribute substantially to meet these grand challenges of our times.

The academic development process (Aarhus University, 2011), the largest organizational restructuring process in the history of Aarhus University, has the objectives of removing organizational barriers to change and innovation, merging research and teaching cultures that work with related issues, and improving conditions for research that cuts across disciplines and research areas.

Regional Developments: The Lisbon Strategy, the European Research Area and the European Higher Education Area

The European Union acknowledges that universities and other institutions of knowledge and education have a central role to play in the future development of Europe. In order to strengthen economic growth, in 2011 the European Council adopted the *Europe 2020 Strategy,* an update of the renowned Lisbon Strategy from 2000, which maintains and reinforces Europe's commitment to: research, innovation and education. The European Research Area was also established in 2000, with aim of fostering robust ground-breaking research through collaborations across the region. From this time onwards, investment in research increased substantially with the allocation of more funding to the European framework programmes for research. In parallel, the European Union has worked to establish a European Higher Education Area (EHEA) (EHEA, 2012) on the foundations of the process which began with the Bologna Declaration of June 1999. In addition, the European Union Commission adopted the Higher Education Modernisation Agenda in 2006. The agenda is a strategic framework for co-operation in education and training in Europe that identifies several areas in need of reform, including a need to develop the three-cycle system (bachelor – master – doctor), which is also a goal of the Bologna process (Commission of European Communities, 2006). This reform is aimed at improving student mobility within the European education area, by establishing shared standards for quality assurance and the structure of degree programmes and thus, increasing the possibilities for cooperation across borders among European educational institutions (European University Association, 2011), following the principles in the European "Magna Charta" declaration. [1] The modernisation agenda also identifies a need to bring the governance structures of European universities up to date, while at the same time guaranteeing their autonomy and freedom of research (European Commission, 2011).

NATIONAL DEVELOPMENTS: THE DANISH GLOBALISATION STRATEGY

At the turn of the century,[2] it became clear that it was necessary for Danish society to reorganize and strengthen its research and education activities in the light of the opportunities and threats represented by global economic developments. Moreover, Denmark, like most other Western countries, must meet the challenge of an ageing population and the fact that the government's profits from the North Sea oil fields are expected to dry up within one or two generations. Therefore, the Danish government adopted a national globalisation strategy[3] in 2006, based on an extensive analysis of the nation's strengths and weaknesses in the global economy. The strategy is aimed at ensuring that Denmark will continue to be one of the world's best countries to live and work in in the coming decades. It has a strong focus on education and research and introduces a number of higher education policy goals, the most significant of which are (Ministry of Science, Technology and Innovation, 2003):

- to increase public investment in research from 0.75% to 1% of the Danish gross domestic product (GDP) by 2010 (meeting the Barcelona target);
- to link the basic public funding of universities more directly to the quality of their activities (aligning outputs and inputs);
- to integrate the government research institutions into the universities (increasing higher education and research system internal efficiency);

- to double the number of PhD students (assuring high quality research staff for expanding the sector);
- to introduce a system of accreditation of all university degree programmes (assuring quality);
- to increase the higher education participation rate from 45% to 50% (extending coverage);
- to stimulate a more rapid throughput of students in tertiary education (rapid increase of labour force qualifications);
- to introduce better and more structured options for Danish students for studying abroad (proactive internationalization).

To realise these policy goals, two major university reforms were necessary: a new University Act to modify the governance structure at Danish universities, in order to grant senior university management more autonomy, and a process to invite universities and sector research institutions to merge in order to produce larger and more powerful institutions.

The first major reform   A new University Act, was introduced in 2003 (Aarhus University, 2003) and modified in 2011. It focused on establishing university autonomy, while at the same time ensuring accountability. The universities were converted into self-governing institutions with university boards, where external stakeholders make up the majority. The board is responsible for appointing the rector and deciding the university budget and annual statement of accounts, as well as other matters of a strategic nature. The rector is responsible for the day-to-day management and leadership of the university under the university board's supervision and represents it to the outside world. The rector appoints deans of the university's main academic areas, who manage their units under the authority of the rector. In short, the reform has contributed to more professional leadership, where the decision-making capacity and the conditions for strategic prioritisation have been significantly improved.

Furthermore, the Danish system for public financing of research was restructured as part of the university reform. Regarding this, an increasing proportion of public research funding has since been provided as competitive grants, and core funding is based on output indicators related to both the quality and quantity of research. Moreover, study programmes are financed by the state through an output based taximeter system (activity level-determined grants based on the calculation of completed student credits).

The second major reform   A few universities and government research institutions were merged in 2007, with the aim being to strengthen and concentrate elite research. That is, these mergers consisted of integration of government research institutions into the university sector and mergers between existing universities, a process through which Denmark went from having 12 to eight universities. The mergers were voluntary; forced mergers would only have been possible through a change in the existing University Act – a change for which there was no majority in Parliament. The mergers were not decided overnight, for comprehensive analyses had to be conducted in 2006 in order to identify complementary research areas and the best opportunities for achieving research synergies. Moreover extensive negotiations involving senior management and the boards of the universities and research institutions were carried out before the final decision of the future Danish landscape of higher education was taken in 2007 (Holm-Nielsen, 2009a).

THE CASE OF AARHUS UNIVERSITY

Aarhus University underwent significant changes in 2006–07 as a result of the merger (Aarhus University, 2008a). More specifically, the university integrated two hitherto independent universities in January 2007 (the Aarhus School of Business and Danish School of Education) as well as the two national government research institutions for the environment and agriculture. With these mergers, Aarhus University grew by 40% overnight and was transformed from a one-campus institution to a nation-wide university with multiple locations and a wider range of research and degree programmes. In addition, the annual budget almost doubled, to approximately EUR 800 million (US$1.05 billion) in 2010, while the number of students increased to about 38,000. The mergers created a much broader scientific and academic resource base, and the addition of new disciplines brought with it a number of promising opportunities for new synergies.

First, a number of obvious possibilities for new collaboration arose among the university's many strong research cultures. Aarhus University, like all research universities, faces the challenge of developing increased interdisciplinary collaboration, in light of the fact that the technological breakthroughs of the future will most probably take place at the intersection of traditional fields of inquiry. That world-class research on neuroscience – as exemplified in the interdisciplinary research framework MINDLab^4 – is taking place at the university is due to the fact that the university has succeeded in bringing researchers together from completely different areas: medicine, computer science, music, psychology, linguistics, physics and many other fields. In sum, the expansion of the university to cover the full range of academic fields has paved the way for similar interdisciplinary research collaborations in a number of areas.

Second, the mergers presented new possibilities for developing new degree programmes and making existing ones more flexible. Moreover, after the mergers the main academic areas of the university spanned the entire research spectrum – basic research, applied research, strategic research and research-based knowledge transfer to public and private sectors. This also meant an increase in the university's interaction with the surrounding society, which in turn has provided even better opportunities for making its intellectual resources available to government, businesses and the population in general.

Whilst the merger strengthened the university considerably, it has also posed a series of new challenges, with, for instance, the increase from five to nine main academic areas creating a range of new internal organizational barriers. There was also overlap between a number of the old and new main academic areas. For example, there were biologists at the "old" Faculty of Natural Sciences and at the "new" National Environmental Research Institute, just as teaching and research on economics took place at both the "old" Faculty of Social Sciences and the "new" Aarhus School of Business.

To sum up, in 2010 Aarhus University was in a new and stronger position as well as a new national, regional and global reality – a reality that both opened up new possibilities and meant increasing competition for research funding and researchers. The scope and impact of the research being performed was greater than ever before, and the university's competitiveness had increased. The challenge was to find a new model for the university which would enable it to exploit the new possibilities and potential to the full, whilst meeting both internal and external challenges. In a few words, the university decided to simplify internal structures, merge academic areas and invest strategically.

THE QUADRUPLE HELIX OF A MODERN UNIVERSITY

Many world-class universities in Europe are built on the Humboldtian tradition of education and research supplemented by a third guiding mission of knowledge exchange.

Aarhus University's strategy, however, consists of four equally important missions on which the organization is built:
- Education
- Research
- Talent development
- Knowledge exchange

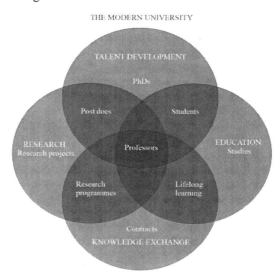

Figure 1. The quadruple helix – the four missions of Aarhus University

It believes that this four-pronged mission, which has been labelled the quadruple helix, to be the answer to the challenges described above. That is, the classical Humboldtian interaction between education and research is here combined with the contemporary emphasis on knowledge exchange and a consistent focus on talent development as a new and fourth dimension, thus making it feasible to combine the quality mass and elite university. In fact, the university considers talent development as the key to university development, for talented young researchers bring new ideas and innovation to the university; they influence education, achieve research results and, when they leave Aarhus University, contribute to the development of an important international network both inside and outside academia. The university has included these four core activities in its strategy since 2008, but with the recent academic development process initiative, it is now fully implementing a management model that puts as much focus on these as on its four faculties.

Education

In an international context, Aarhus University is a large and distinctive educational institution. It constantly assesses and further develops its range of degree programmes in order to meet the requirements of the outside world and the university's own standards of excellence. This academic diversity offers unique opportunities for innovative multidisciplinary degree programmes; however, the internal structures of the organization must also be geared towards promoting this flexibility. One example of the university's active promotion of flexible degree programmes is ECTS Label certification, which few large universities have achieved[5]. The changes being introduced through the academic development process will allow for an even stronger and more flexible inner education market at Aarhus University, which result in it being easier to share and develop degree programmes, courses and teaching resources across the main academic areas, departments and centres.

Research

The expansion through the mergers has enriched Aarhus University by providing it with a wider range of disciplines, and today its activities span the broadest range of research fields of any university in Denmark, which include four faculties: Science and Technology, Business and Social Sciences, Health, and Arts, as well as 26 departments. Moreover, the university's broad academic competences enable it to reach out to all sectors of society and offer a unique opportunity to combine existing academic strengths in new interdisciplinary forms of collaboration in order to create ground-breaking new research results and degree programmes. An important objective in the academic development process at the university is to develop more interdisciplinary research projects and research centres that combine expertise from different fields. That is, interdisciplinarity is what is needed to solve the grand challenges that cannot be solved from the perspective of a single discipline. Two major new initiatives have been designed to further promote interdisciplinary visionary ideas and to support research at Aarhus University, which have been founded through the core budget thanks to internal efficiency gains.

Interdisciplinary centres   Aarhus University is already home to a number of world-class research centres, fifteen of which are basic research centres supported by the Danish National Research Foundation. Several centres are interdisciplinary and have obtained significant research results across traditional research disciplines.[6]To promote further the establishment of interdisciplinary research, the university has allocated resources to support the development of up to ten additional interdisciplinary research centres. These new interdisciplinary centres must span at least two main academic areas and must be based on a strong international academic profile. Besides having two well established interdisciplinary centres in nanoscience (iNano)[7] and brain research (Mindlab),[8] Aarhus University is currently assessing the feasibility of establishing centres in: genome research, neuroscience, register-based research, food, nutrition and health, Arctic research, global change and development.

"Aarhus University Ideas"   For the university, it is paramount that a more strategic use of resources for research does not impede the possibility to pursue the unexpected and for young researchers to establish themselves based on independent research. However, as competition for research funding increases at the national and European level, it becomes increasingly difficult for young researchers without a long track record and just a good idea to win funding. For this reason, Aarhus University has reserved substantial funding for an initiative labelled "Aarhus University Ideas". The aim of the programme is to help visionary and unique ideas towards full implementation though a Research Seed Programme, through which small grants are awarded to young researchers and larger grants are given to projects that hold potential for pushing the knowledge frontier forward in new ways.

Talent Development

As part of its fourth mission Aarhus University strives to offer talented young researchers the best possible conditions for interdisciplinary research and collaboration with leading researchers in relevant fields. The ambition is to support a new generation of researchers born into an interdisciplinary philosophy and practice in relation to research. In fact, in the course of the last five years Aarhus University has doubled the intake of doctoral students and this expansion has included a significant increase in the number of international PhD students at the university. Today, one in five PhD students is of a non-Danish origin and in some disciplines more than 50% of the doctoral students are recruited internationally. This, of course, accentuates the need for services for international researchers and to create optimal conditions for young researchers.

Early recruitment of talent The four graduate schools at the university all offer talent development of an international standard, as PhD programmes are considered an essential element of the university's ambition to achieve excellence (Aarhus University, 2008b). To ensure flexibility in the recruitment of talent and to support young, ambitious potential researchers, it allows admission to its PhD programmes at three different stages.

Table 1. PhD models at Aarhus University

PhD model	Explanation
5 (3+2) + 3 track	In the traditional Bologna model, the PhD student is admitted to three years of PhD studies after completing a master's degree.
4 + 4 track	The 4+4 track allows for early recruitment of students during their master's degree. A 4+4 PhD student has the opportunity to begin research during a master's programme, by combining the research work with a PhD project.
3 + 5 track	On the 3+5 track, the student commences a PhD programme immediately after completing a bachelor's degree.

Aarhus Institute of Advanced Studies Aarhus University has reserved funding to establish the Aarhus Institute of Advanced Studies (AIAS). AIAS will create an inspiring, international environment for exceptionally talented young researchers (junior fellows), guided by world-class professors (senior fellows). Here, they will be exposed to an international and interdisciplinary stimulating environment at an early stage in their careers without the limitation of formal and academic obligations. AIAS junior fellows will cover the entire academic spectrum and bring together academic disciplines and the institute will be located on campus in a dedicated building. In general, this initiative is expected to enable the university to strengthen its international reputation further and to form a strong network of international researchers.

Knowledge Exchange

Services to society are an important responsibility for institutions of higher education and hence, knowledge exchange has been a core mission for a number of years. The changes introduced by the academic development process at Aarhus University will provide the university greater flexibility and capacity to meet better the concrete needs of external stakeholders for knowledge-based solutions. The university has placed the entire breadth of its expertise at the disposal of government, industry and citizens, and offers its external partners clear, easily accessible forms of collaboration and points of contact. This more coherent approach will mean that in the future Aarhus University will be able to deliver more flexible and carefully tailored contributions to all parts of society across the university's four core activities and in particular with respect to complex inquiries related to the grand challenges.

NEW ORGANIZATIONAL STRUCTURE: UNIFIED EXECUTIVE MANAGEMENT
AND NEW UNIVERSITY-WIDE RESPONSIBILITIES

As explained above, Aarhus University has recently undergone a major academic reorganization, with its nine faculties having been reduced to four as well as the number of academic departments cut from fifty-five to twenty-six. The primary objective of this restructuring has been to create larger academic environments that can more easily achieve critical mass and thus make possible more academic specialisation. At the same time, internal barriers that hinder collaboration across academic boundaries have been greatly reduced, creating the right conditions for more interdisciplinary research. The university also wishes to encourage inter-faculty collaboration within the other three of its four core activities: talent development, knowledge exchange and education. All in all the new organizational structure, with fewer and larger units, offers great potential, but also presents a range of possible challenges.

One of the dangers is the possibility of the four faculties developing into four autonomous "universities within the university". The Faculty of Science and Technology, for example, has a turnover so large that if it was an independent university, it would be ranked among the four largest in Denmark and the Faculty of Arts conducts almost 45% of the country's research in arts and humanities. In addition, there is a real risk that management will become isolated from other staff in such large units. In order to fully exploit the potential of the new structure and to overcome the challenges it poses, the university has adopted a new management model, the goals of which are to ensure:

– that there are close links between the senior university management and the management teams in the four faculties, so that the latter work in harmony with the overall strategies of the university, so that these strategies and action plans are based on the strengths of the faculties;
– that there is an increase in the amount of interdisciplinary collaboration, at both the academic and administrative levels;
– that the knowledge and competencies of the staff are taken into account in the overall decision-making and strategic planning of the university as well as during the implementation phase.

In order to achieve these strategic goals, the university has changed its system of governance in a number of ways. First, the senior management team now consists of the Rector's Office (Rector, Pro-Rector and University Director) and the deans of the four faculties. The latter thus participate in the day-to-day management of the university at the highest level, which is a new feature of this system. This ensures that the leadership of the faculties is based on the university's overall strategies and planning, and also that the senior management team is closely linked to academic activities and viewpoints. In order to strengthen the unified nature of the senior management team, the group meets every week, and the deans and their secretariats have now been gathered in the same building as the Rector's Office and its secretariat.

Second, each of the deans has been given responsibility for one of the four core activities, i.e. research, talent development, knowledge exchange or education. This is to ensure that there is more collaborative work and better coordination of activities across the entire university within, for example, research. Each dean discusses strategic initiatives within their specific core activity with a committee consisting of the vice-deans responsible for that activity from each of the four faculties. For example, the Research Committee has responsibility for establishing interdisciplinary research centres and networks at the university, for coordinating large applications for funding to foundations and research councils, and for developing general strategies and plans for joint activities in recruiting, publication, research management, etc. In addition to their responsibilities for joint activities and plans across the university within the four core activities, the four committees are also valuable management forums for discussion, exchange of experiences, and the generation of new ideas and proposals. The Deans will rotate their responsibilities for the core activities on an annual basis, thereby guaranteeing that each acquires great insight into all four core activities, and also that the faculties do not gain "monopolies" over any of these university-wide core activities.

Third, four employee forums have been established, one for each core activity, to warrant that employees' knowledge and skills are brought into play when decisions with significance across the university are made. Each forum has twenty members, consisting of the dean in charge of the core activity, the vice-deans from the four faculties, eight members appointed by the academic councils (two from each council), and seven members appointed by the senior university management. The four forums have quarterly meetings to discuss matters of principle, share experiences with the senior management team as well as to receive advice from the latter and each serves as a university think tank within its field.

From the above it can be seen that the four deans, along with the vice-deans, hold key positions in this new managerial structure. As well as being part of the senior management team, the deans are responsible for the "vertical" management of the four faculties, which includes overall responsibility for its academic and financial administration. At the same time, the four deans are responsible for a long range of cross-cutting activities in the "horizontal bonds" (consisting of managerial committees and employee forums) across the university (see Figure 2).

The new structure has already proved effective in ensuring that the activities of the four faculties are better coordinated, and that cooperation across the faculties is increased.

One important precondition for the reform was the passing in 2003 of the amendment to the *Danish University Act*, which required that university boards should be set up with external members in the majority, and that there should be professional leadership at all levels of the institution (Aarhus University, 2007). This governance model has meant that the university board at Aarhus University is in a position to adopt a clear strategy, in that the rector and other senior managers are selected from the global pool of university leaders, and that the management team has a clear mandate to implement the strategies of the board. As such, the university's academic reorganization is a good example of how the new model

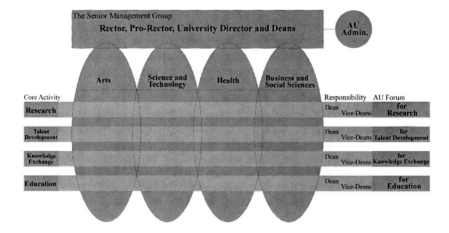

Figure 2. Organigram of Aarhus University. Source: Aarhus University (2011)

initiated by the Danish government can be rolled out in practice in a way that ensures strong leadership governed by a clear mandate.

The rationale for a system of elected managers, which was required until 2003 under the previous *Danish University Act* and which is practised in a number of countries, is that the management is regarded by the rest of the staff as having a high degree of legitimacy. To ensure a continuation of this legitimacy, and also guarantee that the senior management team has access to the best possible advisory support, the four aforementioned four advisory forums have been established, one for each core activity (Holm-Nielsen, 2009b). In addition, the importance of the Academic Councils has been increased. Each of these elects a chair, and together they make up a joint team which can enter directly into discussion with the senior management team, which strengthens the involvement and the influence of the Academic Councils within the university.

CONCLUSION

Denmark has the most satisfied researchers in the world (Russo, 2010), Danish researchers have the world's highest citation rates, and Aarhus University is placed among the world top 100 in most league tables (Times Higher Education, 2010). Thus, the university's situation can in no way be described as a burning platform. However, the demands on universities are increasing, and at Aarhus University we firmly believe that we need to examine our own way of doing our business and organizing ourselves, by designing new and flexible structures that can meet the challenges of the future. The framework conditions resulting from national reforms in Denmark and those at the European level made it possible for the university to act to meet the new challenges and opportunities facing us. In particular, the institutional reforms of Danish universities implemented since 2001 have positively affected their capacity to stave off the financial crisis. That is, by the time the financial crisis erupted, these institutions were strong and independent, which is one reason why, so far, the university sector in Denmark has fared relatively well compared to other European countries. However, if its universities are to maintain this position they will need to be continuously reformed (Milthers, 2011).

Aarhus University's aim with the academic development process is not an attempt to create final optimal structures, for this cannot be achieved once and for all. What is possible and more relevant is to create a modern university that is flexible enough to manoeuvre effectively in a world of change. This perspective will allow the university to remain in the worldwide elite in the years to come. The guiding principles behind the changes are interdisciplinarity, flexibility and interaction with the world based on profound research quality. The lattermost will be achieved owing to fewer and stronger departments and the flexibility will be supported by lean management structures as well as an increased weight being placed on interdisciplinary and university-wide activities. Moreover, Aarhus University expects that these changes will make the university more competitive and attractive to both international and Danish students, international partners, government, industry and organizations, but first of all to new talented people wishing to pursue a career. In sum, the Aarhus University leadership are confident that the university is prepared to meet the global challenges facing the higher education sector and that the process adopted to meet these challenges will actually make us even stronger.[9]

NOTES

[1] Bologna Declaration, please see http://www.magna-charta.org/library/userfiles/file/bologna_declaration.pdf

[2] In 2001 a government commission issued a report sketching the future terms for Danish research and the challenges Denmark faced. It presented a strategy for the development for Danish research. Please see http://vtu.dk/nyheder/pressemeddelelser/2001/forskningskommissionens-betaenkning/ (in Danish).

[3] The strategy was named *Progress, Innovation and Cohesion Strategy for Denmark in the Global Economy*. Please see http://www.globalisering.dk/page.dsp?area=52.

[4] For more information visit http://www.mindlab.au.dk/.

[5] Aarhus University and 28 other European universities have been awarded the ECTS Label by the European Commission in 2009 and 2010 http://eacea.ec.europa.eu/llp/support_measures_and_network/ects_dsl_en.php.

[6] For more information visit http://www.au.dk/en/research/research centres/.

[7] For more information visit http://inano.au.dk/research/annual-reports/.

[8] For more information visit http://www.mindlab.au.dk/.

[9] For more information on of the strategic thinking behind the changes made at Aarhus University, please see Warming, K. C., & Holm-Nielsen, L. B.; (2009). Designing institutional internationalisation policies and strategies. In Internationalisation of European Higher Education Supplement, No.2, Berlin: Raabe.

REFERENCES

Aarhus University. (2003). *Explanatory Notes to the Draft Bill on Universities: The University Act.* Retrieved April 12, 2012, from http://www.ubst.dk/en/laws-and-decrees/ Explanatory%20Notes%20to%20the%20Draft%20Bill%20on%20Universities%20%28The% 20University%20Act%29.pdf

Aarhus University. (2007). *The University Act.* Retrieved April 12, 2012, from http://en.vtu.dk/acts-etc/prevailing-laws-and-regulations/act-on-universities

Aarhus University. (2008a). *Aarhus University Strategy 2008–2012.* Retrieved April 12, 2012, from http://www.au.dk/fileadmin/www.au.dk/strategi/download/strategy2008-2012_02.pdf

Aarhus University. (2008b). Aarhus University – Graduate education at its heart. In G. J. Curtis & A. Bould (Eds.), *Cambridge 800: Cambridge University Students' Union Looks Back on 800 Years of Educational Excellence.* St. James' House: Regal Press Limited.

Aarhus University. (2010). *Tomorrow's Aarhus University.* Retrieved April 12, 2012, from http://www.au.dk/ en/about/changes/

Aarhus University. (2011). *The Academic Development Process.* Working Report, Aarhus University Senior Management Group. Retrieved April 12, 2012, from http://medarbejdere.au.dk/fileadmin/res/fau/ dok/fau_report_chapters1-and-2-UK.pdf

Commission of European Communities. (2006). *Communication from the Commission to the Council and the European Parliament.* Retrieved April 12, 2012, from http://eur-lex.europa.eu/LexUriServ/LexUriServ.do?uri=COM:2006:0208:FIN:EN:PDF

European Commission. (2011). *The Higher Education Modernization Agenda.* Retrieved April 12, 2012, from http://ec. europa.eu/education/higher-education/doc1320_en.htm

European Higher Education Area. (2012). *Bologna Process: European Higher Education Area.* Retrieved April 12, 2012, from http://www.ehea.info

European University Association. (2011). *Statement by the European University Association in Response to the European Commission Consultation on the Modernization of Higher Education in Europe.* Retrieved April 12, 2012, from http://www.eua.be/Libraries/Publications/ EUA_Statement_in_response_to_EC_Consultation_on_Modernisation_of_Higher_Education_in_Eu rope.sflb.ashx

Holm-Nielsen, L. B. (2008). Reforming Denmark's universities for the global market: A report on strategic steps to meet global competition for talent. In *Strategies to Win the Best: German Approaches in International Perspective, the Proceeding of the Second Forum on the Internationalization of Sciences and Humanities.* Berlin: Alexander von Humboldt Foundation.

Holm-Nielsen, L. B. (2009a). Research institutions merging to achieve critical mass: The case of Denmark. *Monografia,* 339–341. Retrieved April 12, 2012, from http://www.fundacioncyd.org/wps/wcm/connect/7 37fa 0042b710f6bb7efb75e36717f7/ MONOGRAF%C3%8DA+ICYD+2009.pdf?MOD=AJPERES

Holm-Nielsen, L. B. (2009b). *Aarhus University in the Global Market: Opportunities, Limits, and Limitations.* Retrieved April 12, 2012, from http://www.au.dk/fileadmin/www.au.dk/ Oplaeg_og_foredrag /2009/Stuttgart_17.09.pdf

Holm-Nielsen, L. B. (2010). Research fundraising strategies. In S. Bergan, E. Egron-Polak, J. Kohler, L. Purser, & M. Vukasović (Eds.), *Leadership and Governance in Higher Education.* Berlin: Raabe.

Milthers, P. M. (2011). Danish universities in the financial crisis: Change and trust. *Higher Education Management and Policy, 23*(1), 1–18.

Ministry of Science, Technology and Innovation. (2003). *Implementation of the Bologna Goals in Denmark.* Retrieved April 12, 2012, from http://www.ehea.info/Uploads/Documents/ DENMARK_2003.PDF

Russo, G. (2010, June 23). For love and money. *Nature, 465,* 1104–1107. Retrieved April 12, 2012, from http://www.nature.com/naturejobs/2010/100624/full/nj7301-1104a.html

Times Higher Education. (2010, June 17). The most cited nations: Data provided by Thomson Reuters from its National Science Indicators, 2005-09. *Times Higher Education.* Retrieved

April 12, 2012, from http://www.timeshighereducation.co.uk/story.asp?storyCode= 412083& sectioncode=26.

AFFILIATIONS

Lauritz B. Holm-Nielsen
Aarhus University, Denmark

MARIJK VAN DER WENDE

AN EXCELLENCE INITIATIVE IN LIBERAL ARTS AND SCIENCE EDUCATION

The Case of Amsterdam University College

INTRODUCTION: JOINING FORCES TO ACHIEVE EXCELLENCE

Amsterdam University College (AUC) was established in 2009 as an excellence initiative jointly undertaken by the University of Amsterdam (UvA) and VU University Amsterdam (VU). AUC is a selective and residential honours college that offers an international liberal arts and sciences bachelor programme, leading to a joint degree from the two founding universities. Both the University of Amsterdam and VU are positioned between 102-150 on the Academic Ranking of World Universities by Shanghai Jiao Tong University (2011), with some 32,000 (UvA) and 25,000 (VU) students, yet quite distinct histories dating back to 1,632 (UvA) and 1,880 (VU). The fact that these two major research universities in Amsterdam joined forces to create AUC and a liberal arts and sciences undergraduate experience was based on the vision that the leaders of the future will have to work together across the boundaries of nationalities, cultures and disciplines, in order to be successful in the globally engaged and culturally diverse society of the 21st century. This paper intends to provide an in-depth analysis of AUC's experience and explain why and how the liberal arts approach is a way to develop excellence in undergraduate education.

From a strategic perspective, the two universities decided to join forces as a way to strengthen excellence, which can be seen as an example of local cooperation for global competition. This approach was supported by the Ministry of Education, the City of Amsterdam, and locally headquartered multinational corporations. Besides and further to this initiative at undergraduate level, cooperation for global excellence between the two universities is being developed or planned for in areas such as graduate education, research, technology transfer, and regional outreach. AUC is considered a successful model in this context since it combines the strengths of both institutions through a process of careful selection and evaluation of students, faculty, staff, and services, based on well-defined principles and criteria for excellence in teaching and learning.

From a systems perspective, the need for an excellence initiative in undergraduate education was fuelled by the general discontent in this area (which will be discussed below), as experienced in virtually all countries with massified higher education systems. The emergence of liberal arts initiatives in Europe can

Q. Wang, Y. Cheng, & N.C. Liu (eds.), Building World-Class Universities: Different
Approaches to a Shared Goal, 89–102.

be seen as a response to the need to differentiate the massified and (overly) egalitarian European higher education systems, by introducing broader curricula and more selective approaches to admission. Known as "University Colleges" they represent in the Netherlands a new branch of excellence in Dutch university education, addressing the situation which was described by the Organization for Economic Co-operation and Development (OECD) as demonstrating an insufficient level of differentiation, where excellence is underrepresented, the international dimension should be enhanced, and too-early specialization should be avoided (OECD, 2008).

UNDERGRADUATE EDUCATION: FROM DISCONTENT TO REDEFINITION

Undergraduate education and its discontent has been intensively discussed and analysed. Central elements of dissatisfaction and critique refer to low performance in terms of retention rates and achieved learning outcomes, student disengagement, stagnant or decreasing graduation rates, and increased time in achieving degrees. These circumstances have come as a result of overcrowded lecture halls, impoverished staff-student ratios, loosening of the research – teaching nexus, and the lack motivation for undergraduate teaching by faculty. Further, despite relentless effort to counter the situation, persistent and/or growing inequalities exist, with higher education being less affordable as a public service. As summarized by Muscatine: "the product of the present curriculum – despite a residue of good learning by good students in good courses – could hardly be called either excellent or economic" (2009:51). Moreover, even in the most elite universities disappointment with the undergraduate achievement has been acknowledged (Bok, 2006).

Contrary to the disappointing record for undergraduate education, research performance has been greatly boosted over the last decades, with growing research dominance to the detriment of undergraduate teaching as a looming consequence. The fact that global rankings seem to enhance this effect has been recognized abundantly (Van der Wende, 2008). Yet, undergraduate education will continue to represent the cornerstone of any higher education system and a key mission of any institution, including research universities. Recognition of the consequent need for reform results in a renewed conversation about the purpose of undergraduate education and the awareness that it is necessary to re-establish a sense of academic mission that emphasizes teaching and the curriculum (Altbach et al., 2009, 2011). Concerns about economic competitiveness and fiscal constraints make a discussion of higher education's accountability with respect to learning achievement largely inevitable (Arum & Roksa, 2011). In addition, the global debate on world-class universities leads to a recognition of the need to re-balance and differentiate institutional missions in terms of requiring a broader range of dimensions for excellence (Van Vught, 2009; Van der Wende, 2011a).

Clearly, the tide is shifting. Re-defining excellence in teaching and learning implies for institutions the development of a vision on what should be learned, why, and how. That is, a future-oriented perspective on the knowledge, values, and skills essential for the 21st century is required and this will be illustrated in the next section by considering AUC's vision and its curriculum design.

A RENEWED FOCUS ON LIBERAL ARTS AND SCIENCES

In the US, inspiring attempts to formulate the way forward were notably led by the "Liberal Education and America's Promise" (LEAP) report on "College Learning for the New Global Century", which embodied an interesting renewed consensus on liberal arts education (the Association of American Colleges and Universities [AAC&U], 2007). Other important contributions to the reinvention of liberal education in the view of new pedagogies were for instance made by Levine (2006). Altbach (2009) underlines the renewed conversation on the value and potential need for liberal education as a more global trend, which emphasizes a broad interdisciplinary curriculum focused on creativity, critical thinking, cultural awareness, problem solving, and communication skills. In Europe, the (re-) emergence of liberal arts programmes was facilitated by the Bologna Process, which recognized undergraduate education as a phase in its own right. Moreover, it can be explained as a response to the need to differentiate the massified European systems (Van der Wende, 2011b). First, in terms of developing broader and more flexible bachelor programmes, with the aim of overcoming the disadvantages of too-early and over-specialization, by re-establishing the balance between breadth and depth of the curriculum, whilst at the same time enhancing learning effectiveness. Second, in terms of establishing more selective branches of higher education, focusing explicitly on excellence, i.e. redefining elite education in overly egalitarian systems.

A prominent example is the Netherlands, where some five liberal arts colleges were established since 1998 as branches of excellence by leading research universities (including Utrecht, Amsterdam, Leiden, and Maastricht). These "University Colleges" recently obtained special status in the higher education legislation, granting them more autonomy than regular university programmes with respect to the selection of students and the level of tuition fees.

AUC capitalized on previous initiatives in the country and mostly on the American experience, but not without a critical stance. It drew on recent accounts – including candid critiques – of the liberal arts tradition (for instance Lewis, 2006) and based on these "lessons learned" it formulated its own vision on why and how liberal arts and science education is most relevant for the 21st century:

– Today's society is in a constant state of flux, and our future leaders need to be flexible, creative thinkers, able to cope with the complexity of the issues facing the world. A liberal arts and sciences education is an excellent foundation in this context.

– In addition to factual knowledge, a liberal arts and sciences education prepares students to become a multilingual, informed and engaged global citizens, with well-developed intercultural competences, able to read intelligently, think critically and write effectively on the processes shaping our world. Students should become better able to make complex connections across disciplines, cultures and institutions; be more creative in their problem-solving; be more perceptive of the world around them; and be more able to inform themselves about the issues that arise in their life, personally, professionally and socially, as well as being equipped to transform such knowledge into practical and ethical action.

– A liberal arts and sciences education enhances their personal development as well as their academic and career development, and provides them with a range of skills that they will be able to use throughout their life.

– In addition, the frontiers of knowledge, both in academia and the world of work, now call for cross-disciplinary inquiry, analysis and application. New pathways across the traditional dividing lines between liberal arts and sciences and the professional fields are needed. Students need to integrate and apply their learning, by addressing the "big questions" in science and society through connecting analytical skills with practical experience, i.e. putting their knowledge into use (AUC, 2011).

AUC's mission: "Excellence and Diversity in a Global City" reflects the belief that both excellence and diversity matter, as both competition and cooperation are key to success in a globalized world. Leadership does not only require excellence, but also the understanding and valuing of diversity. Consequently, AUC's values express a commitment to excellence, diversity, and the global perspective:

– We seek excellence in all that we do and believe that it is not only the responsibility of each individual to strive for his or her best, but also they need to create the conditions for the success of others.

– Diversity is our strength. Different approaches, ideas, and values are integral to the creation of a vibrant and challenging learning environment. Diversity, however, requires tolerance. Tolerance, understanding, and open-mindedness are therefore expected of every member of the AUC community.

– We believe that a global perspective is central to the success of every student. A global perspective requires active engagement with other individuals, communities, and the world. This engagement is celebrated and valued at AUC (AUC, 2012).

AUC'S CURRICULUM CHARACTERISTICS AND LEARNING OUTCOMES

This vision inspired the development of a new curriculum, drawing on eminent scholars in all disciplines from the two founding universities. More specifically, the bare question of what should be taught in order to equip graduates for success in the 21st century led them to outline an engaging curriculum that reaches across disciplinary boundaries, focusing on the "the Big Questions in Science and Society".

The AUC curriculum aims to create an academic community that is rooted in the very best traditions of the liberal arts and sciences, but actively oriented to the demands and challenges of the 21st century. Students live and study on an international campus, following a three-year English-taught bachelor programme that creates new pathways across traditional dividing lines. AUC attracts students from all over the world (50% of its student body is international), who engage on a daily basis in intensive and small-scale seminars with high-calibre international staff (two-thirds have an international background). The curriculum places particular emphasis on:

- Interdisciplinarity: Integrating insights from two or more academic disciplines in order to develop a greater understanding of problems that are too complex or wide-ranging to be dealt with using the knowledge and methodology of just one discipline.
- Scientific Reasoning: The development of academic thinking and strong analytical skills is an integral part of the curriculum for all students. The curriculum offers ample opportunities for students to focus on science and science-related majors in a liberal education context.
- Global Knowledge, International and Intercultural Competence: Understanding of economic forces, interdependence and political dynamics, as well as second-language competence and the ability to respond to cultural perspectives other than one's own.
- Civic Knowledge and Community Engagement: Active involvement with diverse communities and real-world challenges, including in-company internships and off-campus community engagement.
- Research-Based Learning: Multiple opportunities to work, independently and collaboratively on research projects that require the integration of knowledge with skills in analysis, discovery, problem solving and communication, where students are engaged in active learning based on their own questions.

These elements form the main principles of AUC's curriculum, thus shaping a learning experience that aims for the learning outcomes of knowledge acquisition, academic skills, interdisciplinary skills, learning skills, communication skills, engagement at local and global levels as well as personal and social responsibility.

GLOBAL TRENDS AND DRIVERS FOR LIBERAL ARTS EDUCATION
IN THE 21ST CENTURY

The US and European trends are clearly not isolated from each other, as recognized by Rothblatt (2003), who states that the transnational dialogue on liberal education has become more meaningful since basification of higher education in Europe, because this has forced policy makers to consider more differentiated systems of higher education, including specific approaches to undergraduate education such as the liberal arts. Nevertheless, the US and European models for liberal arts contain both similarities and differences (Van der Wende, 2011b). Moreover, the renewed focus on liberal arts is not limited to these two regions, as pointed out by Kirby (2008), who notes that leading Chinese universities share a commitment to general or liberal education with their US counterparts. A commitment to educating the whole person and not just training the specialist may seem counterintuitive in an age increasingly dominated by science and technology and by pressures for ever-earlier and ever-greater specialization. However, this understanding is now the cornerstone of curricular reform in leading universities in mainland China (including Peking, Fudan, Zhejiang, Wuhan, and Sun Yat-sen Universities, with further initiatives announced for Shanghai Jiao Tong and Tsing Hua Universities). In the same region, Hong Kong SAR has benefited from the extension of the undergraduate phase from three to four years to give liberal arts a major role in the first two years of the new bachelor curriculum. Similar approaches are being considered by some leading universities in Japan and China Taiwan. In Singapore, the National University of Singapore recently announced a new liberal arts programme in partnership with Yale University. Also, in other regions, such as the Middle East, such initiatives are being undertaken.

Clearly, the renewed conversation on the value and potential need for liberal arts education can be considered an emerging global trend (Altbach et al, 2009) and as an example of curriculum considerations that take place in the light of globalization and internationalization, is an educational concept that is enjoying global migration itself. What exactly are the main aims and rationales driving this development, how does it relate to developing excellence for undergraduate education in the 21st century, and to what extent is it truly global?

The general underpinnings of liberal arts education are that it should provide students breadth and depth in their academic programmes, ensuring broad knowledge of culture, science and society, as well as in-depth study in a specific area of interest. More specifically, it should help students to develop a sense of social responsibility as well as strong and transferable intellectual and practical skills, including: communication, analytical and problem-solving ability, and a demonstrated competency to apply knowledge and skills in real-world settings (AAC&U, 2007).

Arguments to foster this type of approach to undergraduate education in the 21st century can be described in three broad categories:

− The first type is of an epistemological character and relates to the development of knowledge and the fact that the most exiting science is happening at the interface of the traditional disciplines. That is, the realization that some of the "big challenges" that we face both in science and society are just not solvable by single-discipline approaches and that interdisciplinary work is needed to provide the big breakthroughs. This has led to a substantial focus on cross- or interdisciplinary research into themes, such as: climate change, energy and health and well-being and this needs to be reflected in the curriculum.
− The second type of argument is of an economic and utilitarian nature and relates to the employability of graduates. More specifically, a society characterized by a knowledge economy, innovation, and global competition requires the so-called "21st century skills" which enable graduates to be creative, critical thinkers, and problem solvers who can cooperate in teams and communicate across the boundaries of languages, cultures and disciplines.
− The third category of argument relates to the moral/social dimension and to the humanistic tradition of liberal arts, pertaining to the importance of educating the whole person, including their personal and intellectual development with a view to fostering social responsibility and democratic citizenship.

As depicted in Figure 1, these arguments seem to be to some extent interrelated. It should be noted that the first two categories are strongly driven by the global knowledge economy that is leading to a converging agenda for undergraduate education the 21st century, whereas the third category, the social-moral dimension, may in fact be the most complex one to (re-)define in this "new global century", as it does not seem to be characterized by convergence in the political and ideological sense. Moreover, tensions may arise between the economic and social-moral arguments, as argued by Nussbaum (2010).

The three sets of arguments will be elaborated upon below and illustrated by considering the case of Amsterdam University College.

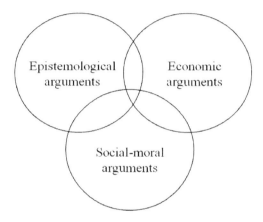

Figure 1. Drivers for liberal arts education in the 21st century

INTERDISCIPLINARITY AND THE ROLE OF DISCIPLINES: COMBINING BREATH AND DEPTH

The focus on interdisciplinarity is recognized as a key component for excellence in undergraduate education. Moreover, the introduction of real-life situations, broad themes and "big questions" from the first year on allows students to develop an expansive intellectual horizon and motivates them to learn, or rather avoid the usual boredom and hence drop out (Elkana, forthcoming). That is, the learning is enhanced, because the students are engaged in the process through the study of challenging problems relating to their backgrounds, history and goals (Muscatine, 2009). Furthermore, this arrangement enables them to decide more effectively upon the subsequent disciplinary courses appropriate for them. However, it is very clear that the interdisciplinary approach cannot replace rigorous teaching of the disciplines, for this type of work requires intelligent collaboration with disciplinary experts, which can only be achieved through in-depth training in at least one (and ideally two) discipline. Or as formulated by Gardner (2008:55) "If no single discipline is being applied, then clearly interdisciplinary thinking cannot be at work". It is therefore recommended to teach from the first year onwards seminars that deal with real-life situations in parallel with rigorous introductory disciplinary courses (Elkana, forthcoming), or a combination of "nuclear (interdisciplinary problem-oriented) seminars" and "planetary courses" (Muscatine, 2009). This combination of interdisciplinary and disciplinary learning relates to the concept of "breadth and depth" as an inherent feature of a liberal arts education and transcends, as such, the discussion on disciplinarity or interdisciplinarity. However, questions of balance, timing and sequence remain important, especially in combination with the notion of student choice which is inherently related to the liberal arts aim for personal development and a broad intellectual horizon.

The AUC curriculum combines breadth of experience with depth of knowledge (see Figure 2). In the first semester of their studies students are expected to think about the "big questions" in science and society, by engaging them in far-reaching themes and broad real-world questions. In fact, Big Questions courses are part of the academic core. Another important aim of these courses is to stimulate students to reflect on their own position with respect to the big questions the world is facing, and how they personally can engage with them. Moreover, the choice of Big Questions courses (Big Question in Science, Big Questions in Society, Big History and Big Books) is independent from the (intended) major. This interdisciplinary approach is motivated by the belief that an education that encompasses different disciplinary perspectives is the best foundation for a broad academic orientation that involves an independent and critical way of thinking. However, the interdisciplinary approach, as explained above, also requires a solid grounding in the separate disciplines, as a substantial depth of knowledge is required for successful interdisciplinary debate. This is conceptualized and depicted in the AUC curriculum circle.

In the AUC curriculum this discipline-based knowledge will mostly be acquired through the major courses in the second and third year. At the end of the first semester, students choose a themed course, which will assist them in their choice for their major course of study. That is, six introductory themed courses are on offer: Energy, Climate and Sustainability, Life, Evolution, and the Universe, Health and Well-being, Information, Communication, Cognition, Social Systems, Cities and Cultures, all of which have a broad interdisciplinary character that introduces students to relevant issues and research questions as well as explaining how different disciplines contribute to it. That is, they offer an orientation and background to the choice of courses for the major, which provides them with the necessary depth of knowledge to engage in the interdisciplinary debate at a more advanced level in their third year and to complete a capstone project.

21ST CENTURY SKILLS AND THE TWO CULTURES OF MODERN SOCIETY

The importance of generic skills is presented above as an economic or utilitarian argument related to employability. Employment in the 21st century is expected to be influenced by more volatile labour markets and careers and a changing demand for skills, i.e. an increasing demand for non-routine interactive and analytical skills as compared to a decreasing demand for routine cognitive and manual skills (OECD, 2010). Typical "21st century skills" would therefore include creativity and innovation, critical thinking, problem solving, communication, collaboration, information, IT, and media literacy, social and cross-cultural skills and leadership and responsibility (Trilling & Fadel, 2009). Regarding these, employers subscribe to the view that graduates need to be creative thinkers, able to communicate, to reason, create, write and speak and to provide leadership. However, many of the skills needed to survive and thrive in modern corporations are those a well-rounded liberal arts education has always provided: depth, breadth, knowledge in context and motion, and the search for deeper understanding. Moreover, liberal arts and sciences graduates are innovative and nimble, can think across platforms, understand society and culture, and see technology as a tool rather than an end in itself (Greenwald, 2010). In the spirit of C.P. Snow (1961), who stated that the breakdown of communication between the "two cultures" of modern society – the sciences and the humanities – was a major hindrance to solving the world's problems, a 21st century liberal arts approach should be able to bridge and integrate these views. It should draw on its origins, when the seven liberal arts were defined as the Trivium (the literary arts) and the Quadrivium (the mathematical arts). Moreover, the humanities, the study of other cultures, languages, and religions, education in moral reasoning and philosophy, is essential for broad development, critical thinking, and ethical judgment. At the same time, young people must learn to think scientifically, i.e. to understand the scientific method and have some mastery of science and technology. Further, mathematics is without no doubt germane to a liberal arts education, for it facilitates quantitative reasoning and statistical literacy.

AUC's Curriculum Circle

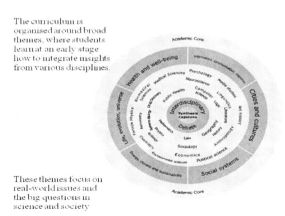

The curriculum is organised around broad themes, where students learn at an early stage how to integrate insights from various disciplines.

At the same time, students achieve depth of knowledge in their chosen major(s), allowing them to participate meaningfully in the interdisciplinary debate

These themes focus on real-world issues and the big questions in science and society

Towards the end of their studies, they bring their knowledge and expertise together in a capstone project.

Figure 2. AUC's Curriculum Circle

97

At AUC, the academic core, ensures that students develop strong skills in mathematics, logic and argumentation, research methods, academic English, a (second) foreign language, and interdisciplinary and intercultural skills. Students take in their first year a set of academic and intercultural skills courses, some of which are compulsory (e.g. Academic English, Logic and Argumentation, and Identity and Diversity in a Global City), or compulsory for specific groups, depending on the intended major (e.g. calculus, statistics or other types of maths courses). A profiling choice made by AUC was to emphasize the sciences and the training of quantitative skills for all students, for in their view the sciences need to be an integral part of an all-round education for the 21st century and they can be successfully taught in a liberal arts context (as demonstrated by Cech, 1999 and Steitz, 2001). Moreover, trends in the Netherlands showed that many potential science candidates are more attracted by broader programmes than by the traditional mono-disciplinary science studies. Producing more science graduates is a strategic need since for AUC's two founding universities and the City of Amsterdam with its major national science research facilities. As many students will later be in a position to make important decisions, whether in business, government, policy, or academia, the scientific way of thinking and approaching life should be valuable if not crucial for their success. Therefore, scientific reasoning, quantitative literacy (numeracy) is part of the academic skills training for all AUC students and consequently, a good level in maths is a key requirement for admission. A high level of proficiency in English is another admission requirement. Regarding this, as the curriculum is taught in English this is not considered a foreign language and so native speakers of English study another language for two or three years. Next to French, German, Spanish and Dutch (not compulsory for international students), the academic core also offers courses in Chinese and Arabic. With respect to the latter two, European students have often learned two foreign European languages already at secondary school relish the chance to acquire these non-European languages. In sum, multilingualism is a genuine notion at AUC.

CITIZENSHIP AND THE NEED FOR A TRULY GLOBAL PERSPECTIVE

The third category of arguments in favour of the liberal arts relates to the moral/social dimension, in particular, to social responsibility and democratic citizenship. The notion of citizenship deserves some particular attention, as clearly it has a strong moral dimension. Elkana (forthcoming) describes the "concerned citizen" in this sense as someone conscious of the major problems that confront humanity today and being aware of the limitations of our existing intellectual tools to cope with these. Moreover, such a person expresses a commitment to contribute to overcoming these problems and limitations and thus to responsible citizenship. In democratic societies it will be taken for granted that this implies democratic citizenship, but this may be less obvious in certain other countries. Questions about the scope of citizenship are of importance as well; should it for instance be national ("citizenship for nation building"), regional (e.g. European or Asian), global, or all of these at the same time? Regarding this, the LEAP report on College Learning in the Global Century (AAC&U, 2007) presented a convincing view on the need for a global perspective for liberal arts education by stating that recent world events have brought into the foreground the importance of linking academic education to issues of democratic citizenship, pluralism, and interculturalism. Influential American scholars also argue that shaping citizens through higher education means that students must be prepared for a culturally diverse and international world, which requires understanding of the perspectives of a wide variety of cultures (Nussbaum, 1997), which fortunately is more evident now as young people rarely leave college as ignorant about the non-Western world as students did some decades ago (Nussbaum, 2010). Moreover, technology has linked humanity in unprecedented ways so we now have a greater opportunity than ever before to become "global citizens" (Gardner, 2011). Nevertheless, accounts on essential learning outcomes in liberal arts demonstrate that intercultural knowledge receives low ratings from both US faculty and students (AAC&U, 2005). In addition, Bok (2006) acknowledges that even the most prestigious US programmes still lack a strong focus on global knowledge, such as foreign languages, international understanding and intercultural awareness. It should be acknowledged, indeed, that the importance of diversity and a global scope in shaping the liberal arts experience in the 21st century has so far been underexposed in the great majority of writings and discussions. It should also be clear that this type of learning can only succeed in a truly intercultural context, which requires a strongly diverse student body and faculty profile, as is illustrated below.

For AUC, the global city of Amsterdam, with its multicultural character (hosting some 180 nationalities) and the strong presence of international businesses and cultural institutions. is a perfect context where excellence and diversity can naturally meet. Its student population (at present 600 in total, growing to approximately 1000 in 2015), as highlighted above, includes 50% international students, from over 35 countries and one third of all the students study for a semester abroad. Over two-thirds of the AUC faculty has an international background (over a third of them hold a PhD from a top-100 university in the Shanghai ranking). Global issues play a central role in the curriculum and the training of intercultural skills is part of the compulsory first year course on Identity and Diversity in a Global City, in which the global city of Amsterdam is actively used as a learning environment. The city features in other courses (e.g. the themed courses on Cities and Cultures, the humanities courses on Literary Cities and Cinematic Cities, social science courses on Urban Life and Society, Urban Economics, etc.) and in community projects that students may undertake in their second or third year. Moreover, AUC benefits from strong ties with the City of Amsterdam authorities, which have resulted in partnerships, opportunities for excursions, guest lectures, internships and community projects. Community outreach is an explicit element of AUC's external strategy and of faculty engagement. However, although AUC was immediately able to generate diversity in terms of a high proportion of international students, attracting minority students from the local setting, proved to be more complicated. Regarding this, AUC is aware that liberal arts education traditionally attracts a white middle-class student population, but feels that this would be an inadequate and in fact, inappropriate student profile, because first and second generation immigrants make up half of the city's population. That is, AUC values diversity as an inclusive and rooted concept that is not limited to the children of the "new cosmopolitans", a global elite that increasingly prefers international and bilingual education (Weenink, 2008). With respect to this, globalization is not only generating cosmopolitanism, but is also bringing migration with its less prosperous dimensions, both of which are integral to global cities and thus, need to be reflected in the student population.

AUC's outreach programme is guided by awareness of the role that cultural capital and social capital may play in admission processes (Reumer & Van der Wende, 2010), in terms of the choice of students for a study programme (minority students tend to prefer professional tracks), and that a residential obligation may be an obstacle for certain groups (e.g. Muslim girls). However, the fact that AUC actually transcends the usual (minority/majority) categories and ethnic divides, as found in Dutch universities, encourages minority students to join. AUC students (some minorities, some not) who voluntarily joined the diversity outreach project have advocated the advantages as being part of a diverse blend meeting in a global context, which allows them to meet fellow students with probably the same convictions and religious beliefs, but from very different cultural or economic backgrounds. Moreover, corporate sponsors of the AUC Scholarship Programme (which supports at present 10–15% of students with a scholarship) are in particular motivated to contribute with these targets in mind. For them, the importance of nurturing a diverse workforce seems to be far more obvious than for certain universities seeing the need to educate a diverse student body. Further, partner schools at secondary level respond positively, enthusiastically participating in joint activities (part of community projects or internships), thus helping to build the necessary bridges step by step, for addressing the shortfall in admissions of local young people. However, this endeavour requires a long-term commitment at the most senior level. Data recently gathered in the context of the survey on "A Student Experience in the Research University" (SERU, administered by the Center for Higher Education Studies at University of California, Berkeley) reflect that students greatly appreciate the international opportunities at AUC, finding that the general climate at AUC is tolerant of diversity (94%), and that diversity is important for themselves (85%). In addition, social integration, the overall social experience and feeling of belonging is reported positively by 85-90% of the students. Finally, AUC students' abilities in intercultural communication are no doubt supported by their strong language skills: 80% master between two to four languages at conversational level (14% three or more) and 62% at least two at the level needed to take up studies in that language (34% three or more). As said previously, multilingualism is a genuine notion at AUC.

CONLUSION: A TREND TOWARDS GLOBAL EXCELLENCE BUT NO PANACEA

In conclusion, the liberal arts model would appear to respond to a variety of demands that define the criteria for excellence in undergraduate education in the 21st century. However, the fact that various trends toward global excellence in undergraduate education seem to amalgamate into a liberal arts approach, as adopted at the forefront of a number of leading systems and institutions, does not imply that this model can be seen as a panacea for all the problems of this context. In particular in this regard, the number of students enrolled in these types of institutions and programmes is quite small, especially outside the US. One of the most pressing questions, therefore, is how can this type of undergraduate experience be provided at scale? Furthermore, the global dimension of liberal arts education deserves more attention and would greatly benefit from a truly global platform for debate on liberal arts and on undergraduate education at large. This debate should be guided by a future-oriented perspective on the values, knowledge and skills essential for the 21st century and how fruitful such a discussion can become at the institutional level, has been illustrated by the case of Amsterdam University College.

REFERENCES

Altbach, P. G., Reisberg, L., & Rumbley, L. E. (2009). *Trends in Global Higher Education: Tracking an Academic Revolution.* Paris: UNESCO and the Center for International Higher Education, Boston College.

Altbach, P. G., Gumport, P. J., & Berdahl, R. O. (Eds.). (2011). *American Higher Education in the Twenty-First Century: Social, Political, and Economic Challenges* (3rd ed.). Baltimore: Johns Hopkins University Press.

Amsterdam University College. (2011). *Amsterdam University College Faculty Handbook 2011–2012.* Amsterdam: Amsterdam University College.

Amsterdam University College. (2012). *Amsterdam University College Mission and Values.* Retrieved May 12, 2012, from http://www.auc.nl/aboutauc/object.cfm/85A5189B-1321-B0BE-A427343001E35A71

Arum, A., & Roksa, J. (2010). *Academically Adrift: Limited Learning on College Campuses.* Chicago: University of Chicago Press Books.

Association of American Colleges and Universities. (2005). *Liberal Education Outcomes. A Preliminary Report on Student Achievement in College.* Washington, DC: AAC&U.

Association of American Colleges and Universities. (2007). *College Learning for the New Global Century. A Report from the National Leadership Council for Liberal Education and America's Promise (LEAP).* Washington, DC: AAC&U.

Bok, D. (2006). *Our Underachieving Colleges: A Candid Look at How Much Students Learn and Why They Should be Learning More.* Princeton: Princeton University Press.

Cech, T. R. (1999). Science at liberal arts colleges: A better education? *Daedalus, 128*(1), 195–216.

Elkana, Y., & Klöpper, H. (forthcoming). *The University in the 21st Century: Teaching the New Enlightenment and the Dawn of the Digital Age.*

Gardner, H. (2008). *Five Minds for the Future.* Cambridge, MA: Harvard Business School Press.

Gardner, H. (2011). *Truth, Beauty, and Goodness Reframed: Educating for the Virtues in the 21st Century*. New York: Basic Books.

Greenwald, R. A. (2010, October 1). Liberal arts II: The economy requires them. *Inside Higher Education*. Retrieved April 10, 2012, from http://wwwinsidehighered.com/views/2010/10/01/greenwald

Kirby, W. C. (2008). On Chinese, European and American universities. *Deadalus, 137*(3), 139–146.

Levine, D. N. (2006). *Powers of the Mind: The Reinvention of Liberal Learning in America*. Chicago: The University of Chicago Press.

Lewis, H. R. (2006). *Excellence without a Soul: Does Liberal Education has a Future?* New York: Public Affairs.

Muscatine, C. (2009). *Fixing College Education: A New Curriculum for the 21st Century*. Charlottesville: University of Virginia Press.

Nussbaum, M. (1997). *Cultivating Humanity: A Classical Defence of Reform in Liberal Education*. Cambridge, MA: Harvard University Press.

Nussbaum, M. (2010). *Not for Profit: Why Democracy Needs the Humanities*. Princeton: Princeton University Press.

OECD. (2008). *Reviews of Tertiary Education – The Netherlands*. Paris: OECD.

OECD. (2010, October). *Globalisation, Competition and Quality in Higher Education: OECD's Insights*. Presentation by Barbara Ischinger at the German Academic Exchange Service (DAAD) Conference on New Horizons for the International University, Berlin.

Reumer, C., & Wende, M. C. van der. (2010). *Excellence and Diversity: Selective Admission Policies in Dutch Higher Education – A Case Study on Amsterdam University College*. University of Berkeley, Centre for Studies in Higher Education. Research and Occasional Papers Series, CSHE.15.10.

Rothblatt, S. (2003). *The Living Arts: Comparative and Historical Reflections on Liberal Education*. Washington, DC: Association of American Colleges and Universities.

Snow, C. P. (1961). *The Two Cultures and the Scientific Revolution. The Rede Lecture 1959*. Cambridge: Cambridge University Press.

Steitz, T. A. (2001). Science Education at Liberal Arts Colleges: Why they do it so well. *Lawrence Today*, Spring 2001 Issue. Lawrence University.

Trilling, B., & Fadel, C. (2009). *21st Century Skills: Learning for Life in Our Times*. San Francisco: Jossey-Bass.

Vught, F. A. van. (2009). (Ed.). *Mapping the Higher Education Landscape: Towards a European Classification of Higher Education*. Dordrecht, Germany: Springer.

Weenink, D. (2008). Cosmopolitanism as a form of capital: Parents preparing their children for a globalizing world. *Sociology, 42*(6), 1089–1106.

Wende, M. C. van der. (2008). Rankings and classifications in Higher Education. A European perspective. In J. C. Smart (Ed.), *Higher Education Handbook of Theory and Research* (Vol. 23, pp. 49–71). Dordrecht: Springer.

Wende, M. C. van der. (2011a). Towards a European approach to ranking. In N. C. Liu, Q. Wang, & Y. Cheng (Eds.), *Paths to a World-Class University: Lessons from Practices and Experiences* (pp. 125–139). Global Perspectives on Higher Education. Rotterdam: Sense Publishers.

Wende, M. C. van der. (2011b). The emergence of Liberal Arts and Sciences Education in Europe: A comparative perspective. *Higher Education Policy, 24*(2), 233–253.

AFFILIATIONS

Marijk van der Wende
Amsterdam University College, the Netherlands
The VU University Amsterdam, the Netherlands

SADIQ M. SAIT

POLICIES ON BUILDING WORLD-CLASS UNIVERSITIES IN SAUDI ARABIA

An Impact Study of King Fahd University of Petroleum & Minerals

INTRODUCTION

The Kingdom of Saudi Arabia's current effort in developing its higher education sector and building world-class universities has drawn international attention. In particular, its higher education reform is aimed at preparing the Kingdom for a future that does not solely depend on its oil resources, and thus strive to assume a key position not only in the Middle East but also the world. With full support from King Abdullah bin Abdulaziz and his government, a range of policies and approaches have been implemented, both at the national and institutional levels, geared to fulfilling these ambitions. Based on this socio-economic context, this chapter provides a review of the current developments and strategies of higher education reform in the Kingdom. More specifically, a case study of King Fahd University of Petroleum & Minerals (KFUPM) is presented to illustrate how these national strategies and policies are being adopted at the institutional level.

THE NATIONAL CONTEXT OF BUILDING WORLD-CLASS UNIVERSITIES

Located between the Arabian Gulf on the east and the Red Sea on the west, the Kingdom of Saudi Arabia is the largest country in the Middle East and it possesses at least 25% the world's oil reserves and is a leader of the international oil industry. Unprecedented economic and social changes have been witnessed over the past forty years. Since the early 1970s, its oil revenues have been utilized to develop its economy, improve social and health standards, and to modernize society (Ministry of Higher Education, 2010a; Al-Mubaraki, 2011).

However, as alluded to above, the government is highly aware that to sustain the nation's development, its future cannot solely depend on its natural resources. This is particularly critical in the context of a global knowledge-based economy, as a nation's sustaining power is increasingly reliant on information, innovation and human capital. To assume a dominant role in the Arab world and to raise its international visibility, the Saudi government believes that higher education will play an indispensable and ever important role in both international cooperation and national competitiveness (Marginson & Van der Wende, 2007). As shown in the *Future Plan for Higher Education in Saudi Arabia*, higher education is designed

Q. Wang, Y. Cheng, & N.C. Liu (eds.), Building World-Class Universities: Different Approaches to a Shared Goal, 103–113.

and evaluated in relation to the overall national development plan, and is considered essential for educating a skilled workforce for its socio-economic development, promoting research and development, and for maintaining its distinctive cultural heritage (Ministry of Higher Education, 2010a). Since 2006, and subsequently as a part of *the Future Plan for Higher Education in Saudi Arabia* (AAFAQ), a variety of policies were designed and are being implemented at promoting excellence in the higher education.

Expanding University Capacities

Higher education in Saudi Arabia has undergone rapid growth in the past few years, with the number of students (both male and female) increasing from 444,800 in 2002 to 903,400 in 2010 (Ministry of Economy and Planning, 2011). In 2009, more than 56.6% of enrolled students were female; male students were 43.4% (Ministry of Higher Education, 2010b). With the establishment of 10 new universities during the past few years, the higher education system now includes 24 government universities, 18 primary school teacher's colleges for men, 80 primary school teachers' colleges for women, 37 colleges and institutes for health, 12 technical colleges and 26 private universities and colleges. Moreover, under the governance of the Ministry of Higher Education, these higher education institutions are distributed across almost all of the country's 13 administrative provinces so as to achieve a regional balance in national growth (Saudi Arabian Monetary Agency, 2007; Onsman, 2011).

The Kingdom currently invests heavily in its education, with the education sector representing over 25% of the total budget (more than US$13 billion), within which more than US$2 billion is spent on higher education annually (Ministry of Higher Education, 2010a). In May 2012, His Majesty King Abdullah bin Abdulaziz is to inaugurate the first phase of the University and Education City projects aimed at creating a world-class higher education infrastructure across the country and boosting research capacities. In fact, a total of US$21 billion will be invested in addition to the regular education expenditure (Arab News, 2012).

Study-Abroad Policy

In addition to higher education expansion, the Saudi government has put in place a variety of scholarship programmes, both government- and university-led, aimed at cultivating a high-skilled national workforce to tackle the pressures of global competition. Such scholarship programmes were initiated in the 1970s, when most students were sent to the US, UK and Canada. This study-abroad policy has been reinforced since 2006 as part of the King Abdullah Programme and within less than four years, more than 40,000 students were sent to universities all over the world, with the main focus being on subject areas that can serve to boost the country's economic development, such as engineering, medicine, information technology and sciences. Moreover, King Abdullah Programme is geared toward developing an internationally competitive workforce and establishing a high calibre base in the domestic universities (Ministry of Higher Education, 2010c).

National Commission for Assessment and Accreditation

To improve the quality of post-secondary education in the Kingdom, the National Commission for Assessment and Accreditation was established, with the responsibility for evaluating universities' academic programmes and curricula against both national and international criteria. The organization not only collaborates with higher education institutions, but also with industry, community agencies, other higher education stakeholders as well as other international quality assurance agencies, so as to ensure its evaluation criteria meet high international standards (National Commission for Assessment and Accreditation, 2010).

THE CASE OF KFUPM

At the institutional level, universities in Saudi Arabia have echoed the government's directives, by implementing different approaches aimed at developing excellence. Among them, KFUPM represents an interesting case, because its exercises have borne fruit in terms of improvements in the quality of education, research and community services. KFUPM, a mainly science and engineering university, was officially established in 1963, and started student admission in 1964, it being a government-supported institution. The vast oil resources of the country pose a complex and exciting challenge for scientific, technical, and management education. To meet this challenge, the university has adopted advanced training and is developing extensive research in the fields of sciences, engineering, and management. Along with other older universities in the Kingdom, KFUPM has a higher status and has better-qualified and more stable staffing. KFUPM graduates are usually preferred by employers of Saudi academics over their counterparts (Onsman, 2011). Since 1970's, the university's enrolment steadily increased and currently there are 8,693 students with a total of 1,702 staff members including both academic and research personnel (Ministry of Higher Education, 2010d). It boasts six colleges (Engineering, Applied Engineering, Sciences, Environmental Sciences, Computer Sciences and Engineering, and Industrial Management), providing both undergraduate and postgraduate level courses.

Strategic Planning Directives and Governance

The Ministry of Higher Education keenly recognized the fact that in their pursuit of enhancing the quality of higher education, leadership was crucial. Consequently, so as to enhance leadership skills, in 2009 the Academic Leadership Centre (ALC) was established to give focus and emphasis to this critical issue. Based on an initial plan, the ALC organized numerous developmental activities serving some of the needs of Saudi higher education institutions and administrators (Academic Leadership Centre, 2012).

Based on the national policy of strong encouragement for rationalized governance, KFUPM was determined from the beginning that it should strive to achieve global excellence in the shortest possible length of time. When the Ministry of Higher Education launched its initiative in 2006 to prepare a modern and a long term plan for university education, *the Future Plan for Higher Education in Saudi Arabia*, KFUPM was chosen to conduct a detailed study for the preparation of an effective plan to achieve a world-class higher education system in the coming 25 years. The plan includes an analytical review of the current conditions and operations and explores the practical development horizon for Saudi higher education to achieve its strategic objectives, as well as ensuring that Islamic values and Arabic cultural heritage are maintained.

Further, it has devoted serious effort in a systematically planned manner, with consecutive strategic plans being prepared and implemented since 2006. The first established goals in five different aspects of provision for the years 2006-2011: to develop excellence in education (producing quality graduates), to develop excellence in research (conducting innovative research with the main focus being on national needs and international trends), to enhance university standing and reputation, to strengthen competitive edge in response to emerging challenges in society, and to provide services to society and the community (creating stimulating campus life and providing responsive services of value to society (KFUPM, 2006). More specifically, the strategic plans set goals for tackling 24 specific issues ranging from improving student motivation, reducing bureaucracy, building alliances, increasing diversity, setting out the research direction, improving human resource policies with respect to retention, competencies, etc., and improving outreach to the community. Having seen the success of this approach in many areas as well as identifying shortcomings, the university leadership decided to develop a second strategic plan, with a longer time horizon, from 2011 to 2020, focused on the adoption of new ideas and technologies (KFUPM, 2011).

In its pursuit of excellence, the university understands the importance of quality assurance and has implemented institutional policies to promote this, by adopting international standards and criteria. As a result, the Accreditation Board for Engineering and Technology (ABET) in the US has declared that its engineering programmes are "substantially equivalent" to similarly accredited programmes in America. In addition, it has recently been accredited by the National Committee for Assessment and Accreditation along with its programmes in sciences and management by the Association to Advance Collegiate Schools of Business.

Human Capital Development

An important parameter that provides for excellence in educating students is the selection of students and faculty and the university believes that an objective mechanism for admitting students is the basis of achieving this goal. In fact, according to the records, a high proportion of the best science students in the

Kingdom join KFUPM. Regarding this, of the approximately 122,000 science students graduating from senior high schools, about 30,000 apply to the university, but only 3,560 achieve the standard required. However, the number of students eventually joining each year at present is about 1,800.

The university has recently embarked on improving its faculty profile by attracting high-level scientists from all over the world, based on the Ministry's direction. More specifically, different schemes have been created under the titles of joint professors, chair professors, and research chair professors. Faculty under the lattermost category are generally selected from the Highly Cited list provided by Thomson Reuters and the total number of Professors attracted thus far to KFUPM in this category is 24 (12 in 2009 and 12 in 2010). The breakdown of these scientists as per the disciplines is: chemistry (3), computer sciences (2), environment (1), engineering (3), material sciences (6), mathematics (6) and physics (3). Moreover, new tracking indicators have been put in place to identify potential researchers with a proven record for hiring and promotion purposes, which has resulted in an increase in the number of excellent postdoctoral researchers and graduate students, helped by the generous stipend on offer.

In addition to the need for such recruitment strategies, KFUPM leaders firmly believe that developing excellence and improving academic skills for faculty members are among the primary goals of academic institutions, as faculty quality is directly related to improving the learning process and thus learning outcomes. Thus, the university has established the deanship of academic development, with responsibility for the continuous enhancement of the quality of its academic system by ensuring that faculty and teaching assistants reach their full potential in teaching and research. Moreover, in order to encourage faculty development, the Ministry of Higher Education holds open competitions covering the whole country regarding proposals for higher education development, as part of the "Development of Creativity and Excellence of Faculty Members in Saudi Arabia". KFUPM has won four programmes to date, including planning and managing e-learning in higher education, e-learning teaching and learning skills for online education, peer consultants in teaching, and developing tests to assess the quality of higher education outcomes, (KFUPM, 2012a).

Research Development and Innovation

Institutional initiatives have been designed and implemented to enhance research excellence, innovation and technology in KFUPM. At a national level, the Saudi government has funded and encouraged universities to establish centres for research excellence. In line with this policy, the university has set up five centres of excellence in the areas of: nanotechnology, corrosion, renewable energy, Islamic finance, and refining and petrochemicals. It has also implemented various internally funded research initiatives covering grants for fast track research and research funds for junior faculty, to name a few. Moreover, in 2008, the Saudi government put out requests for 67 distinct research projects and invited faculty at the country's universities to submit proposals. In all, 37, or more than half of the proposals, were awarded to faculty at KFUPM, the nation's smallest university (KFUPM, 2012b).

The university established Dhahran Techno-Valley (DTV), a high-tech park, on campus, in line with the expressed wish of the Higher Education Ministry. To this, it has succeeded in getting many of the world's leading corporations to establish their research and development (R&D) centres there, thus taking advantage of the proximity to the university engineering labs and faculty and the world headquarters of Saudi Aramco, situated adjacent to the campus. Regarding this, Schlumberger, the world's largest oilfield services corporation, has opened a research centre on the site and since has doubled its business with Saudi Aramco. Moreover, Yokogawa, a Japanese technology company, has also built a research facility and plans to double that space. Further, Baker Hughes, a global oilfield service company, has also inaugurated a research facility to collaborate with Saudi Aramco. Finally, over 10 other multinational corporations have long-term lease contracts in university built facilities in the valley. The main goal behind this setup is to encourage industry-academia interaction focusing on core research helpful for addressing local problems.

Meanwhile, in order to realize its community obligations based on national policy, KFUPM has extended its research dimensions to serve the R&D demands of the nation: industrial, business, and governmental sectors. Regarding this, the university's research institute, with its 30-year history and strong reputation in the region, has been building on its accumulated experience, by playing a central role in the success of numerous industrial and environmental initiatives. This has involved drawing on its strong capability for adapting technologies based on the unique service and operating conditions in the Gulf. An interesting development is the formation of Research Cloud, whereby researchers across the Kingdom's premier universities and institution (such as KFUPM itself, King Abdullah University of Science and Technology and King Abdulaziz City for Science and Technology) can collaborate and use each other's resources electronically through a high speed education network – Saudi Arabian Advanced Research and Education Network.

Table 1 shows that the patent profile of KFUPM has increased by leaps and bounds, a feature that can be accredited to the Kingdom's policies and support in promoting excellence in research. In relation to this, from Figure 2 it is clear that the amount of intellectual property generated in the last couple of years is more than that generated in the previous 20 years.

Collaboration with World-Class Institutions

A strong emphasis of the Ministry of Higher Education is to have research and academic collaboration between highly acknowledged international institutions and the Saudi universities. In relation to this, a trilateral collaboration agreement between Saudi Aramco, KFUPM, and Stanford University aimed at establishing a

Table 1. Patent applications

Total non-provisional patent applications filed (1995–to date)	Current Status	Country filed	Ownership
338	215 pending	204 U.S.	189 KFUPM
			3 KFUPM and Saudi Aramco
			12 KFUPM and MIT
		1 each in Japan, Korea, Eurasia and Norway and 2 each in Europe and China	KFUPM and Saudi Arabia
		2 GCC	KFUPM and 1 with Saudi Aramco, 1 with MIT
		1 India	KFUPM and MIT
	21 abandoned	US	KFUPM
	26 allowed	US	KFUPM
	76 patents issued	71 US	67 KFUPM
			3 KFUPM and Saudi Arabia
		5 Japan	1 KFUPM and Petroleum Energy Centre, Japan
		5 Japan	KFUPM and JCCP Japan

Source: KFUPM (2012c)

strategic relationship in education and scientific research in petroleum engineering and geosciences is a good metric of national policy guiding institutional growth. The university also signed a research collaboration agreement with Massachusetts Institute of Technology in June 2008, which will last for a period of over seven years and will involve the conducting of joint research in the areas of: clean energy and design, clean water, and manufacturing and nanotechnology, and working on educational projects. An increase in the patent profiles as a result of such mutual collaborations is one of the key outcomes.

Information Technology as an Enabler

The Kingdom's policy makers realize the importance of information technology as an enabler of advanced learning and research. In keeping with this, one of the notable advances in technology, a scalable High Performance Computing (HPC)

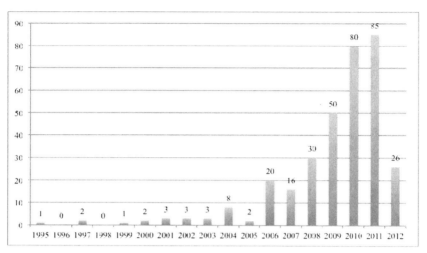

Figure 1. Progress of intellectual property generation at KFUPM, until May 2012. Source: KFUPM (2012c)

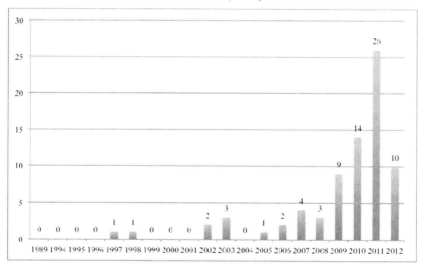

*Figure 2. Patents issued during the last 20 years, until May 2012.
Source: KFUPM (2012c)*

cluster, has been made available to the faculty to improve the effectiveness of advanced research. More specifically, the main benefits to the university in deploying the HPC facility include: increased competitiveness, faster research times and attracting major projects with industry. Furthermore, the e-learning initiative at KFUPM is providing necessary software, including course management systems and authoring and assessment tools for ensuring successful delivery of university curricula and instruction. Regarding the course management systems, these are a major platform for successful course content delivery, assessment, communication and collaboration through the web. In addition, the university's open access initiative is a key driver of the efforts to ensure that all teaching, research and administrative documents are organized, maintained and made available through the web.

The deployment of two enterprise resource planning systems, the Oracle E-Business Suite and the SunGard Banner Student System, was initiated in 2005 with a big bang approach ensuring that all the aforementioned systems went live at once. Moreover, considerable investment was made in making sure that all the major stakeholders were given training and incentives in relation to operating the new software. Further, shared ownership of the data with proper accountability provided validation for its integration into a single system. In relation to the software, a powerful modelling tool was used to cover 160 main business processes in a 24-week time frame, with the entire as-is/to-be cycle being thus completed. However, a careful balance between customized and packaged processes was maintained to ensure best business practices, while adhering to the constraints necessary in a semi-autonomous institution.

Network connectivity available to students has been extended to cover their rooms and dormitories so as to provide them access to the information highway, seamlessly. Further, network storage space is provided to the community in the form of uninterrupted access to their valuable data. In addition, faculty members have round the clock access to computing resources through the high-speed campus network, *Asymmetric Digital Subscriber Line* (ADSL) home network and the *virtual private network* (VPN) for extranet access. The rise in productivity through this all-encompassing connectivity has been phenomenal. Moreover, students can register for courses online from anywhere, conveniently, thereby saving them the burden of having to be physically present. Further, KFUPM has a high percentage of smart classrooms with Internet connectivity to facilitate learning and teaching. In addition, the availability of a digital library service has served to ease the access to learning and research materials. Finally, a major part of the IT budget goes into training and this has resulted in home-grown project completion, and consequent reduction in the cost of exorbitant consultancies.

CONCLUSION

This chapter has reviewed the Kingdom of Saudi Arabia's education policy drivers in relation to building world-class universities and has also presented the KFUPM case to assess its progress to this end. Various strategies and measures have been adopted and implemented at both the national and institutional levels, in particular, in terms of quality assurance, strategic governance and international collaboration. Further, education and research spending has increased massively throughout the country and one impact arising from this is some of its universities now having acquired international visibility in the global rankings. For example, KFUPM entered the Quacquarelli Symonds (QS) World University Ranking in 2008 (QS, 2011) and Academic Ranking of World Universities (ARWU) in 2010 (Shanghai Jiao Tong University, 2011) and its position in both have been continuously improving ever since (see Table 2). To a certain extent, we can argue that the Kingdom of Saudi Arabia's experience in developing academic and research excellence has been successful. The Saudi story also shows that without strong government support and effective management, this could not have been possible.

Table 2. KFUPM's performance on the global university rankings

	2003	2004	2005	2006	2007	2008	2009	2010	2011
ARWU	/	/	/	/	/	/	/	401-500	301-400
QS	/	/	/	/	/	338	266	255	221

Source: ARWU(http://www.arwu.org/);QS(http://www.topuniversities.com/institution/ king-fahd-university-petroleum-minerals/wur)

ACKNOWLEDGMENTS

The author acknowledges King Fahd University of Petroleum & Minerals, Dhahran, Saudi Arabia for all support. Thanks are also due to Syed Tariq Maghrabi, Syed Sanaullah, and Syed Faraz Ahmed for their help in preparation of the manuscript. Special thanks to Nida Chinoy for her immense help in editing and improving the quality of the chapter.

REFERENCES

Academic Leadership Centre. (2012). *Mission and Vision.* Retrieved May 12, 2012, from http://www.alc.edu.sa/Page.aspx?id=6

Al-Mubaraki, A. A. S. (2011). Natioanl and global challenges to higher education in Saudi Arabia: Current development and future strategies. In S. Marginson, S. Kaur, & E. Sawir (Eds.), *Higher Education in the Asia-Pacific, Higher Education,* Dynamics 36. Dordrecht: Springer.

Arab News. (2012, May 2). King Abdullah's SR 81.5 billion to education. *Arab News.* Retrieved May 12, 2012, from http://arabnews.com/saudiarabia/article622349.ece

King Fahd University of Petroleum & Minerals. (2006). *The First Strategic Planning.* Retrieved May 12, 2012, from http://www1.kfupm.edu.sa/opq/

King Fahd University of Petroleum & Minerals. (2011). *The Second Strategic Planning.* Retrieved May 12, 2012, from http://www1.kfupm.edu.sa/opq/ssp/index.html

King Fahd University of Petroleum & Minerals. (2012a). *Development of Creativity and Excellence of Faculty Members in Saudi Arabia.* Retrieved May 12, 2012, from http://www1.kfupm.edu.sa/dad/excellence/

King Fahd University of Petroleum & Minerals. (2012b). *Research Overview.* Retrieved May 12, 2012, from http://www.kfupm.edu.sa/SitePages/en/DetailPage.aspx?CUSTOMID=16& LinkID=Link3

King Fahd University of Petroleum & Minerals. (2012c). *Patent Portfolio.* Retrieved May 12, 2012, from http://dtv.kfupm.edu.sa/IC/patport.html

Marginson, S., & Wende, M. C. van der. (2007). *Globalization and Higher Education.* OECD Directorate for Education, OECD Education working papers series, Working Paper No.8. Paris: OECD.

Ministry of Economy and Planning. (2011). *KSA Economy in Figures.* Retrieved May 12, 2012, from http://www.mep.gov.sa/inetforms/article/Download.jsp;jsessionid=7AFA795010945EE8 F6AC9967BBEBEA36.alfa?Download.ObjectID=181

Ministry of Higher Education. (2010a). *Saudi Arabia: Kingdom of Humanity.* Retrieved May 12, 2012, from http://www.mohe.gov.sa/en/studyinside/aboutKSA/Pages/default.aspx

Ministry of Higher Education. (2010b). *Women in Higher Education: Saudi Arabia Initiatives and Achievements.* Riyadh: Ministry of Higher Education.

Ministry of Higher Education. (2010c). *The King Abdullah Scholarship Programme.* Retrieved May 12, 2012, from http://www.mohe.gov.sa/en/studyaboard/King-Abdulla-hstages/Pages/ default.aspx

Ministry of Higher Education. (2010d). *King Fahd University of Petroleum & Minerals.* Retrieved May 12, 2012, from http://www.mohe.gov.sa/en/studyinside/Government-Universities/Pages/ KFUPM.aspx

National Commission for Assessment and Accreditation. (2010). *Vision and Mission.* Retrieved May 12, 2012, from http://www.ncaaa.org.sa/english/acmspage.aspx?id=4

Onsman, A. (2011). It is better to light a candle than to ban the darkness: Government led academic development in Saudi Arabian universities. *Higher Education, 62*(4), 519–532.

Quacquarelli Symonds. (2011). *Top Universities: King Fahd University of Petroleum & Minerals.* Retrieved May 12, 2012, from http://www.topuniversities.com/institution/king-fahd-university-petroleum-minerals/wur

Saudi Arabian Monetary Agency. (2007). *The 43rd Annual Report.* Riyadh, Saudi Arabia: Research and Statistics Department.

Shanghai Jiao Tong University. (2011). *Academic Ranking of World Universities.* Retrieved May 12, 2012, from http://www.arwu.org.

AFFILIATIONS

Sadiq M. Sait
Department of Computer Engineering, and
Center for Communications and IT Research, Research Institute,
King Fahd University of Petroleum & Minerals, Saudi Arabia

SECTION 3

EVALUATING WORLD-CLASS UNIVERSITIES FROM A RANKING/INDICATOR PERSPECTIVE

SEERAM RAMAKRISHNA

WORLD UNIVERSITY RANKINGS AND THE CONSEQUENT REACTIONS OF EMERGING NATIONS

INTRODUCTION

In today's world of plentiful information and fast paced lives, people tend to rely on readily available and easy to comprehend rankings or ratings when making choices. This is also evident in the rapidly expanding university sector, which has a total enrolment exceeding 150 million students. In particular, the world university rankings, which became available in 2003, are appealing to higher education stakeholders and have prompted increased attention and commitment to the sector, as they are seen by many as proxy indicators of reputation and performance of universities, despite there having been strong criticism regarding the limitations of their methodologies as well as their having had undue influence (Guttenplan, 2011). In the context of the global knowledge economy, the higher education sector is expanding on the backdrop of developed nations pursuing universal higher education, whilst emerging ones are eagerly pursuing mass higher education sectors so as not to be left behind (Marginson, 2007; Altbach, 2011; Ramakrishna & Ng, 2011). This chapter will provide a review of the emergence of world university rankings and the consequent reactions from the emerging countries.

THE EMERGENCE OF GLOBAL UNIVERSITY RANKINGS

A simple web search for meaning of word "ranking" yields varied results which include: "to arrange things in order, classify, establishing social hierarchy", "a listing of items in a group, such as schools or sports teams, according to a system of rating or a record of performance" and "comparison of an investment's performance to others over a given time period" (Merriam Webster Dictionary, 2012). Therefore, in essence it can be taken that "ranking" is a position on a scale in relation to others. It is human nature to compare every aspect that comes to its attention. That is, humans tend to compare intentionally and/or involuntarily as their lives involve making choices, be it the selection of a product, a person or a service. Given the abundance of information, the need to make quick decisions has generated the need for robust measures of reputation and rankings have become central to this process. The higher education sector is no exception to this, for rankings have emerged to serve as a powerful tool for assessing quality, performance and competitiveness of institutions set against the criteria of the

Q. Wang, Y. Cheng, & N.C. Liu (eds.), Building World-Class Universities: Different Approaches to a Shared Goal, 117–128.
© 2013 Sense Publishers. All rights reserved.

global war for talent and excellence (Kehm & Stensaker, 2009; Hazelkorn, 2011; Ramakrishna, 2011a).

In the context of global knowledge economy, higher education is increasingly playing the role of training high-skilled workers for creating knowledge so as to promote economic growth and national security. Since 1960s, in particular in the past two decades, higher education has witnessed unprecedented development, that is, increasing expansion and intensified internationalization activities, in both the developed and emerging countries. As both a public and private good, higher the sector has been promulgated as the means to upward social mobility, employability, higher earnings potential over a person's lifetime and happiness. Having succeeded with their mass higher education goals, the developed nations are now pursuing the goal of universal higher education. Moreover, emerging nations are pursuing the goal of mass higher education to bridge the gap between the developed nations and themselves. On the specifics, the US and European regions are home to about 30 million students each and in recent years China has ramped up its higher education places to about 25 million (the Ministry of Education, 2012). Further, it is estimated that India provides about 15 million higher education places and plans to double the gross enrolment rate to 30% by 2020 (Ramakrishna & Ng, 2011; The Hindustan Times, 2012). In sum, it is estimated that there are more than 20,000 universities worldwide, which are home to nearly 150 million students.

In addition, higher education has continued the process of internationalization, which has been intensified due to a range of drivers: growing demand for talent (e.g. China, India, Qatar, Saudi Arabia, Turkey and Indonesia), expanding access to higher education (e.g. India, China and Singapore), increasing competition to further raise excellence (e.g. Singapore and India), raising opportunities for extra university financial income (e.g. Australia, UK, US, Malaysia, Singapore, Hong Kong SAR China, India and Russia), and global orientation of education (e.g. Japan, Korea, Taiwan China, US, Canada, Germany, Norway, Finland, Russia and Kazakhstan). In general, universities are increasingly acknowledging the need for providing global learning experiences for students in order to prepare them for a future in a competitive yet increasingly interdependent and hyper connected world. This result has been the establishment of a range of international activities, including student exchanges, twinning programmes, double degrees, joint research, and the setting up of overseas branch campuses or even whole universities. It is in these contexts that quality and quality assurance measurement has become the central concern to various higher education stakeholders.

A number of non-profit and for profit organizations, have undertaken the task of comparing substantial numbers of higher education providers in terms of quality and/or excellence. However, comparison and ranking of universities on a global scale has only come into place in recent years (Sadlak & Liu, 2009; Ramakrishna, 2011b), with the Academic Ranking of World Universities (ARWU) being the first published in 2003, by Shanghai Jiao Tong University. Since then, Quacquarelli Symonds (QS), Times Higher Education (THE), the Higher Education Evaluation and Accreditation Council of Taiwan (HEEACT) and Webometrics have also published respective league tables of universities worldwide. According to Hazelkorn's research (2011), today there are 10 different global rankings, and over 50 national rankings in the world, i.e. the obsession with rankings has appeared to now span the globe and their league tables are now released annually with much attention from the media worldwide. As one of the consequences, international conferences are being organized regularly across the globe to discuss the pros and cons of these tables that are seen by many as indicators of performance, in terms of the motives and ethics of ranking universities, the quality and reliability of the data and ranking methodologies and the extent of the openness of the process and the dissemination of information (Hazelkorn, 2011; Ramakrishna, 2011c).

WORLD UNIVERSITY RANKINGS: CRITICISM AND CURRENT DEVELOPMENTS

As the world university rankings gain more and more attention, as pointed out above, there has been closer scrutiny of them, with the key criticisms centring on their methodological limitations, ethical matters, their validity and their overreliance on academic publications.

Methodological Limitations

Universities' missions are diverse, ranging across developing human capital, conducting research aimed at helping the economy through innovation and knowledge-transfer, preparing a workforce of life-long learners equipped for changing economies and societies and building vibrant communities. However, it is impossible to rank all the missions and activities, and consequently difficult to measure and compare diverse higher education institutions using common criteria. As a result, it is hardly surprising that the various rankings have adopted different indicators and applied different weightings to reflect the different aspects of higher education systems. (Marginson & Van der Wende, 2006; Sadlak & Liu, 2007).

Main questions and criticisms arise to methodological limitations, including lacking internationally comparable data as well as favouring English-speaking countries and their institutions. In sum, therefore, the question arises as to whether like is being compared with like especially across the developed and emerging economy divide. With regards to the data collection itself, the statistical significance of data collected from a fraction of stakeholders for determining the ranking indicators, such as "employer surveys" or "academic surveys" have been accused of bias. Others have questioned the fairness of data on daily teaching and research as they are collected by administrators who are at a remote distance from these activities. Finally on this matter, the lack of transparency in the data collection process has been raised as matter, for it is not possible to guarantee that the systems used are robust and not unjustly skewed (Shin & Toutkoushian, 2011).

Another major shortcoming highlighted by a number of scholars is that teaching and other university activities play a secondary role to research in the compilation of university league tables, a matter discussed in detail below. Moreover, it has been argued that current ranking methodologies, because they fail to capture the nature of diverse teaching and learning ecosystems across the globe in terms of what is quality, are inadequate for matching the product with the consumer (Hazelkorn, 2011; Ramakrishna, 2011c). Moreover, not all students want the same learning experience and rather in many cases they seek diverse learning opportunities and value-added experience to prepare them for future careers, which works against the rankings that imply there is only one road to excellence. Consequently, it has been contended that the rankings can mislead potential students in their obtaining a good fit between their optimal needs and a university programme choice.

Methodological limitations may further lead to discomfort and concerns on undue influence on academia as well as knee jerk reaction by university leaders, as there is increasing evidence that university administrators are functioning so as to improve their ranking position and score, which may not be in the best interest of their society that it is serving (Hazelkorn, 2011). Moreover, the league tables are increasingly being associated with successful market performance and consequently, university leaders are diverting their attention to higher rankings, which may also be at the expense of the wider role of an institution In sum, under narrowly defined notions of quality and success, which can be raised as shortcomings of the current rankings, universities may run the risk of over-emphasising their importance to the detriment of a wide range of education and training needs that a higher education system is expected to satisfy (Salmi, 2009).

Over-Reliance on Academic Publications

As can be seen in Table 1, the main university rankings rely heavily on the capturing of research data in the form of academic publications and citations. This is because such information is easier to compile as well as being more universally accepted than that for other types of activities, such as measures of teaching quality. However, regardless of whether this bias towards research accurately reflects performance, it is still problematic. For instance, a university's research performance is aggregated across all its disciplines and subsequently compared and this implies that the top institution is top in all subjects and so on, which is very unlikely to be the case.

Table 1. Comparison of four global university rankings

Ranking	Research Related	Edu-cation	Inter-nationalization	Per Capita Performance	Industry Income	Employer Perception
HEEACT	100%	0	0	0	0	0
ARWU	80%	10%	0	10%	0	0
THE	62.5%	30%	5%	0	2.5%	0
QS	60%	20%	10%	0	0	10%

Source: HEEACT (http://ranking.heeact.edu.tw/en-us/2011/homepage/), ARWU (http://www.arwu.org), THE (http://www.timeshighereducation.co.uk/world-university-rankings/) and QS (http://www.topuniversities.com/university-rankings/world-university-rankings)

However, some of the ranking organizations realized this was a weakness and started to introduce subject specific rankings of universities, which are much more helpful. For example, Shanghai Jiao Tong University started releasing broad subject field rankings in 2007, entitled ARWU-FIELD rankings; and subject area rankings since 2009, termed ARWU-SUBJECT rankings[1] (Shanghai Jiao Tong University, 2012). Similarly QS and THE have published subject specific league tables. Moreover, recently QS has started to publish league tables for indicators, including academic review, employer review, citations per faculty, students per faculty, international students and international faculty. As can be expected these league tables showed that even among the top one hundred institutions, different universities have different strengths and under this broader notion of performance, more universities from non-traditional regions of academic excellence appeared in these specific league tables. Taking a different approach to simply counting publications and citations, Thomson Reuters recently began publishing Global Research Reports (Thomson Reuters, 2012), which identifies strengths and trends of a country and an institution in specific research fields of importance.

Turning to the actual research data collection itself, ranking organizations use information on research publications, such as the number of papers, and the number of citations per paper, which can be extracted from global databases, such as Thomson Reuters's Web of Knowledge and Elsevier's Scopus. However, the current ranking methodologies have yet to be robust enough to deal with such matters as institutional affiliations abbreviated in multiple ways, different authors bearing similar names, citations inflated by self-citations, and negative citations. Moreover, despite these databases giving information on outputs of a research activity i.e. journal papers and citations, what is of much more relevance than hard numbers is the impact of a research activity in the form of value creation, thought leadership, transformative ideas and solutions to the challenges at hand. Perhaps recognizing this, recently the new owner of the Web of Knowledge database, Thomson Reuters, has decided to discontinue maintaining the database of highly cited researchers (Thomson Reuters, 2011), which will have a marked impact on the ranking methodology.

Roads to Excellence for Emergent Universities

Leaving aside the issue of whether measuring research is the most accurate way of measuring performance, it is not likely to be pushed out of the role of being the prime determinant. In light of this, it is of interest to consider the possible stages through which emergent universities from outside the traditional regions for strong higher education provision will need to pass, if they are to achieve higher rankings, as a means of guidance for those who wish to take this path. That is, as illustrated in Figure 1, university based research activities can be grouped into four evolutionary stages. A university that is in the initial stage of transitioning from a primarily teaching institution to one focussing more on research should encourage its members to seek, proactively, competitive research funds as well as to generate conference papers and peer reviewed journal papers. In addition the university leaders need to encourage the provision of consultancies to businesses, and invest limited resources in niche research areas, which are considered areas of strength and/or of relevance to the stakeholders. At the next stage, the emphasis should be on scientific research across the campus in as many disciplines as possible and quality should take precedence over quantity, in the form of high impact journal papers, citations, applications for membership of boards of prestigious international journals and scientific bodies, and licensing and transfer of intellectual property. In the third phase, as the university moves up the ladder of scientific research, it should focus on the peaks of research excellence in niche areas on an international scale, seek election of its faculty members to prestigious national and international academies, gain international recognition in the form of competitive global awards and prizes, and establish substantial academic partnerships with peer world-class universities. The final stage, the acme of scientific research, is characterised by faculty: providing thought leadership on national and international issues and challenges, originating transformative ideas and new disciplines with national and international impact, creating in-tangible and tangible values to the society, and achieving a sustained global reputation. Figure 1 expands upon this trajectory by including other features that should be considered at each stage.

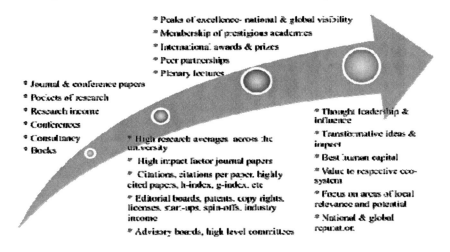

Figure 1. Evolutionary path for achieving excellence in scientific research in higher education institutions.

IMPACT OF THE WORLD UNIVERSITY RANKINGS

However much the global league tables are liked or disliked, world university rankings are here to stay. Released annually with much attention from the media worldwide, the various world university rankings, in a less than perfect way, have exerted huge impacts on higher education and its stakeholders. Moreover, a

122

competitive culture has been injected into and stimulated in global and national higher education systems (Marginson & Van der Wende, 2006). On the part of students, they use rankings to make their study choices, both home and abroad, whilst academics engage with them when making career moves and employers consult them to identify the best sources of talent. Rankings also influence the accreditation of programmes by disciplinary-specific bodies, sponsorship decisions by donors, and universities' willingness to form partnerships. Finally, policymakers in some countries refer to such external information to allocate preferential funding, to foster competition and to influence leadership changes at universities.

Impact on Students

The main consumers of university league tables are students when they make their choice of institutions and subjects to study, as rankings are perceived to reflect the quality and potential value of university qualifications (Hazelkorn, 2011). In reality, a whole range of factors can be of concern to students, including quality of programmes, institutional reputations, learning environment, proximity to home, the availability of bursaries, scholarships and financial support packages, campus life and prospects upon graduation. However, with few reliable quality standards available and little international comparable information, students and their parents are forced to depend on the narrower criteria of the world university rankings when decision making. To address this limitation, there needs to be more avenues for current and past students at universities to inform the ranking organizations about their perceptions of the quality of their educational experience and their future prospects. This could then be included in some form in the ranking data collection process, thereby providing more accurate information for prospective students. In other words, what those responsible for compiling the rankings should extend their concerns to is the value added aspect with regards to the learning atmosphere of the university (Hou, 2010) as told by those who are subject to it.

Impact on Universities and Leadership

The most affected party by the annual release of university league tables could be university leadership, no matter whether they acknowledge it or not. That is, they can see the impact directly in the form of quality and number of students enrolled, which in turn affect their budgets. Some universities discretely discuss the annual league tables and make appropriate adjustments to their policies and practices, where feasible and appropriate, whereas others publicize their performance in their public relations materials and when media opportunities arise. Moreover, of the key players mentioned above, the university leaders, supported by academics and higher education domain scholars, are in better position to understand the implications of the various ranking indicators in terms of their impact on the institution's diverse stakeholders. Consequently, in the interests of transparency and as a means for improving accuracy and trust, ranking exercises should entail consultation with these entities. In addition, from a slightly longer perspective, these people need to establish robust datasets covering a range of issues through inter-organizational agreement that can eventually be employed as indicators in the rankings.

Impact on Policy-Makers and Governments

The emergence of world university rankings has stimulated the awareness of global competition as well as becoming the main method for providing evidence for quality evaluation. Regarding this, Hazelkorn (2011) has argued that university rankings are important because there is a perceived positive correlation between higher education excellence and global competitiveness by governments and organizations at all levels: local, national and even supranational. Moreover, there is widespread evidence, that both governments and higher education institutions, including those in developing countries, are dedicated to having their universities positioned in the global league table (Altbach, 2011). As a consequence, significant restructuring and reform of higher education is being witnessed throughout the globe and a close look at the different global university rankings reveals that the gap between the academic superpower nations and emerging ones has been narrowed.

ACTION TO NARROW THE INFLUENCE GAP AMONGST UNIVERSITIES

To gain a good position in the global rankings, governments and top universities have adopted various strategies to enhance their international competitiveness and three common foci can be identified, that is, competitive funding schemes (see Table 2), internationalization and governance reform at both national and institutional levels. Serendipitously, the global ranking of universities may have helped to narrow the influence gap between universities in academic superpower nations (US and UK) and emerging academic nations.

Until recently, universities with longer and richer histories enjoyed higher esteem in the eyes of the public, potential students, and policy makers, which stemmed from their track record, name recognition, and accumulated good. Some of these older universities contributed to change in their respective societies as well as managing to adapt themselves in response to other societal changes not of their making. More recently founded universities in various nations around the world, in particular those in some developing countries, are making strenuous effort to improve their level of influence and their reputation, both nationally and globally. A closer look at the recent 2011 QS world university rankings, for example, indicates that in criteria such as "academic reputation", "employer reputation", "international faculty", "international students" and "faculty student ratio", universities from outside the academic superpower nations, namely the US and the UK, occupy nearly 50% of the top one hundred positions. The one remaining criteria in the QS ranking, that of "citations per faculty", is yet to yield to a similar

Table 2. Examples of excellence initiatives launched by various nations

Countries	Initiative
Australia	Excellence in Research for Australia Initiative, ERA
Mainland China	The 985 and 211 Projects
France	Grouping of universities and preferential funding of select universities
Germany	Preferential funding of select universities
India	Starting New IITs and IISERs
Japan	Centres of Excellence for 21st-Century Plan; Global Centres of Excellence Programme; and World Premier International Research Centre Initiative
Malaysia	Accelerated Programme for Excellence
Saudi Arabia	World-class infrastructure and talents at public universities
Singapore	Research Centres of Excellence; Competitive Research Programme; National Research Fellowships
South Korea	Brain Korea 21 and World-Class University Programmes
Taiwan China	Development Plan for University Research Excellence
Vietnam	2006-2020 national plan to have at least one university in top 200 of the world by 2020

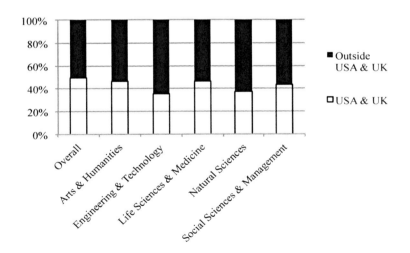

Figure 2. Closing gap among universities in the academic superpowers (US and UK) and other/emerging nations. Source: QS (2011)

position. This is likely to change as the emerging nations are investing more on higher education and scientific research led innovation. The same trend is apparent in the field specific rankings (Figure 2).

Moreover, nowadays the universities labelled as world-class are globally dispersed and this trend is set to continue in the coming decades as the front runners in these regions and their stake holders step up efforts to enhance quality and excellence. In 2012, for the first time, QS published a list of 50 best student cities in the world (Figure 3), with the criteria used for comparison including student mix, employer activity, affordability and quality of living. It can clearly be seen that today the best student cities are globally dispersed.

In sum, generous funding schemes and careful implementation of strategies to root in the culture of excellence by some universities in emerging nations will enable them to move up the ladder of world university rankings. In turn, their increased visibility will enable them to attract top professors, researchers and students, and substantial investment for growth. Moreover, promoting international activities can further invigorate the pursuit of excellence, using strategies such as co-branding and global partnerships in the form of joint education and research programmes with world-class universities in academic superpower nations.

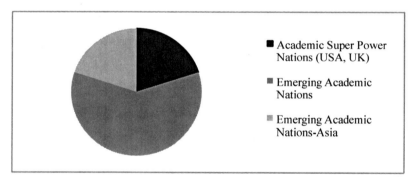

Figure3. Global distribution of 50 best student cities. Source: QS (2012)

CONCLUSIONS

The emergence of world university rankings has enabled students to find suitable schools and subjects to study, helped academics to pursue their careers, provided university leaders benchmark tools for improving quality and performance, and has had an impact on government policies on higher education. However, these rankings, as explained in this paper are subject to limitations in terms of their underlying methodologies, choices of indicators and weightings and quality of data. The previous discussion gives rise to a number of issues that need to be resolved:

– What constitutes quality and relevant higher education?

- What constitutes excellent research?
- What are the roles of universities in scientific innovation?
- What are the roles of universities in a fast paced, globalised cooperative-competitive world?

In my opinion, whilst addressing these questions we need to ensure the following are desired goals or are maintained where they already exist:

- Diversity of universities with different missions is essential for economic and social development.
- Universities must adopt best academic practices and root in a culture of excellence.
- Universities need sustained resources and autonomy.
- Universities are key enablers of scientific research, innovation and entrepreneurship.
- Respected peer review processes and principled research ethics are the basis for effective competition for research funding.
- A national vision for and commitment to higher education.

Regarded as one of the key barometers of global competitiveness, world university rankings have reinforced the agreement that future competitiveness of nations will be based on the availability of highly talented human resources and access to new ideas and intellectual capital (Salmi, 2009). Their publication has led to significant higher education reform and restructuring around the world. Such development, along with fundamental shifts in the global economy, may narrow the long standing influence gap between the academic superpower and emerging nations. Thomson Reuters' Global Research Reports and subject area and indicator specific university league tables substantiate the view that nodes of academic excellence and scientific innovation are now more globally dispersed than ever before. That is, the various contenders can position themselves to compete in niche areas and no longer be seen as laggards.

NOTES

[1] Natural Sciences and Mathematics, Engineering/Technology and Computer Sciences, Life and Agricultural Sciences, Clinical Medicine and Pharmacy, and Social sciences are examples of subject fields. Mathematics, Physics, Chemistry, Computer Science, and Economics/Business are examples of subjects.

REFERENCES

Altbach, P. G. (Ed.). (2011). *Leadership for World-Class Universities: Challenges for Developing Countries*. London: Routledge Publishers.

Guttenplan, D. D. (2011, May 3). Debating the merits of university rankings. *The Global Edition of New York Times*. Retrieved May 12, 2012, from http://www.dit.ie/media/ditresearch/ NYTimes%2030. May.2011.pdf

Hazelkorn, E. (2011). *Rankings and the Reshaping of Higher Education*. London: Palgrave Macmillan Publishers.

RAMAKRISHNA

Higher Education Evaluation and Accreditation Council of Taiwan. (2012). *2011 Performance Ranking of Scientific Paper for World Universities.* Retrieved April 12, 2012, from http://ranking.heeact.edu.tw/en-us/2011/homepage

Hou, A. Y. C. (2010). The development of student learning outcomes based accreditation model in Taiwan higher education. *Asian Journal of University Education, 6*(1), 29–48.

Kehm, B. M., & Stensaker, B. (2009). *University Rankings, Diversity and the New Landscape of Higher Education.* Rotterdam: Sense Publishers.

Marginson, S. (Ed.). (2007). *Prospects of Higher Education: Globalization, Market Competition, Public Goods and the Future of the University.* Rotterdam: Sense Publishers.

Marginson, S., & Wende, M. C. van der. (2006). To rank or to be ranked: The impact of global rankings in higher education. *Journal of Studies in International Education, 11*(3/4), 306–329.

Merriam Webster Dictionary. (2012). Retrieved May 12, 2012, from http://www.merriam-webster.com/dictionary/rank

Quacquarelli Symonds. (2011). *QS World University Rankings: 2011/2012.* Retrieved April 12, 2012, from http://www.topuniversities .com/university-rankings/world-university-rankings

Quacquarelli Symonds. (2012). *QS Best Student Cities in the World 2012.* Retrieved April 12, 2012, from http://www.topuniversities.com/student-life/best-student-cities/2012/

Ramakrishna, S. (2011a, July 15). The global challenge. *Times Higher Education.* Retrieved May 12, 2012, from
http://www.timeshighereducation.co.uk/story.asp?storyCode=412569&sectioncode=26

Ramakrishna, S. (2011b, March 11). Global comparison of universities: Varsity rankings still a work in progress. *The Straits Times,* p. A24.

Ramakrishna, S. (2011c, March 11). Global rankings of universities: The good, the bad and the ugly. In *The Asia-Pacific Association for International Education (APAIE) 2011 Conference.* Taipei.

Ramakrishna, S., & Ng, D. J. T. (2011). *The Changing Face of Innovation: Is It Shifting to Asia?* Singapore: World Scientific Publishers.

Sadlak, J. & Liu, N. C. (Eds.). (2009). *The World-Class University as Part of a New Higher Education Paradigm: From Institutional Quality to Systematic Excellence.* Bucharest: UNESCO-CEPES.

Salmi, J. (2009). *The Challenge of Establishing World-Class University.* Washington, DC: The World Bank.

Shanghai Jiao Tong University. (2012). *Academic Ranking of World Universities.* Retrieved April 12, 2012, from http://www.arwu.org

Shin, J. C., & Toutkoushian, R. K. (2011). The past, present, and future of university rankings. In J. C. Shin, R. K. Toutkoushian, & U. Teichler (Eds.), *University Rankings: Theoretical Basis, Methodology and Impacts on Global Higher Education.* Dordrecht: Springer.

The Hindustan Times. (2012, April 25). 200 Universities across India in Next 5 Years. *The Hindustan Times.* Retrieved April 25, 2012, from http://www.hindustantimes.com/HTNext/Education/200-universities-across-India-in-next-5-yrs-Sibal/Article1-846073.aspx

The Ministry of Education, China. (2012). *Higher Education Statistics.* Retrieved April 12, 2012, from http://www.moe.edu.cn

Times Higher Education. (2012). *World University Rankings 2011–2012.* Retrieved April 12, 2012, from http://www.timeshighereducation.co.uk/world-university-rankings

Thomson Reuters. (2011). *Welcome to Highly Cited Research from Thomson Reuters.* Retrieved May 12, 2012, from http://researchanalytics.thomsonreuters.com/highlycited/

Thomson Reuters. (2012). *Global Research Report Series.* Retrieved April 12, 2012, from http://researchanalytics. thomsonreuters.com/grr/.

AFFILIATIONS

Seeram Ramakrishna
The National University of Singapore, Singapore

128

FREYA MEARNS AND TONY SHEIL

GLOBAL BENCHMARKING AND PARTNER SELECTION USING WORLD UNIVERSITY RANKINGS AND CLASSIFICATIONS

INTRODUCTION TO THE STUDY

One well accepted definition of what constitutes a world-class university has been developed by Alden and Lin (2004). Their list of *Key Characteristics of World-Class Universities* was adopted by Griffith University in Australia in its *Research Plan 2009-2013* to define the cultural shift necessary for advancement; however quantitative evidence of progress is necessary to determine if the university is succeeding, requiring detailed benchmarking of research. Griffith University therefore developed a method, using mainly world rankings and classifications, for the selection of an appropriate grouping of universities upon which to perform global benchmarking of research. The university's specific aim was to identify up to one dozen successful research universities, all from overseas, to gauge whether Griffith University is on a trajectory to become a comprehensive research university of world standing on an internationally accepted range of research performance indicators. This exercise was inspired by the story of the Academic Ranking of World Universities (ARWU), established by the Graduate School of Education at Shanghai Jiao Tong University, which itself began life as an attempt to establish the global standing of Chinese universities (Liu, 2009).

At the turn of the century, the Australian government promoted the use of benchmarking to help university leaders compare the performance of their institutions with others and determine how their performance could be improved (McKinnon, Walker & Davis, 2000); however, at that time few useful international rankings were available to assist such endeavours. Hazelkorn (2011) points out that recently "benchmarking has transformed institutional comparison processes into a strategic tool" (p. 42) and that in the global era of higher education, rankings and classification systems have encouraged more data exchange, thus allowing institutions to undertake extensive analysis. It is therefore disappointing that most institutions currently use the available rankings data for little more than superficial analysis of their own performance and to scan the results of competitor institutions.

This chapter outlines the method employed by Griffith University which led to the eventual identification of five successful research universities against which to benchmark research performance, to determine whether Griffith University is on a similar trajectory to become a world-class research university represented on all major world university rankings. The analysis of world rankings and classifications

Q. Wang, Y. Cheng, & N.C. Liu (eds.), Building World-Class Universities: Different Approaches to a Shared Goal, 129–143.
© 2013 Sense Publishers. All rights reserved.

also provides Griffith with the foundation for future research benchmarking using these internationally successful universities that should help answer questions such as:

– At what point in their histories did similar universities to Griffith University make the transition from being merely good to great research universities?
– What "breakthrough" strategies were in place at critical junctures in these universities' histories?
– What are the lessons from others founded during the same era as Griffith University and what structures, organizational arrangements, missions, and supporting strategies are taking them forward?
– What expectations should be placed on institutions at Griffith University's stage of development with respect to their research performance?
– What investment is required to produce "step change" and lift "Griffith-like" universities to the next stage of development?

A central objective of this chapter is to demonstrate that analysis of world university rankings and classifications can allow benchmarking which extends an institution's understanding of itself and others, thereby allowing it to set achievable targets and deliver strategic outcomes. In discussing the development of world-class universities, Salmi (2009:71) states that "each country must choose, from among the various possible pathways, a strategy that plays to its strengths and resources". The approach for identifying benchmark institutions that is outlined in this chapter has potential for use both by institutions and governments to inform national dialogue, thus allowing decision-makers to choose appropriate strategies rather than embarking on potentially misplaced quests to develop "world-class" institutions in the absence of evidence that this is achievable.

ABOUT GRIFFITH UNIVERSITY

Griffith University is named in honour of Sir Samuel Walker Griffith (1845-1920), a former Premier and Chief Justice of Queensland and the first Chief Justice of Australia. The year 2011 marked the 40th anniversary of the passing of the *Griffith University Act 1971*. It followed closely in the footsteps of numerous Australian and overseas universities established in a period of global higher education expansion between 1960 and the mid 1970s (Quirke, 1996).

The university comprises five campuses located in the rapidly growing population corridor linking the cities of Brisbane and the Gold Coast. Enrolling more than 43,000 students, with one-quarter of these from overseas, Griffith University is one of Australia's largest and most international universities and it also ranks among Australia's top 10 research universities, according to in-house analysis of the Government's *Excellence in Research for Australia 2010* results, where it was rated world-standard or better in 45 fields of research.

Griffith University has an international reputation in the arts, humanities and social sciences, with a range of highly regarded programmes in law and criminology, education, political sciences, business and psychology. It is nationally preeminent in the creative and performing arts as host to the Queensland College of

Art, the Griffith Film School and the Queensland Conservatorium. Since its foundation the university has been strong in environmental sciences and aspects of physical and chemical sciences, but until recently has had little presence in health and medical sciences, engineering, and information technology. However, in response to demographic change and population growth in South-East Queensland, it has more than doubled in size since 2002 through expansion of existing areas and by developing a significant presence in medicine, dentistry, allied health, architecture, and branches of engineering and information technology. A new health precinct, developing around the Gold Coast campus, includes a $150 million Griffith Health Centre and the AUS$1.76 billion (about US$1.8 billion), 750 bed Gold Coast University Hospital, both of which are scheduled for completion in early 2013.

This rapid expansion has significantly improved the rate of output, quality and international visibility of research undertaken at Griffith University. In 2011, it secured a top 500 position on the ARWU ranking for the first time, becoming only the second university in the State of Queensland to be ranked on the ARWU, QS World University Rankings and the Times Higher Education World University Rankings.

The *Griffith University Strategic Plan 2009-2013* announces its vision to be "recognised as one of the leading universities of Australia and of the Asia-Pacific region" (p. 2). Benchmarking Griffith University's research performance trajectory against comparable universities that are currently outperforming Griffith University on world rankings should not only help it to track its progress, but also to identify strategies to help achieve its vision.

UNIVERSITIES OF THE 1960S AND 1970S

In the lead up to and following the *Robbins Report* (1963), the United Kingdom more than doubled the size of its university system from 20 to 43 universities. This period of higher education expansion commenced with Sussex in 1961 and included the universities of East Anglia (1963), York (1963), Lancaster (1964), Warwick (1965), Bath (1966) and Surrey (1966). Following the *Martin Committee on the Future of Tertiary Education in Australia,* Australia followed suit in 1964 by establishing Macquarie University, then Newcastle in 1965, Flinders (1966), La Trobe (1967), James Cook (1970), Griffith (1971), Murdoch (1973) and Deakin (1974). Universities with an explicit mandate of offering wider access to higher education, and in several cases supported by an interdisciplinary research focus, were also established in countries such as Sweden (Umeå), Denmark (Odense), the Netherlands (Maastricht), Canada (Simon Fraser), and Israel (Ben Gurion), to name just a few.

There is less evidence of an organized widespread trend in establishing new universities in the US during this era; however there was significant investment in research and development (O'Mara, 2005) and in higher education, including the establishment of new campuses of existing universities and new buildings on older campuses to accommodate a ballooning of student numbers (Thelin, 2004). The

State of California, though, did produce a Master Plan in 1960 (California State Department of Education, 1960) and, in fact, the best example of a 1960s research-led institution that has gone on to achieve world research leadership is the University of California, San Diego which, according to its website, is "renowned for its collaborative, diverse and cross-disciplinary ethos that transcends traditional boundaries in science, arts and the humanities".

There is little evidence of deliberate systematic expansion in countries outside Europe, Australia and North America during the 1960s and 1970s; however, there are some universities established during this era that are performing very well, including in Japan (Tsukuba University) and Brazil (State University of Campinas).

Several of the universities from the 1960s and 1970s era have developed into leading research universities, including the previously-mentioned University of California, San Diego, which is positioned in the world top 20 as a global research powerhouse. Those ranked in the top 200 universities worldwide on the major university rankings include the universities of Warwick, Maastricht, Sussex, Tsukuba, and the University of California, Irvine. Others, such as Simon Fraser, East Anglia, Southern Denmark (formerly Odense), Umeå, and Campinas appear poised to make the transition to top 200 status. These universities demonstrate that while it is difficult to compete in world rankings against universities with much longer histories, it is not impossible to do so.

PREVIOUS BENCHMARKING OF GRIFFITH UNIVERSITY'S
RESEARCH PERFORMANCE

In 2009, Griffith University identified the University of Warwick as a potential benchmark university and analysed its history to determine what breakthrough strategies had led to its rise through the world rankings. The purpose of the exercise was to determine whether Griffith University could use any of Warwick's strategies to propel its own improvement in performance, and to provide targets for research output and other measurable indicators.

The University of Warwick, established in 1965, is an outstanding institution where excellent research and teaching outcomes have seen it accepted in recent years as a member of the prestigious Russell Group of universities. It was established only a few years before Griffith University and is similar in numerous ways, but outperforms Griffith University on all major world rankings, appearing in the top 150-300 in both the Academic Ranking of World Universities (ARWU) and the Higher Education Evaluation and Accreditation Council of Taiwan (HEEACT) listings and reaching top 50 status in the QS World University Rankings, 2011.

Warwick provides a potent example of a university with a strong social sciences profile, similar in this respect to Griffith University, which has succeeded in climbing onto the higher rungs of the research ladder. Griffith University is now producing the same number of research outputs as Warwick did around 2000, which might suggest that it, having commenced teaching in 1975, is approximately a decade behind Warwick in its development. The fact that Warwick has achieved a doubling of research outputs since then also suggests that Griffith University needs to sustain its recent growth well into the future, if it is to become "the next Warwick".

Warwick has several attributes that have positioned it extremely well over time including its location in a population catchment of almost 10 million people in the British midlands; its proximity to some of Britain's leading company headquarters and industry; and an abundance of developable land. The university's bold vision and strong leadership over many years, combined with good access to the centres of power in London, are widely acknowledged as the essential ingredients of its success.

The University of Warwick is also a useful example in developing landmark facilities over time, which has led to significant growth in research and teaching profiles; slowly but surely positioning the university to become the institution it is today. These include the Arts Centre (1974), the Science Park (1984), the Warwick Business School brand (launched 1984), the Conference Centre (mid-1980s), and the Medical School (2000). Moreover, it is beginning to attract philanthropic income and has set a £50 million (about US$81 million) fundraising goal as part of its *50 Forward* fundraising campaign.

While Griffith University lacks the vast tracts of developable land, the large population base and co-location with corporate headquarters enjoyed by Warwick, it does have features that even Warwick lacks, such as the co-location of the AUS$1.76 billion (about US$1.8 billion) Gold Coast University Hospital, due for completion in early 2013 and the attractiveness of its location in Brisbane and the Gold Coast to international staff and students. Whether Griffith University can become "the next Warwick" remains to be seen; however, this initial benchmarking exercise serves as the basis for a more detailed future initiative, tracking Griffith's future progress alongside Warwick and other identified benchmark institutions.

Other universities, such as Simon Fraser University in Canada and Monash University in Australia, were identified as potential benchmarks for Griffith University and proved to have many similarities to it, though outperforming it on all world rankings. In fact, Griffith University's benchmarking analysis of the former highlighted many shared research discipline strengths, as well as a number of areas in which Griffith University and Simon Fraser University may be able to provide useful strategic advice to each other on areas they wish to develop. On the basis of this benchmarking, Griffith University approached Simon Fraser University about the possibility of developing a strategic partnership – such a partnership was put into effect in May 2010 when the two presidents signed an institutional memorandum of understanding, committing to joint activity in research as well as learning and teaching. This initiative was extended in 2011 with the launch of the Griffith University – Simon Fraser University Collaborative Travel Grants Scheme.

These recent benchmarking exercises proved very useful; however, Griffith University wished to look beyond the English-speaking universities so as not to limit the lessons that could be learned from benchmarking, and therefore decided to develop a systematic approach to identifying other benchmark universities.

METHOD – FILTERS USED TO INFORM THE CHOICE OF OTHER BENCHMARK INSTITUTIONS

Starting from a list of approximately 17,000 universities and institutions of higher education (International Association of Universities [IAU], 2004), the eventual choice of other benchmark institutions came down to the application of seven filters, which made these universities comparable to Griffith University. Wary of the tendency in Australia for comparisons to concentrate mainly on institutions in the US and UK, a fundamental principle of the exercise was to identify a truly international list of prospective benchmark universities.

The following "filters" were applied before arriving at the short-list of five institutions; they are also outlined in Figure 1.

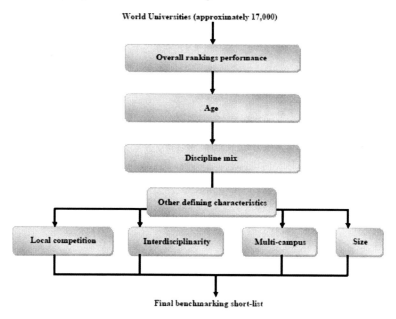

Figure 1. Filters for identifying benchmark universities

Overall Rankings Performance

Appearing on any one of three selected world rankings   The first hurdle was that selected universities should be listed on at least one of three world university rankings in 2010, two of which are founded upon research performance:
– Academic Ranking of World Universities (ARWU);

- Higher Education Evaluation and Accreditation Council of Taiwan (HEEACT) Performance Ranking of Scientific Papers for World Universities;
- QS World University Rankings.

Griffith University's vision to be recognised as a leading university in the Asia-Pacific region necessitates international recognition of the quality of its research and influenced the choice of which rankings to use. When the analysis began in 2010, seventeen Australian universities were ranked on the ARWU, accounting for almost half of the university sector and Griffith University's absence from that ranking before 2011 was seen as a significant weakness hindering the achievement of its vision. The institution ranked highly on "volumetric" rankings such as the Scimago Institutional Rankings,[1] however, fell down when "quality" indicators (such as papers in *Nature* and *Science*) were introduced. While the university's lower rank on unadjusted indicators, such as citations per paper, reflected Griffith University's social sciences orientation, to some extent, it was agreed that relatively new offerings in professional areas including medicine, dentistry, health services, engineering and architecture, should rapidly improve its standing. The university needed to understand the impact that these developments would have on its research performance and its attractiveness to both staff and students, especially from overseas, as well as determine whether there were additional strategies available to further strengthen performance. Therefore, two rankings (ARWU and HEEACT) on which it was not listed were chosen and a third (QS), in which it had been listed for several years.

Griffith University remains highly conscious that "international rankings in their present form only cover a very small percentage of the world's 17,000 universities, between 1% and 3% (200-500 universities), completely ignoring the rest" (Rauhvargers, 2011:7). However, with a good resources base and annual institutional budget in the region of US$800 million, it was thought that it had the scale and the emerging quality to confine benchmarking to the three chosen rankings systems. At the time of analysis there were 737 universities listed on at least one of these three rankings in 2010, including Griffith University, which was ranked at 323 in the 2010 QS World University Rankings.

Appearing on all three rankings   The list that resulted from the first step of the analysis showed that 361 universities were represented on all three selected rankings and therefore this filter was chosen as a refinement to ensure that the final short-list included only universities that were of a uniformly higher standing to that of Griffith University, which was listed on only one of these major rankings in 2010.

Appearing in the top 300 for the QS World University Rankings   Universities that appeared in the QS World University Rankings at a position outside of the top 300 were excluded as an additional refinement. This refinement was used to again ensure the benchmark universities were ranked higher than Griffith University and this reduced the list to 259 universities.

Age – Identification of Universities Established between 1960 and the Mid 1970s

Examination of the list of 259 universities suggested that Griffith University was very different culturally to most of these institutions, many of which were steeped in tradition with a long, distinguished research and education history.

Our analysis found that few top 50 universities (2010 edition of each of the three rankings) were founded post 1920:
- ARWU: The University of California, San Diego (1960), the University of California, Irvine (1965) and Université Paris-Sud (1965);
- HEEACT: Osaka University (1931), the University of Texas MD Anderson Cancer Center (1941) and the University of California, San Diego (1960);
- QS: Osaka University (1931), Seoul National University (1946), Australian National University (1946), University of New South Wales (1949), the Chinese University of Hong Kong (1963, although an amalgamation of three extant colleges) and the Hong Kong University of Science and Technology (1991).

Indeed, other research has shown a link between age of institution and performance in world university rankings and that institutional age affects the measured institutional research performance (Sheil, 2008; Sowter, 2008; McMillan, 2010). Therefore, it was important to ensure that benchmark universities were of a similar age to Griffith University to ensure they provided realistic research performance goals and the application of an age filter to limit benchmarks to universities established during the 1960 to mid-1970s period of higher education expansion reduced the list to 25.

Discipline Mix – High Quality Social Sciences Research

Griffith University is distinctive amongst Australian universities in that greater than 40% of its research has a social sciences orientation, therefore a decision was taken to remove institutions not ranked in the QS World University Rankings 2010 – Social Sciences and Management (top 400) – this reduced the list to 20. This decision to filter based on the high social sciences focus of Griffith University has since been supported by the QS Social Sciences subject rankings in 2011, in which the University was one of only eight Australian universities to appear in the world top 200 in at least four of the six focussed social sciences subject rankings.

Other institutions using this method might have different discipline mixes or research focuses and therefore use different discipline rankings to filter for appropriate benchmarks. Why is discipline mix important? An essential objective of benchmarking is to compare "like with like" and while Griffith University is developing rapidly across a range of health, science and engineering disciplines, it could not ignore its current disciplinary strengths. The objective, therefore, was to identify benchmark institutions against which Griffith University could model its own progression in the coming five to 10 years, whilst ensuring that observations were not distorted by differences in disciplinary practices.

Non-ranking indicators – Size, competition, interdisciplinarity, and multi-campus attributes

At this point we asked four defining questions that encapsulate important environmental and mission-based factors faced by Griffith University. Institutions not meeting at least three of the criteria for selection were removed, these being:

- Is the university classified as at least as big as "M" (medium sized) in the QS Classifications? ("M" is the classification given to universities with ≥ 5000 students, "L" is assigned to universities with ≥ 12000 students, "XL" to universities with ≥ 30,000 students; Griffith University has a student population of approximately 30,000 FTE.)
- Is there a local (<100 km) competitor institution that is much older and considered world-class?
- Does the university espouse being inter- or multidisciplinary, both in teaching and research?
- Does it have substantial parts of its student load spread across multiple campuses?

Other institutions using this method might need to choose different non-ranking indicators as filters, but the end-goal should be the same: to identify benchmark institutions that have similar defining characteristics. Such indicators require investigation beyond the current World University Rankings, although enhanced rankings and classifications are being developed, such as the European Commission-funded U-Multirank, and updated formats of more-established rankings are beginning to consider such characteristics (e.g. the QS classifications and the ARWU Global Research Universities Profile project).

Eleven short-listed universities met at least three of these four defining characteristics and this penultimate list of 11 included representation from eight nations: Brazil, Canada, Denmark, Japan, the Netherlands, Sweden, Spain, and the United Kingdom – they are listed in Table 1 and are considered to be Griffith University's broader short-list of benchmark universities. Interestingly, this list includes the previously-identified University of Warwick and Simon Fraser University.

Five of these short-listed institutions (italicized in Table 1) matched on all four non-ranking indicators and are therefore the universities that will be used for the first round of benchmarking.

DATA SOURCES

The filtering technique used to narrow the search for compatible benchmark institutions from 17,000 candidates to five necessitated access to extensive amounts of data, much of which would have been unavailable or difficult to acquire before the establishment of world university rankings and classifications (see Table 2).

Table 1. Short-list of benchmark universities

University	QS classification of size	Local, older, well-respected competitor	Espouses to be inter-disciplinary	Multi-campus university
Autonomous University of Barcelona, Spain	L	Yes	Not obviously	Yes
Maastricht University, The Netherlands[**]	L	Yes	Yes	Yes
Simon Fraser University, Canada[**]	L	Yes	Yes	Yes
State University of Campinas, Brazil[**]	L	Yes	Yes	Yes
Umeå University, Sweden	L	No	Yes	Yes
University of East Anglia, UK	L	Yes	Yes	No
University of Southern Denmark, Denmark[**]	M[*]	Yes	Yes	Yes
University of Sussex, UK	M	Yes	Yes	No
University of Tsukuba, Japan[**]	L	Yes	Yes	Yes
University of Twente, The Netherlands	M	Yes	Yes	No
University of Warwick, UK	L	Yes	Yes	No

Note: [*]While classified as "M" by QS, the University of Southern Denmark reports a student count of 20,000 on its website, which suggests it should fall into the "L" category according to QS's definition of size.
[**]Shortlisted universities for benchmarking.

Rankings provided the starting point for narrowing down the initial pool, which potentially included all institutions listed in the "World List of Universities and Other Institutions of Higher Education" (IAU, 2004). The primary rankings used were the ARWU, HEEACT and QS world university rankings and these were supplemented by the use of the QS university classifications. The second most important source of strategic and statistical data was taken from the universities themselves by accessing their websites and brochures. Moreover, only publicly available information and data were used; no contact was made with the

Table 2. Data sources used to inform filtering

Filter	Data Source(s)
Overall rankings performance	Academic Ranking of World Universities 2010
	QS World University Rankings 2010
	Higher Education Educational Accreditation Council of Taiwan Rankings 2010
Age	QS Top Universities Guide
	Institutional websites and brochures
Discipline mix	QS World University Rankings 2010 – Social Sciences and Management
Size	QS World University Rankings 2010 classifications
Competitive environment	Scan of local universities to identify world-leaders
Mission and campus arrangements (e.g. multi-campus)	Institutional websites and brochures

universities themselves. Some bibliometric analysis, using both the Thomson Reuters' Web of Science and Elsevier's Scopus databases, has since been undertaken to observe changes in research performance over time in response to historical turning points, such as the establishment of a medical school; however these databases were used after benchmark selection had been carried out, thus they were not used to filter results or inform the final choice of benchmark institutions.

The final selection of short-listed benchmark universities included several institutions already well-known to Griffith University and others with which we were unacquainted. Preliminary analysis of each institution involved identifying their respective missions, organizational structure, current and historical highlights, research strategy, key statistics, bibliometric data, discipline mix, and international partnerships. Only a few preliminary observations are summarised below and the full findings will be provided in a detailed follow-up exercise.

OBSERVATIONS FROM PRELIMINARY EXAMINATION OF THE BENCHMARK UNIVERSITIES

The preliminary examination of the leading universities in the broader benchmark group suggested that institutional histories are punctuated by "breakthrough" highlights every five-ten years, such as: amalgamations, university rebranding, expansion into new disciplines, or a dramatic increase in capital funding, investment or donations. These breakthroughs often translate directly into research outcomes, however, this is not always immediate and the delay between strategic action and measurable performance improvements can lag by several years. It was noteworthy that, on the whole, research strengths are persistent over time, with the same strengths prevailing now as they did 30-40 years ago during establishment.

However, this has not prevented institutions from expanding and most in the benchmark group are indeed becoming more comprehensive over time.

Like Griffith University, some of the benchmark group have accepted the reality that in the medium term they will be unable to develop international leadership in all research areas, and so are focussing on building upon areas of established research excellence. Whether these are called Thematic Areas of Research Strength (Simon Fraser) or Research Themes (Maastricht), they have the same objective and involve between four and 12 areas, usually selected from between 20 and 40 research centres and institutes.

Ambition and bold strategic vision appear to be hallmarks of institutions in the benchmark group. For example, Simon Fraser University aims to be "the most research-intensive comprehensive university in Canada" (Simon Fraser University, 2011), while the University of Tsukuba aspires to be "a frontrunner in the university reform in Japan" (the University of Tsukuba, 2011). All have a strong commitment to interdisciplinary and multidisciplinary research and an equally strong drive to break with tradition, by providing an innovative alternative to more established universities. In sum, this is a reminder that there are numerous institutions with ambitious plans and that the race to become a top 200 or even top 400 global research university is intense.

ADDITIONAL USES OF THE METHOD – DEVELOPMENT OF STRATEGIC PARTNERSHIPS

Simon Fraser University was one of the final five short-listed universities resulting from this systematic method. As this university was one previously (independently) identified by Griffith University as a highly compatible partner, this result suggests not only that the filtering method does lead to sensible outcomes, but also that it might be used by institutions wishing to develop strategic international partnerships with compatible universities. In fact, Griffith University has used the outcomes of this exercise to begin negotiations with other potential global partners, with very favourable initial responses. A by-product of this exercise is, therefore, the development of a novel method for university partner selection.

TRANSFERABILITY OF THE METHOD FOR USE BY OTHER INSTITUTIONS

This benchmark short-listing method, with some adjustment, should be applicable for use by administrators in any university currently listed, or close to being listed, in world university ranks. This method will be most useful where the goal is to benchmark with higher performing institutions that have similar defining characteristics, such as age, size, discipline mix, mission and competitive environment. Of course, the particular defining characteristics used as filters 2 to 7 in the method will need to be adjusted to suit the university wishing to benchmark; however, such adjustments should be easy to implement.

At the time of undertaking the exercise, Griffith University was performing against the relevant indicators at a level just outside the top 500 universities in the

ARWU and HEEACT rankings and so felt these were appropriate sources for identifying suitable benchmarks. For filter 1 (overall rankings performance), however, some universities might find broader rankings, such as Scimago (which ranks more than 2,000 institutions), more useful than those used by Griffith University. Additionally, the authors note that universities from developing nations often rank higher in world rankings that include reputational factors (e.g. QS World University Rankings and Times Higher Education World University Rankings) and so the use of such rankings in filter 1 might allow identification of more suitable benchmarks for universities in these nations.

Institutions in some nations might not be well-placed to use this method, if their mission is focused on local engagement, national capacity building and acting as the catalyst for social change, rather than internationally-renowned teaching and research, as the current world rankings do not measure appropriate indicators to judge the success of such missions very well. However, Australia has a well-developed university system, an international focus, and comparably high levels of investment in higher education, so Griffith University is well-placed to aim for global impact on current international scales.

CONCLUSION

The lessons learned in this exercise were numerous and provided Griffith University with the foundation for further analysis to determine how it might develop its research profile and performance to grow from a good university to a great one. The technique described also has enormous potential to be used by universities as a basis for the development of strategic relationships, because it can provide guidance for almost any research active university to engage in a similar exercise. This would not have been possible before the establishment of world university rankings and classifications, which has led to increased transparency, accountability and accessibility of data. By sharing this experience we aim to promote a more rational and constructive use of world university rankings that are so often misused in a one-dimensional way.

ACKNOWLEDGEMENTS

The authors of this paper acknowledge the contributions of Karen Moorehead and Dr Heidi Russo of the Research Policy Team at Griffith University to developing benchmarking templates and to data collection for the benchmarking of the University of Warwick before the development of the described method for short-listing other benchmark institutions. Additionally, they contributed to data collection for the benchmarking of Simon Fraser University before the establishment of the memorandum of understanding with Griffith in 2010.

NOTES

[1]   Griffith University ranks at 167 in the world and 7th in Australia in the 2010 edition of the Scimago Institutional Rankings World Report – Social Sciences and Humanities.

REFERENCES

Alden, J., & Lin, G. (2004). *Benchmarking the Characteristics of a World-Class University: Developing an International Strategy at University Level*. London: Leadership Foundation for Higher Education.

Committee on the Future of Tertiary Education in Australia. (1964-65). *Tertiary Education in Australia: Report to the Australian Universities Commission* (Chairman: L. H. Martin). Melbourne: Government Printer.

California State Department of Education. (1960). *A Master Plan for Higher Education in California, 1960–1975*. Sacramento: California State Department of Education.

Committee on Higher Education. (1963). *Higher Education: Report of the Committee Appointed by the Prime Minister under the Chairmanship of Lord Robbins 1961–63*. London: HMSO.

Griffith University. (2009). *Strategic Plan 2009–2013*. Retrieved May 8, 2012, from http://www.griffith.edu.au/about-griffith/plans-publications/pdf/strategic-plan.pdf

Hazelkorn, E. (2011). *Rankings and the Reshaping of Higher Education: The Battle for World-Class Excellence*. Basingstoke: Palgrave Macmillan.

International Association of Universities. (2004). *World List of Universities and Other Institutions of Higher Education* (24th ed.). Basingstoke: Palgrave Macmillan.

Liu, N. C. (2009). The story of the academic ranking of world universities. *International Higher Education, 54*, 2–3.

McKinnon, K. R., Walker, S. H., & Davis, D. (2000). *Benchmarking: A Manual for Australian Universities*. Canberra: Department of Education, Training and Youth Affairs.

McMillan, C. (2010). Building the world-class university of the future: Impact of age on institutional research performance. In *The 6th Annual QS-Apple Conference and Exhibition*. Singapore.

O'Mara, M. P. (2005). *Cities of Knowledge: Cold War Science and the Search for the Next Silicon Valley*. Princeton: Princeton University Press.

Quacquarelli Symonds. (2011). *QS World University Rankings by Subject Social Sciences*. Retrieved July 1, 2011, from http://www.topuniversities.com/university-rankings/world-university-rankings

Quirke, N. (1996). *Preparing for the Future: A History of Griffith University 1971–1996*. Brisbane: Boolarong Press.

Rauhvargers, A. (2011). *Global University Rankings and Their Impact*. Brussels: European Universities Association.

Salmi, J. (2009). *The Challenge of Establishing World-Class Universities*. Washington, DC: The World Bank.

Sheil, T. (2008). Size does matter: Strategic research policy options for small nations and their institutions in response to world university rankings. In *OECD Conference: Does Size Matter? Universities Competing in a Global Market*. Reykjavík.

Simon Fraser University. (2011). *Strategic Research Plan*. Retrieved August 22, 2011, from www.sfu.ca/vpresearch/docs/SRP2010_15.pdf

Sowter, B. (2008). World university rankings: Beneath the surface. In *The 4th Annual QS-Apple Conference and Exhibition*. Seoul, Korea.

Thelin, J. R. (2004). *A History of American Higher Education*. Baltimore: The John Hopkins University Press.

University of California, San Diego. (2011). *UC San Diego Campus Profile*. Retrieved March 23, 2011, from http://ucsdnews.ucsd.edu/about/index.html#institution

University of Southern Denmark. (2011). *About the University of Southern Denmark.* Retrieved August 22, 2011, from http://www.sdu.dk/Om_SDU

University of Tsukuba. (2011). *Mission Statement.* Retrieved August 22, 2011, from http://www.tsukuba.ac.jp/english /about/objective.html.

AFFILIATIONS

Freya Mearns
Policy Officer, Research Excellence,
Griffith University, Australia

Tony Sheil
Research Policy and Strategy,
Griffith University, Australia

DANIE VISSER AND MARILET SIENAERT

RATIONAL AND CONSTRUCTIVE
USE OF RANKINGS

A Challenge for Universities in the Global South

INTRODUCTION

This chapter considers how the rankings can be used in order to address challenges faced by universities in the developing world. There is in many quarters an assumption that the international ranking of higher education institutions is irrelevant to research planning at universities located in developing economies, where there is limited scope and resources to produce internationally competitive scholars and cutting-edge research. In this chapter it is argued that, although one would not deny that the agenda of universities located in the global South is clearly not specifically contemplated when the various international rankings are constructed, these rankings can play an important role in steering research in universities in the developing world, if research managers were to use the league tables in a rational and constructive way. Through a case study of the University of Cape Town, this chapter attempts to demonstrate how the challenge of using the rankings appropriately in a university located in a developing economy was turned into a catalyst to crystallise a set of goals that now drives the research planning as well its monitoring and evaluation. It is believed that this particular experience may provide a global model for meaningful engagement with the ranking systems, with special relevance for institutions in the global South.

Placed in the context of South African higher education, the case study describes a series of ongoing interventions between research management and faculty that fostered collaboration between the different parties to achieve a common set of goals. Taking a range of ranking system indicators as point of departure, evidence-based debate was fostered to focus on the need to demonstrate the impact of research. This in turn led to structured activities whereby field-specific plans were put into place to enhance excellence, incentivise quality and build the next generation of academics.

The impact of our engagement with the global ranking systems must be understood in the context of the power relations between universities in developing economies and the ranking phenomenon, and this is briefly described at the end of next section. In closing, and in order to move the impact of this exercise from its narrow institutional perspective to one that is more general and transferable to

Q. Wang, Y. Cheng, & N.C. Liu (eds.), Building World-Class Universities: Different Approaches to a Shared Goal, 145–159.

other institutions – and especially those based in the global South – a summary is provided of the most important lessons learnt in the process.

CRITICAL ENGAGEMENT WITH RANKING SYSTEMS

Higher Education in South Africa: Changes since the New Democracy (1994)

Higher Education in South Africa has undergone significant changes since 1994 when the Apartheid regime, under which the majority of the country's population was denied the right to vote, came to an end. The new democracy was faced with myriad challenges to address the inequities of the past. Not the least of these was the education system where access under the earlier regime was administered along racial and ethnic lines. As a result, there were marked differences in quality between the "historically black" and the "historically white" institutions (schools as well as universities), with limited access to education for disadvantaged groups. Viewing the education system as a key instrument to achieve equity across all population groups, South Africa has been overhauling it since 1994 and continues to strive towards an integrated and coordinated system. However, much work still needs to be done and large numbers of students that gain access today are still wholly under-prepared for higher (post-secondary) education.

Higher Education Institutional Mergers

An important aspect of the reconstruction process was the merging of institutions that took place in 2005 and 2006. 36 higher education institutions (consisting of 21 universities and 15 technikons) were reconfigured into a new public higher education system consisting of 11 universities; five "universities of technology" and six "comprehensive institutions". Technikons offer applied disciplines and are now called "universities of technology"; "universities" offer a wide range of degree programmes in both arts and science disciplines at both the undergraduate and graduate level; whereas "comprehensive universities" are hybrid institutions that resulted from the merging of traditional universities with technikons. These offer programmes and degrees in the traditional arts and science disciplines as well as the applied disciplines offered by the universities of technology. Key developments since 1994 can thus be summarised as a shift towards an integrated and coordinated higher education system, with a blurring of the rigid boundaries between institutional types. Programme and qualification offerings in the curriculum have evolved (Council for Higher Education, 2004:41) but challenges related to equity, throughput and attrition have escalated rather than been resolved. As a result, research capacity in the majority of institutions has been compromised, particularly in the science and technology fields. This is also evident in the low participation rates by international standards of doctoral students, a factor that is exacerbated by the perceived unattractive prospects of a career in the academy. Heavy teaching loads have further compromised the system, with student-to-lecturer ratios worsening steadily every year.

In addition to the above challenges experienced by all the institutions affected by the mergers, some of these new institutions now operate at a scale the country has not experienced before. In all the merged institutions the leadership struggle to reconcile different organizational cultures. Differences in academic orientation, political affiliations and student profiles further complicate their work. On the one hand, institutions that led the research field in the past were only nominally or not at all affected by the mergers and continue to perform well. The University of Cape Town falls into this category. On the other hand, most of the merged institutions struggle to build capacity in the face of their complex structures and diversity of programmes that have differential entry and exit requirements and that require complex articulation between levels (Breier & Mabizela, 2008:297).

As a result, South Africa is lagging behind, "with a 17% gross participation rate in higher education; a research output of all universities combined (8,200 publications a year) less than that of the single University of Sao Paulo in Brazil (9,000); only 34% of academics have doctoral degrees ... production of only 28 doctorates per million people per year compared to 569 in Portugal, 288 in the United Kingdom and 187 in South Korea" (Makgoba, 2011).

Developing a Differentiated System with World-Class Centres and Programmes

The education section of the recent *National Development Plan: Vision for 2030* (National Planning Committee, 2011) still regards higher education as an equity instrument but for the first time links knowledge production and equity within a more differentiated system. For the first time – and this is a radical shift – there is recognition that "you can only have equity, or social justice *and* high-level knowledge production within a differentiated system" (Cloete, 2011). This is understood as a distinction between high-quality education and training skills on the one hand, and knowledge production on the other, with an emphasis on the concentration of resources, for example through the establishment of world-class programmes and centres of excellence that straddle more than one institution. However, for the moment, knowledge-production capacity remains unevenly distributed in an inherently differentiated system that is contested by those institutions that carry the brunt of the backlog in student and staff capacity. This is measured through indicators such as student graduates in relation to enrolments, proportion of staff with doctorates and the quality of publications. In terms of an analysis carried out by the Centre for Higher Education Transformation (CHET), four universities are in the high knowledge-producing category, five other universities are in the medium category, whilst the two remaining universities and all the universities of technology are in the low knowledge-producing grouping (Badsha & Cloete, 2011).

Although there is now an emerging consensus that South Africa requires differentiation in its higher education institutions to meet the range of student needs and also for effective knowledge production and socio-economic development, there is no consensus on how this differentiation should be approached. The government's views on the importance of world-class universities are of crucial importance in any developing country. In South Africa, the *National Development Plan*, issued on 11 November 2011 by the National Planning Commission, reveals an important difference with the approach to such universities in many other developing countries. It formulates the government's ambition as follows (National Planning Committee, 2011:278):

> A few world-class centres and programmes should be developed within both the national system of innovation and the higher-education sector over the next 20 years. These should be in areas of competitive and comparative advantage, including indigenous knowledge systems.

In other words, whereas the strategy in countries such as China is to create a set of world-class universities, the South African government's approach is not to develop specific universities as world-class centres, but rather to develop world-class centres *within* universities across the spectrum. This ties in with the general approach of the National Research Foundation (NRF) to create, in co-operation with the Department of Science and Technology (DST), a series of DST/NRF Centres of Excellence in various fields in different universities, with each such university drawing in researchers from other universities in a hub-and-spoke model. The DST/NRF South African Research Chair initiative, modelled on a Canadian example,[1] is an extension of this approach and also seeks to create, in a manner of speaking, mini centres of excellence spread across the university system. The common denominator in the strategy of all the relevant government departments, including the Department of Higher Education, is to increase the efficiency of the higher-education system, but at the same time to level the playing fields. As explained above, South Africa's universities are divided into three categories, namely high, medium and low knowledge-producing institutions (National Planning Committee, 2011:273). The government's strategy not to entrench the power relations of the status quo is driven by the desire above all to overcome the country's divided past. The government's thinking is evidently that, if it were to pick a few universities to develop into truly world-class institutions, it would be seen as compounding the historical imbalances that existed in Apartheid South Africa. Not everyone agrees and the Vice-Chancellors of the University of the Witwatersrand, Johannesburg, Professor Loyisa Nogxa and the University of KwaZulu-Natal, Professor Malegapuru Makgoba, have each argued in favour of lifting out certain universities to build on the strengths that already exist, for the benefit of the whole nation.

The debate is not over and those who believe that international competiveness for the country is better achieved by holistically developing a few universities into world-class institutions will continue to make their case. And it is important that it be done, for the right level of government involvement in a developing country's universities is crucial. Mahmood Mamdami has convincingly shown that significant distortions can develop if a government in such a country were to decide "that higher education is more of a private than a public good" (Mamdami, 2007:ix). However, for the moment the upshot of the South African government strategy is that a university in this country that aspires to being world-class cannot rely on government pumping resources into it to achieve this. Such a university may of course boost its quest for world-class status by competing successfully for some of the centres of excellence sponsored by the government, but in the end will have be creative in finding alternative sources of funding to achieve this ambition.

In a developing democracy, the imperative for a good education *as well as* for social justice and equity is not negotiable, regardless of where institutions find themselves within the differentiation debate. The imperative for "responsiveness to local, national and regional needs" and "the strengthening of relationships with community, civic, government, business and industry partners for local and regional development" (Gibbon, 2004:5) is part and parcel of institutional mission in the context of developing economies such as those in the global South. It is in this light that the following case study of the University of Cape Town should be considered.

Engaging with the Rankings

Universities in developing countries have especially complex roles. Although social responsiveness increasingly forms a central part of the mission of universities in the developed world, the imperative to react to the demands of their country and society is especially strong in respect of universities in the developing world. The limited resources for planning in such countries place a moral duty on universities, where much of these resources are typically concentrated, to address the specific challenges with which the societies in which they operate confront them. And this inevitably implies a lesser freedom to pursue an open research agenda; it also implies, often, the necessity to do policy and planning work for government, with a concomitant reduction in the time and inclination to share the research results in international publications. Academics understand, of course, that this slant on research in developing-world universities does not mean that international recognition and excellence are unimportant in such universities. They know that it is only through excellence – and through communicating that excellence internationally – that they will be able to attract the best students and the best teams to create the intellectual environment that enables novel solutions to problems. What they do not easily accept is that the ranking tables are relevant to their situation and that they have something meaningful to say about the degree of excellence of their research.

How then, to persuade academics in a global South university that the rankings are relevant to them as well?

First, it is important not to set advancement in the international league tables as a goal in itself. This would be counterproductive, since the best people produce their best when they feel that they are building something valuable, that they can change minds, and that they can make the world a better place – not to occupy a particular place on a ladder that they are not so sure that they should be climbing. So the key is to convince the university community that, although the individual rankings do not measure every aspect of excellence, they each give a particular view of the cathedral of excellence – and that it is worthwhile to know where the cutting edge is (Baty, 2009).

Therefore it is important to present academics with a sophisticated picture of the ranking systems; the different goals and philosophies that they have; their advantages and limitations; flaws and biases (and that the people who create the ranking systems understand the inevitable limitations of the systems) – but also their impact on funders and policy makers. Academics that understand that their university will not dictate behaviour simply to comply with the pressures of ranking will – together with the administrators – think beyond the competitive nature of the systems to trigger a fresh approach to research planning. In doing so, an analysis and combination of indicators emerge that provide a proxy of research excellence for each discipline and research field offered at the institution. Our analysis also reveals that some of the indicators of excellence agreed upon by faculty through the process of engagement and debate (that will be described below) are indeed embedded in the rankings systems (such as publication in journals of truly international repute) and that some are not (such as the uptake of research findings by civic society in the immediate vicinity of the university). Either way, engagement with the ranking system raises awareness of the critically important nature of comparative data and focuses faculty plans on *defining and measuring excellence* in ways appropriate to their disciplines.

How Researchers at the University of Cape Town Were Drawn into the Debate about Rankings

In 2008, the task of constructing a framework for engagement with the ranking systems was undertaken during a one-day symposium for the University's leading researchers as well as those that serve on the cluster of research-related committees. This was soon after the University of Cape Town became the only university in Africa to be ranked in (as it then was) the Times Higher Education – QS World University Rankings (THE-QS) 2009 system top 200. More recently, as we are all aware, the World Best Universities (run under the auspices of the US News and World Report together with Quacquarelli-Symonds) has taken over the former THES-QS ranking system, whilst the Times Higher Education (THE) has teamed up with Reuters in the Thomson Group to produce a new ranking system, called the Times Higher Education World University Rankings. The U-Multirank project has also been launched in the meantime. This so far consists of a feasibility study funded by the European Commission, to design and test a multi-dimensional global university ranking. The aim of the 2008 the University of Cape Town symposium was to consider the two ranking systems leading the field at the time, namely the Shanghai Jiao Tong University's Academic Ranking of World Universities (ARWU) and the Times Higher Education system and to debate the way in which the University should position itself in relation to these systems. The symposium devoted a session to each of the following topics:

Rationale and indicators   The rationale for the existence of the above two ranking systems, the indicators of excellence that they use and examples of the resulting league tables over the preceding three years were presented and discussed in some detail. It was explained that indicators were selected to measure the institution's setup (input variables), function and efficiency (process variables), and productivity and impact (output variables) – relative to the performance of other universities (Salmi & Saroyan, 2007).

Benefits and limitations   A discussion of the advantages and limitations of both systems, with a detailed analysis of their flaws and biases but also their impact on society, raised considerable debate. Drawing on ranking analysis and criticism[2] such as the work of Marginson (2007) and Altbach and Salmi (2011), researchers were reminded that most countries with large higher education systems devise national ranking systems driven by the press, departments of education, grant councils, accreditation agencies or other organizations and that the ranking of academic institutions is essentially driven by the public who have a keen interest in the quality of universities as publicly funded institutions. It was pointed out that the quality of universities cannot be precisely measured by mere numbers, nor can the quality of world universities be accurately compared because of the huge differences of various types of universities in different countries. The choice of indicators and their weights make significant differences to the final ranking results. In addition, some systems (such as ARWU) have a bias against Humanities and Social Sciences, young universities, and disciplines not related to awarding fields; there is also a bias towards English institutions in English-speaking countries and towards large and comprehensive universities. Additional notes of caution against self-evaluation through the ranking system lens included the danger that rankings become an end to themselves; the fact that they largely disregard vocational diversity; that those rankings that draw on reputational assessment may produce ill-grounded and circular results; that they do not take account of the challenges faced by under-resourced institutions (i.e. those in the global South); and, most importantly, and controversially, through their emphasis on bibliometric analyses, they do not acknowledge our mission as a higher education institution responsive to our socio-economic environment.

Evidence was also produced that reputational advantages flow from high rankings and that the results impact on public opinion, government and industry. Worldwide, most universities and policy-making constituencies are taking the results very seriously and league tables are being embedded into strategic decision-making and structural and organizational changes. Examples were given of ranking criteria that change institutional behaviour, with institutions changing in response or anticipation to what is measured. Ultimately, it was agreed that although league tables are flawed, they seem to be here to stay (Hazelkorn, 2007; Leach, 2005).

Other institutional and national imperative   A reminder of the other institutional and national imperatives that by necessity had to drive institutional performance was also brought into the discussion. In South Africa at present these include the

National Research Foundation's new programme on social responsiveness; the national Department of Science and Technology's (DST's) Human Capacity Development strategy and the focus on PhD recruitment and throughput as a primary driver; focus on growing the pipeline of graduate students; equity imperatives; and the improvement of local journals. However, it was agreed to lobby government with renewed vigour to invest more in research and development, as there was a direct correlation between the percentage of gross domestic product (GDP) invested in research and development (R&D) and the number of world class universities in a country.

Positioning the university in relation to the systems   In the debate about how the University should position itself in relation to the systems as expounded above, the university community agreed that chasing the rankings is meaningless in itself, but that the mirror the rankings hold up to the university provides the means of evaluating one's own performance in relation to the goals that one has set. In this process, an important realization was that the common denominator of world-class universities is their excellence in relation to the impact of their research. Where universities' researchers publish, and who they collaborate with, are keys to their success.

THE FRAMEWORK FOR ENGAGEMENT

Although most academics were indifferent or opposed to the ranking systems at the outset of the symposium, the consensus was that the information available through the ranking systems provided an important planning tool and as a result, a "framework for engagement" with the ranking systems was formalised within the University structures. It was based on the following principles that guide individual researchers as well as the research committees responsible for research planning, monitoring and evaluation:

Ongoing Engagement with the Ranking Systems and Their Indicators

As an institution, it was agreed to remain mindful of the combination of indicators which the ranking systems uses to arrive at a proxy of excellence. In order to influence the choice of indicators, there is a need to engage with the agents that drive these systems, such as the IREG Observatory on Academic Ranking and Excellence (2009) and the newly established Times Higher Education Survey Platform Group. The latter should be supported in their efforts to refine the indicators and devise measures to evaluate research performance in the Humanities. Participation in the Thomson Reuters Global Institutional Profiles Project (2010) aimed at building comprehensive profiles of academic institutions across the world to facilitate comparisons would also be a positive way of engaging with the systems.

The Need to Develop Our Own Discipline-Specific Indicators of Excellence

Understanding international ranking systems, and working to the best advantage within them, does not mean eschewing debate within the University about indicators. On the contrary – developing faculty-specific[3] indicators of excellence and impact is a vehicle for making patent the unarticulated assumptions about quality and making it possible to debate them. In some faculties, some or all of the indicators of the various international rankings will be fully relevant. In others, these indicators will not help to ascertain the quality of the enterprise or its impact – and in respect to these faculties, there was agreement to re-think ways in which the disciplines that they comprise can best evaluate the impact and visibility of research, and to put in place steps to improve performance in this regard.

Symposium participants were urged to take the principles of the Framework back into their disciplinary units and to engage with it in discipline-specific ways. The cluster of research committees were given a time-line for providing the central research committee with continuous feedback on how their engagement with the Framework might influence the planning as well as monitoring and evaluation of their own research.

Responses from the Faculty Research Committees indicate that knowledge of the ranking systems is focusing the minds of researchers on the impact of their research. There is consensus that the impact of research translates differently across the disciplines and there is no "one size fits all" way of measuring and evaluating outputs across the board. Rather than blindly trying to improve performance by emulating institutions at the top of the league tables, there is a concerted effort to identify indicators that are appropriate to the research area and the context in which research has to be applied. Partner institutions from across the globe are also being identified by sectors within faculties for benchmarking purposes (comparing apples with apples). On the whole, a key outcome has been raised awareness of the value of benchmarking research productivity against comparable international peers (selected on a discipline-specific basis by individual departments) and to draw on the findings to enhance monitoring and evaluation practices.

FURTHER INSTITUTIONAL RESPONSES TO THE FRAMEWORK

As a result of the framework for engagement with the ranking systems, the faculties continued to develop ways in which the framework could be used to balance the seemingly competing agendas that pull universities in opposite directions – namely to do cutting-edge research while at the same time being socially responsive. Through various forms and with a range of constituencies within the institution, it was agreed that universities can no longer limit themselves to their own backyard, since the source of students, funds for research, and collaborative opportunities are in certain contexts just as much outside as inside the borders of the country in which a particular university is situated. At the same time, however, this need to strengthen international linkages (including with Africa beyond our borders) is complicated by the parallel imperative to work for the public good, especially in relation to the community in which a university is situated.

One approach to producing internationally competitive research, which, wherever possible, also benefits society, is to reject the binary opposition of cutting-edge research and social engagement. If researchers are encouraged to monitor the potential social benefit of their work, social innovation becomes an integral part of the University's research activity. Consequently, the University can excel internationally and still fulfil its mission to be socially engaged. Support should not, however, be limited to socially responsive research only, but opportunities for social innovation through research should not be missed. It was agreed that, as public institutions, universities have a duty to use their resources responsibly. This implies that it would be wasteful not to bring to fruition the social benefits inherent in research. However, there is a fine line between this and wasting resources by doing what any non-governmental organization (NGO) could do. Higher education institutions should focus their efforts at social engagement by making a contribution that NGOs are not so equipped to achieve, viz. bring new solutions to societal problems through the agency of research and training. There are many examples of social innovation which emphasize that excellent research and social engagement are inter-related rather than opposing goals: the human trials of the first two candidate vaccines against HIV-AIDS to be developed in Africa come to mind, as does the research on "resurrection plants" that can tolerate extreme water loss ($\geq$ 95% of total water content) for extended periods of time and which impacts directly on food production in arid areas, to name but two examples.

IMPACT OF THE FRAMEWORK ON CURRENT EVALUATION PRACTICE

The conclusions reached through critique of the ranking systems culminated in an institutional concept paper (Visser, 2010) that now drives the institutional strategy for research. The 2008 workshop was followed-up with a major Research "Indaba" (Symposium) in May 2010 to take stock of progress since 2008 in benchmarking ourselves against international standards and to explore how to improve our research cooperation nationally and internationally. Most importantly, this gathering led to each faculty formally working out a detailed formal plan to enhance the quality and impact of its research. These plans have in common a commitment to playing in a much higher league of global research.

The following themes evolved out of the debate on the ranking systems, each of which is linked to a specific type of evaluation practice.

The first theme to evolve was the need for increased focus in areas that can offer something unique thanks to our specific location in Africa, and thus create intellectual hubs that draw both students and researchers to the University. A number of modalities were developed or embraced to achieve this, namely research chairs; institutional cross-disciplinary signature themes that are united around an interlinked set of research questions; centres of excellence, institutionally recognised and accredited research groupings such as units, centres and institutes united around a common theme; and a number of select partnerships with other institutions or research councils, once again united around a common research agenda. Evaluation of these modalities has been institutionalised through peer-review based on a self-evaluation portfolio and site visit, using quantitative and qualitative indicators.

A second theme to evolve out of the ranking systems debate was the renewed focus on international co-operation, including collaboration with other countries in Africa. Analysis of the ranking systems' indicators shows that strategic partnerships are critically important to enhance the global impact of research. This approach has since been strengthened through a bibliometric analysis of the University of Cape Town's scientific publications in journal articles carried out by the Centre for Research on Science and Technology (CREST) in South Africa that demonstrates higher citation rates when researchers co-author with international colleagues. Evaluation and benchmarking of the University's research have now evolved to include a database to track the extent and nature of collaboration with institutions in other countries (including other countries in Africa) in order to assess how well synergies are optimised. Mapping the diversity of the student body and staff to inform recruitment practices have also been put in place. New initiatives include incentives to encourage publications based on international collaboration, benchmarking the uptake of mobility grants and assessing the outputs that result from grants and fellowships abroad.

A third theme to evolve is the drive to increase the visibility of what is already being achieved in terms of research but which is not always accessible in the public domain. There is a need to interrogate current dissemination strategies to ensure that the University's research output is visible, both to researchers worldwide and to the communities that could benefit from it. In order to do this the power of the internet must be embraced as a tool to showcase our research and connect our researchers to the rest of the world. If not, the impact of the institution's research will remain below its potential and the communities in our own region that could benefit from the research will not know how some of the findings can impact on their lives. Renewed awareness of the role played by dissemination has led the institution to sign the Cape Town Open Education Declaration, a ground-breaking initiative that aims to promote open resources, technology and teaching practices in education. Drafted in January 2008, the declaration springs from a meeting convened by the Shuttleworth Foundation and the Open Society Institute in Cape Town in September 2007. Although the commercialization of intellectual property remains a challenge, universities thrive on making knowledge freely available and the Cape Town Open Education Declaration establishes important principles for ensuring this. The renewed focus on internationalization has also led to an institution-wide Enterprise Content Management (ECM) project that includes an interactive research portal as well as the implementation of a virtual "science shop" (Living Knowledge: The International Science Shop Network, 2012) for engagement with communities.

The fourth theme to evolve is that of increased support to all levels of researchers, from emerging researchers, through to mid-career and internationally established staff. This includes support along the full innovation chain in respect to patentable inventions and other research with marketable potential.

Evaluation of progress in this regard is done through quantitative and qualitative indicators applied to the outcome of research development initiatives such as the University of Cape Town's Emerging Researcher Programme and the Supervision Training Programme (University of Cape Town, 2012); the implementation of new mechanisms to support large international grants; internal projects to enable and support large-scale cross disciplinary collaboration as well as an audit of the current state of our laboratories and research infrastructure.

SUMMARY OF LESSONS LEARNT

First, it is important to engage academics in an open debate about the value of the rankings. By not dictating behaviour simply to achieve a higher ranking, researchers will come to understand that some of the indicators of excellence are embedded in the rankings systems (such as publication in journals of truly international repute) and that some are not (such as the uptake of research findings by civic society in the immediate vicinity of the university), but that, either way, engagement with the ranking system makes faculty aware of comparative data and focuses their plans on defining and measuring excellence in ways appropriate to their disciplines.

Secondly, bringing the analysis of ranking data to the attention of faculty highlights the importance for authors to target journals and book publishers that have the highest impact – and therefore best *visibility* – in their particular field. This information also makes faculty more selective when forging collaborative partnerships by ensuring they select those that will raise their own (and the institution's) visibility. Analysis of the ranking data further emphasizes the necessity to produce graduates who can hold their own in world-class institutions, thus strengthening curricular evaluation, postgraduate supervision and the need for effective mentorship. By focusing the attention on these attributes and by providing appropriate incentives, academic behaviour can be modified to focus effort and concentrate resources to benefit the university enterprise as a whole.

Thirdly, by focusing the minds of researchers on the *impact* of their research, field or discipline-specific indicators emerge that are appropriate to each particular research area (such as the creative and performing arts). This encourages faculty to identify and engage with counterparts at institutions they claim to be comparable with (comparing apples with apples), thus benchmarking against appropriately challenging and competitive sectors at other universities and strengthening their monitoring and evaluation practices in ways that are appropriate to their fields.

Fourthly, as shown by the University of Cape Town case study, engagement with the indicators of the ranking systems can be a catalyst for the formalization of a research strategy that not only optimises institutional strength but that capitalises on researchers' buy-in to the notion of strategic publication, collaboration and "packaging" of their efforts. This awareness in turn strengthens the nexus between administration and the researchers. Rather than seeing research administration as a limiting managerial force to contend with, there is a sense of partnership and collaboration to make the most of existing strengths and capacity. This partnership between research managers and faculty greatly facilitates the development and implementation of mechanisms whereby research excellence can be further enhanced, such as the establishment of an office of research integrity, an integrated information management system and research portal. Faculty buy-in and cooperation with institution-driven quality assurance reviews and audits by external experts are further spin-offs that help to ensure world-class infrastructure and practice.

CONCLUSION

In view of the controversy surrounding ranking systems, it is almost ironic that the University of Cape Town's engagement with ranking systems became the catalyst for achieving the common sense of purpose encapsulated in the Concept Paper alluded to above. Under the current executive leadership, the framework for engagement with the ranking systems focused minds and helped crystallise a set of goals that continue to inform practice. Rather than blindly investing its resources and energy to achieve excellence as defined by the league tables, the University is using its understanding of the rankings to focus on the principles that – specifically for a university in the global South – enable excellence in an increasingly globalised and competitive world.

NOTES

[1] The Canada Research Chairs programme was created in 2000 and consists of 2000 research professorships that are central to the country's national research and development strategy. An investment of CAN$300 million (about US$304 million) per year has succeeded in recruiting some of the world's finest minds as Chairholders that are appointed across the disciplinary spectrum to include engineering and the natural sciences, health sciences, humanities, and social sciences. The purpose of the programme is to enhance knowledge creation and quality of life, strengthen Canada's international competitiveness, and help train the next generation of highly skilled people through student supervision, teaching, and the coordination of other researchers' work. (http://www.chairs-chaires.gc.ca)

[2] Today one would draw on a host of new literature in the field, including Jamil Salmi and Philip Altbach's *The Road to Academic Excellence: The Making of World-Class Research Universities.* Washington, DC: The World Bank, 2011.

[3] In South Africa, the word "faculty" is more regularly used not in the American sense of "academic staff" but refers to a grouping, school or division of cognate disciplines that are clustered together for administrative purposes, under the leadership of a dean. Examples include Faculty of Humanities, Faculty of Health Sciences, etc.

REFERENCES

Altbach, P. G., & Salmi, J. (2011). *The Road to Academic Excellence: The Making of World-Class Research Universities.* Washington, DC: The World Bank. Retrieved April 03, 2012, from http://issuu.com/world.bank.publications/docs/9780821388051?mode=embed&layout=http://skin.issuu.com/v/light/layout.xml&showFlipBtn=true

Badsha, N., & Cloete, N. (2011). South Africa: Differentiation consensus emerges. *University World News: The Global Window on Higher Education*, (200). Retrieved April 03, 2012, from http://www.university worldnews.com/article.php?story=20111202222305300

Baty, P. (2009). Rankings 09: Talking points. *Times Higher Education: World University Rankings*. Retrieved April 03, 2012, from http://www.timeshighereducation.co.uk/ story.asp?storycode=408562

Breier, M., & Mabizela, M. (2008). Higher education. In A. Kraak & K. Press (Eds.), *Human Resources Development Review 2008: Education, Employment and Skills in South Africa*. Cape Town: HSRC Press.

Canada Research Chairs. (2011). *About Us*. Retrieved April 03, 2012, from http://www.chairs-chaires.gc.ca/about_us-a_notre_sujet/index-eng.asp

Cloete, N. (2011). South Africa: Radical new plan for higher education. *University World News: The Global Window on Higher Education*, (200). Retrieved April 03, 2012, from http://www.universityworldnews.com/ article.php?story=2011120222252975

Council on Higher Education. (2004). *South African Higher Education in the First Decade of Democracy*. Retrieved April 03, 2012, from http://www.che.ac.za/documents/d000081/

Gibbon, T. (2004). *Creating Comprehensive Universities in South Africa: A Concept Document*. Commissioned report, Department of Education. Retrieved April 03, 2012, from http://www.info.gov.za/view/ DownloadFileAction?id=70361

Hazelkorn, E. (2007). The impact of league table and ranking systems on higher education decision making. *Higher Education Management and Policy*, *19*(2), 87–110.

IREG Observatory on Academic Ranking and Excellence. (2011). *IREG Observatory: University Rankings Under Scrutiny*. Retrieved April 03, 2012, from http://www.ireg-observatory.org/index.php?option=com _content&task=view&id=66&Itemid=2

Leach, J. (2005). Tables: They may be flawed but they're here to stay. *The Guardian*. Retrieved April 03, 2012, from http://www.guardian.co.uk/education/2005/nov/29/ universityguide.highereducation/print

Living Knowledge: The International Science Shop Network. (2012). *Frequently Asked Questions*. Retrieved April 03, 2012, from http://www.livingknowledge.org/livingknowledge/science-shops/faq

Makgoba, M. (2011). South Africa: Universities must build winning nation. *University World News: The Global Window on Higher Education*, 200. Retrieved April 03, 2012, from http://www.universityworldnews. com/article.php?story=20111202221544907

Mamdani, M. (2007). *Scholars in the Marketplace: The Dilemmas of Neo-Liberal Reform at Makerere University, 1989–2005*. Dakar: Codesria. Retrieved April 03, 2012, from http://www.codesria.org/IMG/article_PDF /article_a945.pdf

Marginson, S. (2007). Australia: The power of rankings. *World University News: The Global Window on Higher Education*, (05). Retrieved April 03, 2012, from http://www.universityworldnews.com /article.php?story=20071108143650369

National Planning Committee. (2011). *The National Development Plan: Vision for 2030*. Retrieved April 3, 2012, from http://www.npconline.co.za/medialib/downloads/home/NPC%20National %20Development %20Plan%20Vision%202030%20-lo-res.pdf

Salmi, J., & Saroyan, A. (2007). League tables as policy instruments: Uses and misuses. *Higher Education Management and Policy*, *19*(2), 31–68.

Shanghai Jiao Tong University. (2009). *Academic Ranking of World Universities: Ranking Methodology*. Retrieved April 03, 2012, from http://www.arwu.org/ ARWUMethodology2009.jsp

Reuters, T. (2012). *Global Institutional Profiles Project*. Retrieved April 03, 2012, from http://www.science.thomsonreuters.com/globalprofilesproject/.

Times Higher Education – QS World University Rankings. (2009). Top 200 World Universities. *Times Higher Education*. Retrieved April 03, 2012, from Retrieved from http://www.timeshighereducation.co.uk/Rankings2009-Top200.html

158

University of Cape Town. (2012). *Research Development Emerging Researcher Programme and the Supervision Training Programme.* Retrieved April 03, 2012, from http://www.researchoffice.uct.ac.za /research_development/erp/overview/

Visser, D. P. (2010). *A Vision for the Development of Research at the University of Cape Town: Greater Impact, Greater Engagement.* Paper presented at the Research Indaba Symposium: READ (unpublished), the University of Cape Town, South Africa.

AFFILIATIONS

Danie Visser & Marilet Sienaert
University of Cape Town, South Africa

GERARD A. POSTIGLIONE AND JISUN JUNG

WORLD-CLASS UNIVERSITY AND ASIA'S TOP TIER RESEARCHERS

INTRODUCTION

University league tables and policies aimed at world-class standing are adopted in promoting excellence in universities both at a national and an institutional level. With a focus on the research productivity of academics, the connection between research productivity and university policies such as personnel policy and funding allocation has been raised a big issue. How this phenomenon of building world-class universities has impacted on the research productivity of academics and, in particular, highly productive academics? This empirical study of research productivity in four Asian higher education systems, that is, mainland China, Hong Kong Special Administrative Region (SAR) China, Japan, and South Korea, uses data from the Second International Survey of the Academic Profession and measures research productivity by number of scientific journal publications over a three-year period. It identifies and analyses commonalities shared by the most highly productive Asian researchers, including their individual attributes and perceptions as well as factors associated with their affiliated universities.

RESEARCH BACKGROUND

Asian universities are on the rise (Levin, 2010). This is not surprising since countless indicators point to a rapid jump in research productivity rates among Asian academics. Hong Kong SAR, mainland China and South Korea have experienced an unprecedented increase in research productivity. While Japan's rate of productivity has levelled off somewhat, its academic productivity rates are among the highest in Asia. Mainland China has climbed the global league tables by massively boosting scientific publications. In 2008, Chinese researchers published 204,000 papers in peer-reviewed journals that had abstracts in English. Mainland China's global knowledge share rose from 4.4% in 1999 to 10.2% in 2008, with a very strong showing in engineering subjects, including nano-technology. Only the US has a larger share. Moreover, mainland China's spending on higher education has grown by 20% per year since 1999, and is now over US$100 billion. Most of the funding is funnelled to the elite institutions, which helps explain why the number of Chinese universities in the 500 globally ranked institutions published in the Academic Ranking of World Universities

Q. Wang, Y. Cheng, & N.C. Liu (eds.), Building World-Class Universities: Different Approaches to a Shared Goal, 161–181.

increased from 14 in 2003 to 22 in 2010 (Shanghai Jiao Tong University, 2010). Hong Kong SAR and South Korea have been equally impressive, though their university systems are smaller and their percentage of gross domestic product (GDP) for research pales in comparison to Japan and mainland China. According to the U.S. National Science Board, between 1995 and 2007, the number of papers produced each year in mainland China grew by 16.5% a year, South Korea by 14.1%, Singapore 10.5%, Taiwan China 8.6%, and Thailand 14.5%. Between 1995 and 2007, mainland China's annual number of research papers rose from 9,061 to 56.806, moving past the UK and Germany. In 1995 the output of international science and technology papers in India and mainland China was about equal. By 2007 research output in mainland China was three times that of India, while the number of papers from South Korea surpassed that of India, (even though India has more than twenty times the population). The number of researchers per million is 3,187 in South Korea, 708 in Mainland China, and 199 in India (Agarwal, 2009).

Table 1. Comparative performance of selected countries and regions in relation to share of publication volume and share of highly cited articles[*], all fields, 1998 and 2008

	Share of all articles		Share of 1% most cited articles		Index of highly cited articles	
	1998 (%)	*2008 (%)*	*1998 (%)*	*2008 (%)*	*1998 (%)*	*2008 (%)*
United States	34.0	28.9	62.0	51.6	1.83	1.78
European union	34.6	33.1	25.1	29.6	0.73	0.89
China	1.6	5.9	0.1	2.5	0.07	0.42
Japan	8.5	7.8	4.3	4.5	0.50	0.58
Asian-8[**]	3.6	3.6	0.3	2.2	0.08	0.32

Note: [*] The index of highly cited articles is the share of the world's top 1% cited articles divided by the share of world articles. 1.00 = a share of the world's most highly cited articles on in proportion with the share of all articles. An index number of more than 1.00 constitutes relative high performance in this respect.
[**] Asian-8 = India, Indonesia, Malaysia, Philippines, Singapore, South Korea, Taiwan, and Thailand.
Source: National Science Board, US (2010). Science and Engineering Indicators

Several East Asian countries continue to invest heavily, though selectively, in the infrastructure and research of top universities. In order to sustain large gains in global research capacity, they are prepared to continue to support increases in research funding. The countries of most interest are those with a national policy to establish world-class universities. These include mainland China's 211 and 985 Projects, Korea's Brain 21 Program, and Japan's Global Centres of Excellence. Despite having three of its universities in Asia's top 10, the relatively tiny Chinese territory of Hong Kong has not set forth any specific policy to boost its university rankings.

Table 2. Science and engineering papers[*]*: All nations over 10,000 papers and Asia-Pacific countries and regions*[**] *over 1,000 papers in 1995 and 2007*

	1995	2007	Annual change (%)		1995	2007	Annual change (%)
United States	193,337	209,695	0.7	China	9,061	56,806	16.5
United Kingdom	45,498	47,121	0.3	Japan	47,068	52,896	1.0
Germany	37,645	44,408	1.4	South Korea	3,803	18,467	14.1
France	28,847	30,740	0.5	India	9,370	18,194	5.7
Canada	23,740	27,799	1.3	Australia	13,125	17,831	2.6
Italy	17,880	26,554	3.3	Taiwan	4,759	12,742	8.6
Spain	11,316	20,981	5.3	Singapore	1,141	3,792	10.5
Netherlands	12,089	14,210	1.4	New Zealand	2,442	3,173	2.2
Russia	18,603	13,953	−2.4	Thailand	340	1,728	14.5

Notes: [*] In all fields (includes social sciences).
[**] Excluding West Asian countries and regions.
Source: National Science Board, US (2010). Science and Engineering Indicators

An increasingly popular explanation being put forward is that those East Asian systems with a Confucian heritage are characterized by similar patterns and policies tied to their cultural heritage (Marginson, 2011; Yang, 2010). These include favouring investment in science and technology to the detriment of the humanities and the social sciences, and similarly in applied and commercial research over academically-controlled basic research.

In spite of the impressive research performance of academics in East Asia, there is a lack of research on their background, academic activities, and institutional factors that drive their productivity. We are left with popular stereotypes of Asian academics as diligent and hard working. To a large extent, this paper's data supports this stereotype (see Table 3). Asian academics involved in the Second International Survey of the Academic Profession report a more robust professional profile in respect to working hours. It is believed,

Table 3. International comparison of hours on academic activities*

	Teaching	Research	Total		Teaching	Research	Total
Canada	20	16	51	Japan	20	17	51
US	21	12	49	South Korea	21	18	53
Finland	17	16	43	Hong Kong	20	14	50
Germany	16	16	45	Mainland China	19	14	41
Italy	19	17	45	Malaysia	18	7	36
Netherlands	20	10	39	Argentina	14	16	38
Norway	13	14	35	Brazil	20	9	39
Portugal	20	13	41	Mexico	21	9	45
UK	18	12	45	South Africa	21	9	42
Australia	18	14	46				

Note: * Arithmetic mean of hours per week.
Source: International Centre for Higher Education Research Kassel (2011)

however, that the explanation is far more complicated than just a matter of time on task, however significant that may be. For example, while Hong Kong academics are highly productive researchers, their work hours profile has a much greater emphasis on teaching than their counterparts in Japan or South Korea.

It stands to reason that academics in systems with higher research productivity would have a strong affiliation to their field/academic discipline than to their department or institution. This is particularly true in Japan, which has the strongest research output, and also in Hong Kong, which has a highly mobile academic profession.

Thus, the purpose of this study is to reflect the impact of world-class university policy on research productivity of academics, to analyse the profile of highly productive academics in selected Asian countries and to explore the common factors that appear to be drivers of that productivity. This study asks the following questions:

- How have the research activities of academics changed since the introduction of a university ranking system or world-class university policy?
- Who, broadly speaking, are Asia's highly productive scientists? What are the characteristics of their profile?
- What factors explain their productivity in contrast to that of the larger population of researchers in Asia?
- More specifically, this research investigates:
- What are the demographics and academic background indicators of Asia's most highly productive faculty?

- What are the features of their academic activities in comparison with low productive faculty?
- What characteristics of the most highly productive faculty can be attributed directly to their affiliated institutions?

Table 4. International comparison of importance of affiliation[*]

	Discipline[**] (%)	Department (%)	Institution (%)
Japan	93	62	63
South Korea	89	89	74
Hong Kong	90	72	60
Mainland China	80	73	68
Malaysia	96	87	87
Canada	91	68	59
US	93	77	59
Finland	89	72	68
Germany	92	51	45
Italy	78	59	57
Netherlands	88	71	49
Norway	96	69	47
Portugal	79	59	66
UK	82	56	38
Australia	89	67	50
Argentina	94	84	87
Brazil	94	73	79
Mexico	97	90	93
South Africa	93	76	60
Argentina	94	84	87

Note: [*] Question: Please indicate the degree to which each of the following affiliations (Discipline, Department, and Institution) is important to you.
[**] Percentage (%) of "strongly agree" and "agree" in five scales.
Source: International Centre for Higher Education Research Kassel (2011)

IMPACT OF WORLD-CLASS UNIVERSITY POLICY ON ACADEMICS

World-class universities, usually taken to mean leading research universities, conduct cutting-edge research and contribute to technical innovations through patents and licenses (Salmi, 2009). The World Bank (2002) explains that research universities play a critical role in training the professionals, high-level specialists, scientists, and researchers needed by the economy and in producing new knowledge with a support of national innovation systems. There is no doubt that one of the key features of the world-class university is highly qualified faculty and their excellence in research (Altbach, 2004; Khoon et al., 2005; Niland, 2000). In this context, ranking indexes, including the Times Higher Education World University Rankings and the Academic Ranking of World Universities produced at Shanghai Jiao Tong University, also consider influence of faculty by measuring research performance or citations.

165

The key research universities in Asia have tried to establish world-class universities and support possible strategies and pathways for such universities. Universities in Asia are under pressure to benchmark according to "international standards" and academics are being urged to publish in internationally recognized journals (Deem et al., 2009). How do those changes impact on academics and how do they respond to attempts to steer research activities?

As Hazelkorn (2008) indicated, competitive rankings and research output metrics have been quickly adopted in the missions and performance measurement institutional system. Research should not be oriented merely towards problem solving for local contexts anymore but should focus on issues relevant to a wider context and publication in top international journals (Reale & Seeber, 2011). Lucas (2006) noted that academics are in competition with one another at the levels of discipline, institution, system, and international system.

Evident in these changes, universities are intent on improving their research positions. Deans and faculty are increasingly sensitized to ranking results and underlying indicators are considered in the formulation of new structures (Hazelkorn, 2009). Many universities have recruited "star" faculty to enhance the productivity and research income of universities, rewarded faculty for publication in highly cited journals, instituted performance pay and created stricter standards for appointment/promotion and even the identification of weak performers.

How do academics respond to these environments? The academic profession is coming under intense pressure to alter the way in which it has traditionally performed. There has been increased awareness of the importance of publishing high quality research for academics. Academics publish in international journals with consideration of Impact Factor in order to increase their reputation and their capability to attract funds (Reale & Seeber, 2011). Individual faculty may earn bonuses or performance-related pay depending upon research success. As well, there are emerging pressures on funding, knowledge production and decision processes which may convince professors to change their research interests and to join bigger groups (*ibid*). Increased incentives for research performance have altered the traditional roles of academics, affecting the balance of teaching and research (Dill, 2009).

RESEARCH PRODUCTIVITY OF ACADEMICS

All of the available data, including the tables above, focus on academics within a system. The aim of this chapter is to narrow that focus to the top tier of researchers in each of the selected university systems to understand better why some faculty are more prolific in research publication than others, and to generalize their profile, perspectives and the institutional features they believe account for their success. Unfortunately, past literature tells us little, though it strongly hints that highly productive faculty collaborate more than their counterparts. While existing studies focus on averages to compare faculty performance, our paper examines extreme differences between the most and least productive academics. Past empirical research on research productivity has been mostly confined to academics in developed countries, such as the US, UK, and Australia. Much less is known about the variety of factors influencing Asia's research productivity, as measured by journal publications, in different nations (and especially in those with emerging economies). It is difficult to obtain a comparative perspective from existing single-nation studies, since there are large variations in terms of disciplinary field, time span, and other independent variables. In Asia, neither the comparative literature on the professoriate in general, nor the literature dealing specifically with publication productivity in single-nation studies has provided a reliable basis for predicting publication productivity across countries.

One needs to find key differences between productive and unproductive researchers. Differences in ability, energy, creativity, motivation, ambition and self-discipline are considered to be important factors in distinguishing between productive and unproductive researchers. To a certain extent, productive researchers are strategic, that is, they give priority to producing short articles which can be published quickly, interspersed occasionally with a number of high quality papers. Several academics identified the stringency of the university's requirements for promotion as the main reason for why they academics employ gamesmanship in their approach to research (Wood, 1990).

Productive and unproductive researchers also exhibit different attitudes as to scholarship and academic activities. Their productivity may be associated with certain behavioural habits and patterns which act as tools or devices for accomplishing tasks (Fox, 1983). For example, the highest levels of productivity seem to result from mixed research activities, though this is less the case with applied and developmental research than with basic research (Prpic, 1996b)

Finally, the literature tells us that top tier researchers tend to be more collaborative. This elite group of top researchers are not only far more internationally networked, but they are also more involved in teamwork and other forms of regular scientific cooperation. In short, there is a high degree of scientific collaboration and international involvement among eminent scientists (Prpic, 1996a). Playing roles in a wider scientific activity (regional and international), such as editor, reviewer, mentor, examiner, etc. is indicative of the highly productive researcher, and significantly influences the development of each scientific field. For this reason, academics often struggle with time allocation in their workload. Also, the productivity of the respondents who started their career in academic science is seen to be higher than respondents who, prior to employment in science, had worked in non-science institutions (Wood, 1990).

Several studies have attempted to examine those institutional factors that contribute to research productivity. Institutional characteristics such as organizational structure and leadership, size of program and faculty, control by private sector, amount of university revenue, availability of technology and computing facilities, and the number of books and journals in libraries affect research productivity of academics. As well, workload policies, availability of leave, travel, institutional funds for research, the number of students financially supported for research, availability of star faculty and the institutional availability of nongovernmental research funds can encourage or discourage of academic activities (Dundar & Lewis, 1998). The culture of a department or institution also has been found to be an important factor determining the research performance of individual faculty. Culture relates to shared attitudes and values in academic unit (Cresswell, 1985).

Not surprisingly, positively perceived academic environments are conducive to higher research outputs. Some research points to the importance of researcher perception of clear organizational goals, a climate of respect, participative governance, and resource availability in achieving optimal conditions for professional activity and productivity (Bland & Ruffin, 1992). As well, Prpic (1996a, 1996b) indicates that the institutional factors are more pronounced within the elite group of researcher than within in the non-productive group.

Other studies have looked into the influence of organizational freedom on productivity. While the findings are somewhat mixed, they tend to suggest that higher levels of academic freedom support publication productivity (Fox, 1983). Productivity is supported where scientists have flexibility and freedom with ideas, and where organizational goals do not conflict with individual interests and aspirations for basic research (*ibid*).

Pressures to publish for promotional purposes are claimed by some academics to be anathema to some types of research. Colleagues who can provide stimulation and challenge are as important, though the influence of collegiality in the work environment is variable (Wood, 1990).

In order to better understand the scientific productivity of first-class scientists in Asian universities, this research will examine selected aspects of their profile and perspectives on academic work and their institutional environments.

METHODOLOGY

This study uses data from the international survey of "The Changing Academic Profession" conducted in 2007–2008 (Research Institute for Higher Education, 2008). This is the second such international survey, the first was coordinated in 1993 by the Carnegie Foundation for the Advancement of Teaching. The second international survey included 20 countries. The survey questionnaire is composed of over 200 questions about demographics, academic career, perception of scholarship, workloads, perception of work environment, attitudes toward teaching, research, and institution, and a series of academic issues. Each country team obtained a national representative sample of its academic profession. In order to allow international comparisons, all countries addressed the core questions. In order to minimize measurement bias across countries, country teams maintained a high level of standardization in terms of question order, question wording, response options, reference periods, and layout and formal design. Due to the absence of national lists of members of the academic profession, a one-stage simple random sample was not possible for most countries. Instead, most national studies applied a two-stage cluster sample. At the first stage, a random selection of institutions was drawn. At the second stage, individual academics within each institution were selected at random; several strata (groups of academics by discipline, gender, and ethnicity, if applicable) were differentiated (*ibid*).

In this particular phase of the research, this research will analyse the characteristics of academics in four higher educational systems: two of China's systems (mainland and Hong Kong), Japan, and Korea. To examine and compare research productivity, this research identified two groups: the 10% of each of the most and least productive academics based on the number of journal publication. First, their demographics profile is analysed by gender, age, and the country where their doctoral degree was obtained. Second, their perceptions related to scholarship (teaching, research, and service) are analysed. Finally, we examined the different institutional characteristics that align with academic productivity. Thus this research relies on three sets of factors: those concerning researcher profiles, researcher perceptions, and institutional factors (institutional profiles and researcher perception on them).

FINDINGS

Research Productivity of Academics in East Asian Countries and Regions

Existing studies of research productivity have mainly used the mean score to compare faculty performance. However, there are extreme differences, namely among the most and least productive academics. Most publications are produced by a small number of academics, while many faculty members produce few or none at all. The distribution of publications is heavily and negatively skewed. Therefore, before comparing the characteristics of the most and least productive group, we examined the research productivity of all academics in the sample survey. Table 5 presents the patterns and quantity of productivity of Asian academics.

Research productivity was classified into five types: authored or co-authored books, edited or co-edited books, articles, reports written for a funded project, and conference presentations. As Table 5 demonstrates, the proportion of academics with zero publications is very high as well as is the number with close to the median number of publications. In the case of authored or co-authored books and edited or co-edited books, about 70–80% of academics sampled had produced only a nominal number.

Looking at the differences across academic systems, the productivity of academics in South Korea, Japan, and Hong Kong towers above that of mainland China. Academics in Japan and South Korea publish more co-authored books than those in the other three systems. Academics in mainland China and South Korea publish more co-edited books than those in the other three places. The number of books produced by academics in Hong Kong is lower than that in the other countries and the ratio of non-publishing faculty is high. However, Hong Kong academics publish more articles and reports for funded projects. In addition, more of the work of South Korean and Hong Kong academics is presented at conferences.

Table 5. Research productivity of academics in 4 higher education systems

		Mainland China	Hong Kong SAR	Japan	South Korea
(Co) authored books	Mean	.85	.48	1.59	1.03
	Median	.0	.0	1.0	.0
	Non-publication	1,196 (65.5)	473 (70.0)	576 (43.3)	463 (51.6)
(Co) edited books	Mean	.84	.44	.46	.67
	Median	.0	.0	.0	.0
	Non-publication	1,129 (61.8)	491 (72.6)	1.039 (78.2)	637 (71.0)
Articles	Mean	8.54	9.55	9.23	10.64
	Median	6.0	6.0	5.0	7.0
	Non-publication	310 (17.0)	53 (7.8)	167 (12.6)	20 (2.2)
Report written for a funded project	Mean	1.43	1.61	1.21	2.63
	Median	.0	.0	.0	2.0
	Non-publication	1,179 (64.6)	350 (51.8)	729 (54.9)	222 (24.7)
Conference presentations	Mean	2.58	7.50	5.43	7.59
	Median	1.0	5.0	2.0	4.0
	Non-publication	839 (45.9)	64 (9.5)	508 (38.2)	145 (16.2)
Total N		3,612	811	1,408	900
Missing		1,786	135	79	3
Valid data N		1,826	676	1,329	897

Given the risk of working with mean scores to determine patterns of research productivity, faculty has been separated into high and low productivity groups. Among the five types of research publication, journal articles are the most common indicators used to calculate research productivity. Thus, three groups (high-performance, middle group, and low-performance) were constructed based on their number of journal publications in a three-year period. As Table 6 shows, the top 10% of the Asian academics have published an average of 20 articles each in the last three years, while the bottom 10% of faculty members have not published any journal articles over the three year period. This trend is similar across each of the four systems of higher education. Yet, South Korean academics stand apart from the others in one respect – even low productivity academics still published about three articles each in the last three years, which includes international and domestic journal articles.

Table 6. Comparison of research productivity

		Top 10%	Middle	Lower 10%
China	Number of articles	>20	1–19	<0
	Number of faculty	186 (10.2)	1,330 (72.8)	310 (17.0)
Hong Kong	Number of articles	>20	2–19	<1
	Number of faculty	86 (12.7)	487 (72.0)	103 (15.2)
Japan	Number of articles	>22	1–21	<0
	Number of faculty	136 (10.2)	1,026 (77.2)	167 (12.6)
Korea	Number of articles	>21	4–20	<3
	Number of faculty	91 (10.1)	648 (72.2)	158 (17.6)

Demographics and Academic Background

In the analysis of demographics factors, this research has identified the following patterns that differentiate high and low productivity groups:

First, the ratio of male academics exceeds that of women in the highly productive group, and the ratio of the latter is higher than the former in the low productivity group. In short, women academics are less productive. This finding merits very careful interpretation, however. Male academics are likely more highly distributed among highly productive fields such as medical science and engineering. In contrast, women academics have higher representation in fields such as the humanities, where journal article production is less characteristic of the field. This gender gap is especially egregious in Japan, where male academics constitute about 99% of the highly productive group.

Second, while it is assumed that senior academics are more productive than junior academics, the data undermines this assumption. There is a high ratio of young academics in the highly productive group in both South Korea and mainland China, systems that are both in a period of rapid expansion and which draw upon a large group of young scholars who were sent overseas to earn their highest academic degree. In these countries, the most highly productive academics are in their 30s and 40s. Thus, among the so-called emergent systems of mainland China and South Korea, the research productivity of junior academics is relatively high, and it can be expected that this group to remain productive for quite some time. These countries have instituted policies and initiatives to enhance research productivity of young academics, and they seem to be working.

Third, with respect to where qualifications were earned – domestically or abroad – both South Korea and Hong Kong have about a third of their faculty with overseas doctorates, while most academics in Japan and mainland China earned domestic doctorates. Yet, this does not seem to matter in respect to journal productivity. There is no discernible pattern that indicates that the most productive academics earned their doctorates overseas.

Fourth, we examined whether highly productive academics are distributed in research (intensive) universities as it is known that experienced and well qualified academics became harder to recruit and retain because they tend to seek positions at universities with high rankings (Dill, 2009). Due to data limitations, only the Hong Kong and South Korea cases were analysed. As expected, a high proportions of productive academics are working in research universities; however, considerable proportions of leading scholars are also working in other types of universities.

Fifth, regarding academic discipline, most highly productive academics are in hard disciplines including engineering, natural science, and medical science. Further research is needed to reflect differences in research style and publication preference and to try to separate analysis between academic disciplines.

Finally, highly productive academics seem to have accumulated research experience from various institutions during longer periods. Longer prior experience in different institutions translates into higher productivity.

Perceptions about Scholarship

To examine perceptions about scholarship, this research used the "discovery" dimension of Boyer's (1992) four types of scholarship (discovery, application, integration, and teaching). Overall, the most and least productive researchers in the four higher education systems under study have contrasting perceptions of scholarship, with the top 10% emphasizing discovery and basic/theoretical research. Also, the most productive group perceives social responsibility as a key dimension of scholarship. There were no significant differences between the two groups in their perception of scholarship as application and integration. For top academics in mainland China, discovery was seen as far and away the most important dimension of scholarship. They perceive scholarship as highly aligned with international research, commercial-oriented research, and multidisciplinary research. This might be interpreted as the result of mainland China's undergoing market reforms. In general, academics agree on the importance of fundamental research even if some of them timidly underline the "peculiarity" of research (Reale & Seeber, 2011). However, changes in the performance funding context are valuable for pushing some researchers to shift their research agenda towards more applicative, interdisciplinary, emerging fields (*ibid*).

Table 7. Summary of research: sample total, top 10 % academics and lower 10% academics

		Sample total*				Top 10%				Lower 10%			
		CH	HK	JP	KR	CH	HK	JP	KR	CH	HK	JP	KR
Gender	Male	2,005 (62.9)	536 (67.3)	1,266 (91.0)	734 (81.6)	149 (82.3)	74 (89.2)	134 (98.5)	69 (75.8)	182 (60.1)	59 (59.0)	142 (85.0)	123 (77.8)
	Female	1,302 (37.1)	261 (32.7)	125 (9.0)	166 (18.4)	32 (17.7)	9 (10.8)	2 (1.5)	22 (24.2)	121 (39.9)	41 (41.0)	25 (15.0)	35 (22.2)
Age	Up to 35	1,346 (39.7)	104 (13.7)	57 (4.2)	47 (5.2)	32 (18.0)	5 (6.5)	2 (1.5)	3 (3.3)	94 (32.3)	23 (24.7)	3 (1.9)	10 (6.3)
	36-45	1,430 (42.1)	231 (30.5)	330 (24.3)	398 (44.3)	92 (51.7)	21 (27.3)	24 (17.8)	49 (53.8)	140 (48.1)	19 (20.4)	21 (19.3)	48 (30.4)
	46-55	492 (14.5)	299 (39.4)	437 (32.1)	366 (40.7)	40 (22.5)	40 (51.9)	52 (38.5)	31 (34.1)	45 (15.5)	31 (33.3)	46 (28.6)	75 (47.5)
	56-65	115 (3.4)	116 (15.3)	473 (34.8)	84 (9.3)	12 (6.7)	10 (13.0)	53 (39.3)	7 (7.7)	11 (3.8)	18 (19.4)	69 (42.9)	23 (14.6)
	66 and elder	10 (0.3)	8 (1.1)	63 (4.6)	4 (0.4)	2 (1.1)	1 (1.3)	4 (3.0)	1 (1.1)	1 (0.3)	2 (2.2)	12 (7.5)	2 (1.3)
Country getting doctoral degree	Own country	979 (93.5)	172 (26.6)	1,019 (96.7)	502 (57.0)	105 (91.3)	25 (31.3)	124 (91.2)	55 (60.4)	54 (96.4)	19 (23.8)	86 (94.5)	88 (60.7)
	US	8 (0.8)	185 (28.6)	17 (1.6)	261 (29.6)		16 (20.0)		29 (31.9)		25 (31.3)		41 (28.3)
	UK		139 (21.5)				19 (23.8)				20 (25.0)		

173

Table 7. Continued

Institution	Research (intensive) University	409 (50.0)		327 (36.0)			53 (61.6)	49 (53.8)			41 (40.0)	42 (27.0)
	Non-research (intensive) University	402 (50.0)		568 (63.0)			33 (38.4)	42 (46.1)			62 (60.0)	116 (73.0)
Discipline	Teacher Training	260 (8.0)	103 (7.6)	113 (12.6)	4 (2.3)	1 (0.8)	3 (3.7)	5 (5.5)	21 (7.7)	16 (16.7)	21 (13.5)	26 (16.5)
	Humanities	483 (14.9)	125 (9.2)	152 (16.9)	6 (3.4)	0 (0)	5 (6.2)	4 (4.4)	32 (11.8)	24 (25.0)	25 (16.1)	49 (31.0)
	Social Science	637 (19.6)	159 (11.8)	208 (23.1)	22 (12.6)	4 (3.1)	4 (4.9)	5 (5.5)	69 (25.3)	32 (35.4)	18 (11.6)	35 (22.2)
	Natural Science	885 (27.3)	225 (16.6)	158 (17.5)	68 (38.6)	20 (15.4)	22 (27.2)	23 (25.3)	72 (26.5)	5 (5.2)	15 (9.6)	22 (13.9)
	Engineering	713 (22.0)	257 (18.9)	147 (16.3)	59 (33.5)	27 (20.8)	20 (24.7)	26 (28.6)	62 (22.8)	2 (2.1)	30 (19.4)	20 (12.7)
	Medical Science	110 (3.4)	255 (18.8)	78 (8.7)	5 (2.8)	51 (39.2)	26 (32.1)	19 (20.9)	5 (1.8)	8 (8.3)	21 (13.5)	1 (0.6)
Experience**	Project	677 (61.7)	202 (18.6)	515 (58.7)	75 (64.7)	31 (24.0)	45 (55.6)	66 (72.5)	31 (54.4)	27 (34.2)	15 (15.6)	68 (46.9)
	HEI	11.3	17.7	11.0	14.7	20.9	16.8	11.1	12.5	10.3	19.1	13.2
	RI	0.3	1.6	1.0	0.5	1.5	0.7	1.5	0.3	0.4	1.5	0.5

Note: *CH: Mainland China, HK: Hong Kong SAR, JP: Japan, KR: South Korea.
**Project: research project experience (%), HEI: Higher Education Institutions experience (duration), RI: Research Institute experience (duration).

Table 8. Perceptions on scholarship (% of agreement)

		Mainland China	Hong Kong	Japan	Korea
Discovery	Sample	54.1	81.3	77.4	77.6
	Top 10%	57.8	90.6	83.6	71.4
	Lower 10%	52.8	80.8	68.7	80.4
Application	Sample	81.5	78.7	74.9	83.1
	Top 10%	83.5	82.4	69.6	84.6
	Lower 10%	82.5	80.8	81.5	83.5
Integration	Sample	76.0	73.3	80.6	90.6
	Top 10%	78.0	75.3	80.6	84.6
	Lower 10%	77.3	70.7	79.4	91.0
Social responsibility	Sample	70.5	63.8	64.8	76.2
	Top 10%	75.8	71.8	66.4	84.4
	Lower 10%	64.2	59.6	62.1	70.9
Commercially-oriented	Sample	50.3	10.8	21.8	19.4
	Top 10%	53.0	23.7	29.6	32.9
	Lower 10%	50.6	9.2	13.7	13.4
Multi-/ interdisciplinary	Sample	80.1	67.3	53.1	53.2
	Top 10%	91.1	82.6	65.4	58.6
	Lower 10%	75.5	53.2	42.2	51.3

Academic Activities

This research categorizes academic activities into three types: teaching, research, and service. The participation rate of specific kinds of activities was examined by the amount of time allocated to each. First, as expected, highly productive academics spent much more time on research rather than teaching. Academics have to deal with a wide range of tasks. They may research, teach and conduct external work; rules may not always encourage involvement in research activities (Reale & Seeber, 2011). Academics who invest much more time for research may produce more publications, however, the time allocation varies according to university mission. Second, highly productive academics collaborate more than others, particularly in the international domain.

Institutional Characteristics

Research productivity is also dependent upon institutional characteristics, and can be gleaned from the academics' perception of how their institutions operate. We categorized institutional characteristics into two types; aspects of institutional academic culture and performance-based institutional management.

Table 9. Academic activities

			Mainland China	Hong Kong	Japan	Korea
Time allocation	Total	Sample	33.2	44.2	48.0	52.2
		Top 10%	44.3	49.3	51.3	53.4
		Lower 10%	32.8	45.0	46.5	48.5
	Time spent teaching	Sample	19.2	19.8	20.3	21.1
		Top 10%	17.4	13.3	15.9	18.6
		Lower 10%	19.3	23.4	23.1	20.4
	Time spent research	Sample	13.5	14.8	16.7	18.1
		Top 10%	21.6	19.7	21.1	22.0
		Lower 10%	12.1	11.2	13.6	15.4
Research Collaboration	Institutional collaboration	Sample	37.0	54.9	51.5	65.0
		Top 10%	61.6	77.6	74.3	90.0
		Lower 10%	30.7	39.4	32.9	43.8
	International collaboration	Sample	12.6	60.2	23.8	29.5
		Top 10%	33.0	85.9	49.3	51.1
		Lower 10%	9.0	38.4	7.8	12.4

First, with the exception of Korea, the top tier researchers, more than the lower tier, perceive both the protection of academic freedom as well as a strong emphasis on institutional mission as important. Top tier Korean academics seem to view their institution's commitment to academic freedom as inadequate (see Table 10).

Second, performance-based management matters greatly to top tier academics. The most productive academics perceive their institutions as making decisions about personnel and funding allocation on the basis of performance based criteria (see Table 11).

Table 10. Institutional culture (% of agreement)

		Mainland China	Hong Kong	Japan	Korea
The administration supports academic freedom	Sample	53.3	53.8	56.1	50.4
	Top 10%	58.4	65.1	63.6	49.5
	Lower 10%	46.8	53.6	50.6	55.1
A strong emphasis on the institution's mission	Sample	64.7	62.5	59.4	50.3
	Top 10%	68.9	62.2	62.1	51.6
	Lower 10%	61.2	60.2	56.5	51.9

Table 11. Performance-based management matters (% of agreement)

		Mailand China	Hong Kong	Japan	Korea
Pressure to raise external research funds	Sample	57.3	78.1	79.8	58.2
	Top 10%	66.3	90.7	84.2	69.2
	Lower 10%	49.0	53.3	69.1	54.5
A strong performance orientation	Sample	60.1	65.4	52.3	62.8
	Top 10%	69.5	67.9	61.7	64.8
	Lower 10%	56.5	63.9	40.0	59.9
Performance based allocation of resources to academic units	Sample	49.6	58.3	31.2	34.1
	Top 10%	52.9	56.6	39.6	40.7
	Lower 10%	49.6	57.0	23.4	33.1
Considering the research quality when making personnel decisions	Sample	56.3	69.3	59.7	33.0
	Top 10%	58.0	72.8	62.4	36.6
	Lower 10%	52.9	71.3	53.5	22.4

CONCLUSIONS

This study was initiated to explore how world-class university policy has impacted on the research productivity of academics, in particular highly productive academics. Academics in many Asian universities have attained a high level of research productivity in a short time. This study uses data from the Second International Survey of the Academic Profession to examine the common factors correlated to the support of top tier researchers in four Asian university systems: China (Hong Kong and mainland) Korea, and Japan. Three sets of factors were examined: demographic, perspectives on academic work, and perspectives on institutional context. Regarding age, the common assumption that senior academics are more productive than junior academics does not hold in the emergent systems of Korea and China. These countries have instituted policies and initiatives to enhance research productivity of young academics. Another common assumption is that attaining doctorates in Western countries equates with higher research productivity. While only a small proportion of top tier Japanese and Chinese academics earn doctorates overseas, a significant proportion (about one third) of South Korean and Hong Kong academics earn overseas doctorates, mostly in the US. In all cases, the assumption about overseas-earned doctorates and academic productivity is not supported by the data. One might speculate that those who returned to their county were less productive than those who remained employed overseas. More research is necessary on this important point. The most and least productive researchers show different perceptions about scholarship and academic activities. For example, highly productive academics emphasize discovery and basic/theoretical research as well as perceiving social responsibility to be a key dimension of scholarship. They are highly collaborative in their work orientation. There is also a high degree of international scientific collaboration and involvement among productive academics. Finally, the most productive researchers differ from the rest in their perception of institutional factors. The most productive academics are more likely than others to perceive their institutions as making decisions about personnel and funding allocation on the basis of performance based criteria. With the exception of South Korean academics, who seem to expect more, the most productive academics in Asia view their institutions as protecting academic freedom, more than other academics do.

While this preliminary study has broadened our understanding of the characteristics and determinants of the most highly productive academics in four Asian systems of higher education, nevertheless, there are issues which need to be explored further in order to reach more specific conclusions. While a set of predictors has been identified through descriptive analysis in this research, more in-depth examination is needed of how much each predictor is a significant determinant of research productivity in each higher education system. More comparative analysis of predictors of research productivity in advanced Western higher education systems is needed to find the unique characteristics of Asian systems.

ACKNOWLEDGEMENT

We would like to thank Professor Jung Cheol Shin (Seoul National University, South Korea) for his ideas, meaningful suggestions and comment.

REFERENCES

Altbach, P. G. (2004). The costs and benefits of a World-Class Universities. *Academe, 90*. Retrieved April 10, 2012, from http://www.aaup.org/AAUP/pubsres/academe/2004/JF/Feat/altb.htm

Agarwal, P. (2009). *Indian Higher Education: Envisioning the Future*. New Delhi: Sage.

Bland, C. J., & Ruffin, M. T. (1992). Characteristics of a productive research environment: Literature Review. *Academic Medicine, 67*(6), 385–397.

Boyer, E. L. (1992). *Scholarship Reconsidered: Priorities of the Professoriate*. Princeton, NJ: Princeton University Press.

Cresswell, J. W. (1985). Faculty research performances: Lessons from the science and social sciences. In *ASHE-ERIC Higher Education Report, 4*. Washington, DC: Association for the Study of Higher Education.

Deem, R., Lucas, L., & Mok, K. H. (2009). The "world-class" university in Europe and East Asia: Dynamics and consequences of global higher education reform. In B. M. Kehm & B. Stensaker (Eds.), *University Rankings, Diversity, and the New Landscape of Higher Education* (pp. 117–134). Rotterdam: Sense Publisher.

Dill, D. D. (2009). Convergence and diversity: The role and influence of university rankings. In B. M. Kehm & B. Stensaker (Eds.), *University Rankings, Diversity, and the New Landscape of Higher Education* (pp. 97–116). Rotterdam: Sense Publisher.

Dundar, H., & Lewis, D. (1998). Determinants of research productivity in higher education. *Research in Higher Education, 39*(6), 607–631.

Fox, M. F. (1983). Publication productivity among scientists: A critical review. *Social Studies of Science, 13*(2), 285–305.

Hazelkorn, E. (2008). Learning to live with league tables and ranking: The experience of institutional leaders. *Higher Education Policy, 21*, 193–215.

Hazelkorn, E. (2009). Attitudes to rankings: Comparing German, Australian and Japanese experience. In S. Kaur, M. Sirat, & W. G. Tierney (Eds.), *Addressing Critical Issues on Quality Assurance and University Rankings in Higher Education in the Asia Pacific*. Penang, Malaysia: University Sains Malaysia.

International Centre for Higher Education Research Kassel. (2011). *The Changing Academic Profession: Main Survey Results*. Unpublished reports. Kassel: University of Kassel.

Khoon, K. A. Shukor, R., Hussan, O., Saleh, Z., Hamzah, A., & Ismail, R. (2005, December). Hallmark of a world-class university. *College Student Journal*. Retrieved April 10, 2012, from http://findarticles.com/p/articles/mi_m0FCR/is_4_39/ai_n16123684/

Levin, R. C. (2010, February 1). *The Rise of Asia's Universities*. London: Speech to the Royal Society. Yale University Office of Public Affairs. Retrieved April 17, 2010, from http://opa.yale.edu/president/message.aspx?id=91

Lucas, L. (2006). *The Research Game in Academic Life*. Maidenhead: SRHE and Open University Press.

Marginson, S. (2011). Higher education in East Asia and Singapore: Rise of the confucian model. *Higher Education, 61*(5), 587–611.

National Science Board, US. (2010). *Science and Engineering Indicators 2010*. Retrieved April 10, 2010, from http://www.nsf.gov/statistics/seind10/

Niland, J. (2000, February 3). The challenge of building world-class universities in the Asian Region. *Online Opinion*. Retrieved April 10, 2006, from http://www.onlineopinion.com.au/view.asp?article=997

Prpic, K. (1996a). Characteristics and determinants of eminent scientists' productivity. *Scientometrics, 36*(2), 185–206.

Prpic, K. (1996b). Scientific fields and eminent scientists' productivity partners and factors. *Scientometrics, 37*(3), 445–471.

Reale, E., & Seeber, M. (2011). Organization response to institutional pressures in higher education: The important role of the disciplines. *Higher Education, 61*(1), 1–22.

Research Institute for Higher Education. (2008). The changing academic profession in international comparative and quantitative perspectives. *Research Institute for Higher Education International Seminar Reports, 12*. Hiroshima: Hiroshima University.

Salmi, J. (2009). *The Challenge of Establishing World-Class Universities*. Washington, DC: The World Bank.

Shanghai Jiao Tong University. (2010). *Academic Ranking of World Universities – 2010*. Retrieved May 8, 2012, from http://www.arwu.org

The World Bank. (2002). *Constructing Knowledge Societies: New Challenges for Tertiary Education*. Washington, DC: The World Bank. Retrieved December 2, 2008, from http://go.worldbank.org/N2QADMBNIO

Wood, F. (1990). Factors influencing research performance of university academic staff. *Higher Education, 19*(1), 81–100.

Yang, R. (2010). Advanced global strategy in China: The case of Tsinghua. In S. Marginson, S. Kaur, & E. Sawir (Eds.), *Higher Education in the Asia-Pacific: Strategic Responses to Globalization*. Dordrecht: Springer.

AFFILIATIONS

Gerard A. Postiglione & Jisun Jung
Faculty of Education,
The University of Hong Kong, Hong Kong SAR

SIMON M. PRATT

THE GLOBAL INSTITUTIONAL PROFILES PROJECT

A New Approach to Evaluating Academic Institutions

INTRODUCTION

Universities have multiple and varied missions and the stakeholders in university evaluation have differing objectives to their evaluation. University rankings are inflexible because they dictate the evaluation methodology to the user of the ranking regardless of their evaluation objective. Furthermore, a single ranking position cannot represent the complex nature of universities and their multiple missions. The Global Institutional Profiles Project is an initiative by Thomson Reuters to profile the world's higher education and research-intensive institutions. This "profiling" approach facilitates a multidimensional evaluation that captures the multiple missions of the institution but also the various objectives of the stakeholders in evaluation. This paper presents some of the preliminary results of the project and profiles the performance of leading institutions against international peers.

UNIVERSITY RANKINGS: ISSUES AND CHALLENGES

Before one considers the question of how to evaluate a university it is worth taking a moment to consider three fundamental questions to set the context of the evaluation. Firstly, what are the objectives or missions of a university? Secondly, how can one measure success of an institution in achieving those objectives? Finally, what is the purpose of the evaluation? These may seem simple questions but the answers are not straightforward.

With regards to the objectives and missions of the university, this is perhaps the most fundamental but hardest question of all. Every university will have multiple missions such as teaching, research, knowledge transfer, innovation and public engagement (Boulton & Lucas, 2008) and the importance placed on those missions will vary from region to region and institution to institution.

One way to broadly classify the objective of a university is to consider universities as knowledge brokers; they impart knowledge upon those people and entities with which they interact. Whether this is in the case of students learning knowledge and skills during their time at the university, the transfer of highly trained graduates from education into the labour market, the transfer of knowledge

Q. Wang, Y. Cheng, & N.C. Liu (eds.), Building World-Class Universities: Different Approaches to a Shared Goal, 181–196.

to the broader research community through research outputs such as articles and books or knowledge transfer of intellectual property to the commercial sector.

Universities also create new knowledge through the research they conduct. Most universities will have research activities at the very core of what they do and will dedicate a significant proportion of their resources to the research mission. One can see that in many university ranking initiatives, or exercises measuring the public perception of universities, it is the research-intensive universities that are most readily recognized. It is through their research activities that a university builds its reputation and therefore attracts the best scholars and faculty. Research, however, is not the only thing that universities do. Unlike dedicated research institutions universities also teach and train people. Research creates a knowledge-rich environment in which able minds are able to flourish.

A further important activity for universities, although perhaps not an activity that is normally considered a mission, is the finance-raising activity of the institution. In the age of austerity that we live in today, the financial sustainability of higher education and research institutions is challenged. One can therefore observe an increasing importance placed on the fundraising activities of universities through a variety of channels such as; philanthropy by alumni, consultative services and the management and commercialization of intellectual property.

The importance of the missions and objectives of a university will vary. The direction that a university will take may be influenced by internal and external factors, such as government policy, the needs of the local community and commerce, the history of the university and the culture of the university's faculty. For example, universities in rapidly developing countries tend to focus on physical sciences, engineering and technology that support the unique social and economic challenges of their local environment.

One can frequently see activities that serve multiple objectives. In fact cross-over activities are the unique component that sets a university apart from a teaching institution or research facility. For example consider research-based doctoral programmes, they are both teaching and research yet at the same time the outcomes of the research and the knowledge and skills that the individual student gains and carries with them into the labour market are drivers of social and economic advancement.

The outputs and outcomes of the various university missions may not be tangible and it will often be impossible to measure success. For example, given the huge variation in the structure of undergraduate degrees from region to region and between subjects, one cannot systematically evaluate the teaching performance of universities globally. It is not reasonably feasible to conduct direct measurement of teaching outputs such as exam results and therefore one must rely on proxies and indicators such as the reputational standing of the university, staff student ratio, employability and student satisfaction.

Some missions are even harder to evaluate, for example who can say that a piece of music produced by the music department of one university is better than another? Clearly it is not possible to make a judgment about subjective choice in an objective way.

Every university will have special cases that also need to be taken into consideration. For example, King's College London has been selected to provide the anti-doping laboratory for the London 2012 Olympic and Paralympic games (King's College, 2012). It is challenging to evaluate the social and economic impact of this particular activity and impossible to compare to the activities of other universities around the world in a fair and relevant way.

Conversely, some activities of universities are relatively easy to measure. For example the main output of scientific research is the journal article; by counting articles one can reliably measure the volume of research activity. Furthermore by counting the citations to those articles and the citations per paper one can measure the impact of that research upon the global research community. This type of analysis works best when using homogenous data, for example within the same subject and time period. There are established methodologies to benchmark research within its own discipline and make relevant comparisons about the relative performance across disciplines. It is not so clear, however, how one can measure the impact of research on society. For example, it is difficult to compare the social and economic impact of a particle physics experiment that furthers our understanding of the physical world to a breakthrough in cancer research that may lead to new treatments.

The purpose of an evaluation is entirely dependent on the stakeholder and there can be many different types of stakeholders. For example the parents of potential students, a research funding body looking to assign funding, a university planning department looking for new collaborators, a professor searching for a new post or a university leader trying to make better informed decisions.

Rankings aim to make order out of this chaotic environment. They enforce a defined set of evaluation criteria and use indicators and proxies of performance to distil the multiple missions of the universities into one single ranking number. The end results of ranking exercises are simple and easy to understand which means that rankings are popular with the layperson and media. By enforcing a common set of evaluation criteria upon all universities they may miss aspects that are of particular importance to that individual university. Thomson Reuters works closely with Times Higher Education to develop their World University Ranking to be as good as it can possibly be (Baty, 2011). There is, however, a problem: a single ranking position can never accurately describe the multiple missions of the university nor the multiple requirements of the stakeholders in evaluation.

GLOBAL INSTITUTIONAL PROFILES PROJECT

The Thomson Reuters approach is one of profiling with the objective of creating informative profiles of universities that are rich in robust data from multiple sources and cover the multiple aspects of a university mission. The intention is to leave it to the user of the profiles to decide which data they are interested in but, then, to provide analytical tools to help the user understand performance indicators in context of the global environment. Adding value to the data, such as benchmarking and normalization to show relative performance of the university regardless of its subject specialization, converts the data into actionable knowledge that can help the user make better informed decisions.

In 2009 Thomson Reuters launched the Global Institutional Profiles Project with the long-term objective of profiling 1,000 higher education and research organizations. The project started with an extensive survey of stakeholders to better understand what the requirements and challenges are (Adams, Baker & Smith, 2010). In the summer of 2011, second cycle of the project was completed with over 600 participating institutions.

There are three major sources of data:
– Results of the Thomson Reuters Annual Academic Reputation Survey, which demonstrates the reputational standing of institutions in the global academic community;
– Data provided by the universities themselves on students, staff and funding, which provides the context of the university, how large the university is, what its focus is and how well resourced it might;
– Bibliometric data from the Web of Science, which shows the research output and performance in terms of scholarly articles.

There are multiple intentions in capturing three different data sources. Firstly it is beneficial to have an overall picture of the institution to better understand the different performance indicators in context of each other. For example an institution that is strongly focused on undergraduate education will not have as many resources available to dedicate to research and therefore its publication output may be lower. Secondly, by having three different types of data from three different sources one can build a more accurate picture of performance and have greater confidence in the results. All indicators will have anomalies of one type or another and there will be varied levels of confidence in each one, but if all three types of data are showing the same type of performance one can have a high degree of confidence in the results of the evaluation.

Future directions of the project include: expanding the scope to include other types of research intensive organizations such as government research facilities; an expansion of the content types to better describe the multiple missions of participating institutions (in particular a focus on industry interaction); continued enhancement to the way data is analysed and presented to improve understanding.

ACADEMIC REPUTATION SURVEY

Annually Thomson Reuters conducts a web-based survey of academics and researchers asking them to provide feedback about what they consider to be the best institutions globally within their subject area. The survey is carefully designed to collect as robust data as possible. Some of these features include:
– A clear distinction between reputation for research and reputation for teaching;
– A hierarchal subject classification scheme so that academics can accurately reflect their specialization;

- A policy of participation by invitation only to prevent manipulation of the results;
- Structured distribution of the invitations to provide a fair balance between subjects and geographical regions;
- Translations into multiple languages to overcome English-language bias.

One of the many challenges faced with conducting the survey concerns the creation of an authoritative list of universities globally. A university will have an official name but the names by which they are colloquially known may be varied. Because the participants in the survey may use a wide variety of names to describe the same institution, an automated lookup system was developed to encourage the survey participant to select a university from a pre-defined list of names. This lookup system ensured clean data and prevented survey participants from making trivial errors such as spelling mistakes. A manual write in option is also available if the institution was not available from the automated lookup system.

A pre-requisite to the lookup system is an authoritative index of university names that the system can draw upon. The initial generation of the index in 2009–2010 relied on publicly available lists of universities. These lists were found to contain errors, particularly for institutions from non-English speaking countries, and to be too broad in scope. The inclusion of minor institutions created noise in the results, for example "Cambridge College" in the US is easily confused with the "University of Cambridge" in the United Kingdom. There are also cases where it is beneficial to have more than one variant of a university name to be included in the index to improve lookup recall; this is particularly true of universities from non-English speaking countries. For example the "University of Vienna" has a local language name of "Universität Wien". Once the survey has been completed the variants are unified to get consistent results.

After the first survey was completed in May 2010 the results of the survey were used to inform decisions about the inclusion and exclusion of universities in the index for the survey in 2011. There were two major changes to the index: the exclusion of the generic system names, for example "University of Illinois" to better identify which specific university in the system the survey participant intended to choose; and the addition of university name abbreviations. For example "Massachusetts Institute of Technology" was changed to "Massachusetts Institute of Technology (MIT)".

In 2011 the second survey was completed with over 17,500 respondents from more than 130 countries. Combined with the results from 2010 this comes to 31,000 unique responses. Over 90% of the respondents declared their role as that of academic staff, institutional leader or researcher. This is clear evidence of the authority of this excellent resource (Pratt, 2010).

DATA COLLECTION FROM THE PARTICIPATING INSTITUTIONS

Working directly with participating institutions, factual data about their activities was collected. Thomson Reuters has made considerable efforts to collect high quality, internationally comparable data while keeping the work burden for the participating institutions to a minimum. There are a number of features that facilitate this. Existing data sources are used where available, for example the UK Higher Education Statistics Agency (HESA) data is used to pre-fill the profiles for UK institutions. A comprehensive manual describing the data submission process, which includes a set of common data definitions for all institutions, has been created.

There is a strong support structure to help the participating universities submit accurate data; this includes detailed documentation, tutorials and webinars. In 2010 a series of 15 webinars was conducted with several hundred attendees. There is also a team of dedicated data editors, based on region, to answer questions and help participating institutions, including local language support when available. Universities are requested to submit subject area breakdowns of their data and as the subject classifications are the same as those used in other parts of the Global Institutional Profiles project, this facilitates relevant comparisons between data types.

As the universities submit data, a comprehensive data validation cycle is performed including comparisons to third party data, comparisons to previously submitted data and statistical analysis to identify anomalies.

Data supplied by the institution include, but are not limited to:
- Numbers of academic staff,
- Numbers of students at various education levels,
- Funding information, and
- International diversity information.

As anticipated, the largest challenge in collecting the data from the universities was getting their agreement to participate. This was achieved through a number of means such as promotion of the project through the media and at academic conferences and direct communication through e-mail and telephone to explain the benefits of participation with the universities. The support of our partner Times Higher Education was fundamental in achieving this success. Although there was a number of universities that were unable to participate in the first year, currently more than 95% of the primary target institutions are actively participating in the project.

BIBLIOMETRIC DATA

The third component of data, bibliometric data, relies on the publications authored by the academics and researchers of the institution. The data is sourced from the Thomson Reuters Web of Science^{SM}, considered the gold standard by many evaluation bodies globally.

For each institution, detailed unification of their institutional name variants is performed to ensure that all of their papers are captured. A wide variety of data for each institution is produced such as: number of papers, number of citations, citation impact (or citations per paper) and the proportion of papers with an international co-author.

Data for each of the six subject areas used in the profiles project is also extracted. These subjects are: Arts and Humanities; Clinical and Pre-clinical Health; Life Sciences; Physical Sciences; Engineering and Technology; and Social Sciences.

DATA ANALYSIS

Factual data on its own is a valuable resource but one can also perform several analyses to turn the data into actionable knowledge about the institutions.

There are several different approaches that are used. Firstly, compound indicators are created to overcome size dependence. For example, instead of looking at the total number of papers produced by an institution we look at the number of papers per academic staff member. This gives us an indication of the productivity of the institution regardless of size (see Figure 1 for an example). The universities shown in the diagram, Durham University, the University of Manchester, the University of Tokyo and Pohang University of Science and Technology (POSTECH), were chosen for diversity of institution type and geography.[1]

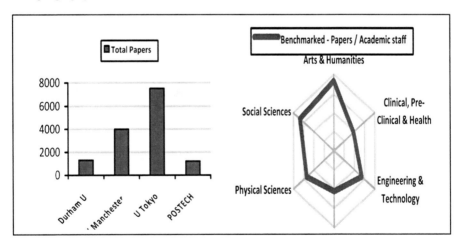

Figure 1. A comparison of two indicators of performance: Total papers vs. papers per academic staff member. (Data from 2008)

It is also possible to develop novel indicators combining data from two different data sources. For example, the number of papers per unit of research funding, considered an output/input indicator and may be an indicator of how efficient the institution is at conducting research. These types of compound indicator are unique to the Global Institutional Profiles project.

NORMALIZATION

Another important area is that of benchmarking to overcome inherent differences in performance across subject areas. For example, there is a large difference in productivity, as measured by papers per academic staff member, between the life sciences and the social sciences. To better understand the performance, one can benchmark the value for one university against the average value for all universities in the same subject area and year. This provides an indicator of relative performance. As can be seen in Figure 2, the difference is striking.

By "benchmarking" against a subject average one can establish the relative performance in the context of the subject. By taking an average of the "relative performance" across the subjects it is possible to establish a normalized performance indicator for the institution as a whole that overcomes subject bias. A weighted average is used so that the subjects with the greatest volume of activity contribute the most to the outcome.

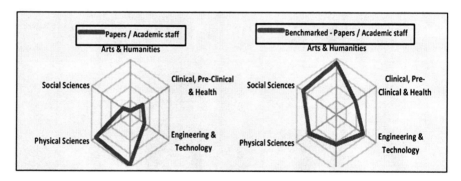

Figure 2. A comparison of six subject areas for the indicator "papers per academic staff".
(Data for the University of Manchester, 2008)

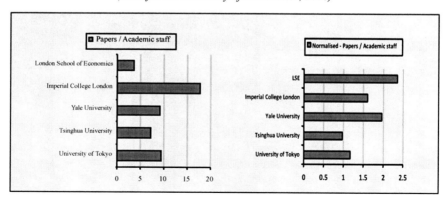

Figure 3. An example of the results of subject normalization. Papers per staff member

Figure 3 shows the results of this subject normalization for selected institutions. The London School of Economics, with its focus on the social sciences, has a low number of publications per staff member. Their relative performance is, however, high.[2]

RESULTS

This next section presents some of the findings from the Global Institutional Profiles project 2011.

The analysis shows a huge difference in the size of universities (see Figure 4). The Japanese and Chinese universities are notably large compared to international peers. The University of Toronto and Harvard University are also very large.

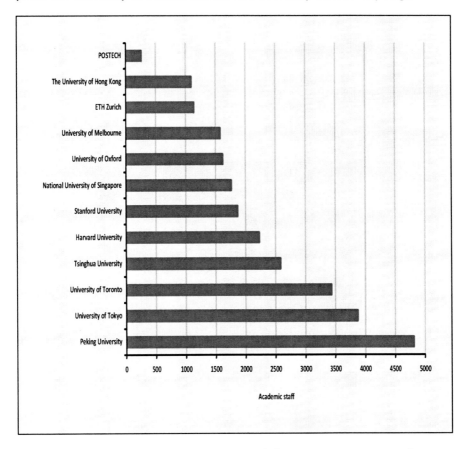

Figure 4. The relative size of selected world-class universities as measured by the number of academic staff

Figure 5 shows the overall income and research income of the same group of universities. The income figures have been modified by purchasing power parity (PPP) to convert to a common currency base and take into account differences in the costs of living.

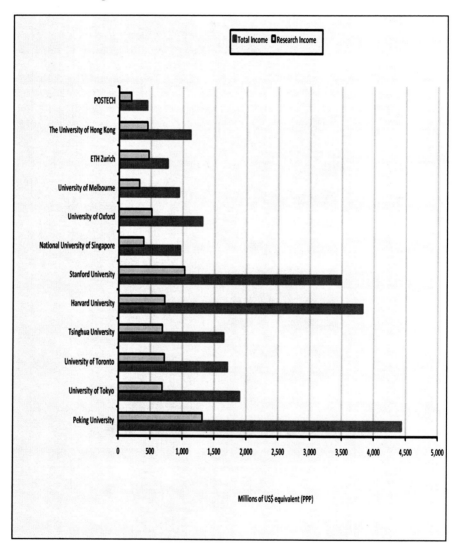

Figure 5. The total income and research income for selected institutions (2009) in millions of US$ equivalent modified by Purchasing Power Parity

The research funding scaled for institution size is shown in Figure 6. Research income normalized for subject and scaled for size is listed in Figure 7. These indicators overcome the differences in the size of the institutions and difference in the subject specialization of the institution. The Chinese and Korean universities have substantial funds at their disposal but the University of Tokyo has surprisingly little. These observations may in part be a consequence of the PPP modification but are largely driven by investment policy in those countries.

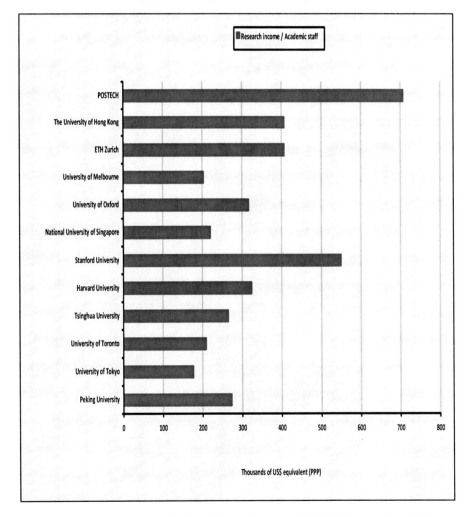

Figure 6. Scaled research funding. (Research income [US$ PPP] per staff member)

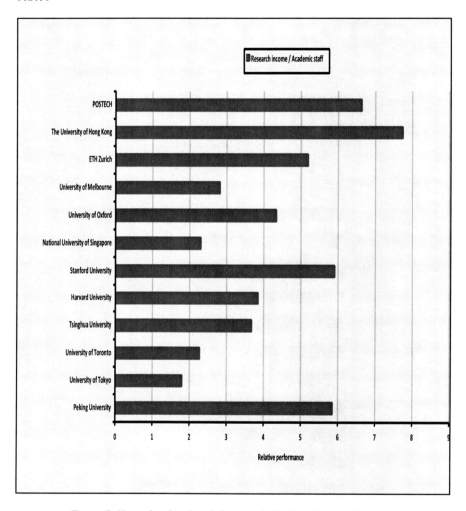

*Figure 7. Normalized and scaled research funding. (Research income
[US$ PPP] per staff member)*

Figure 8 reflects the performance of selected universities for various indicators. Each indicator is scaled for the size of the university and normalized for subject distribution, with the exception of the reputational standing which is not normalized.

The indicators compare the performance of a university to the distribution of performance for all 600 universities in the Profiles Project. This is a useful approach to make the different indicators comparable even though the data behind the indicators are very different.

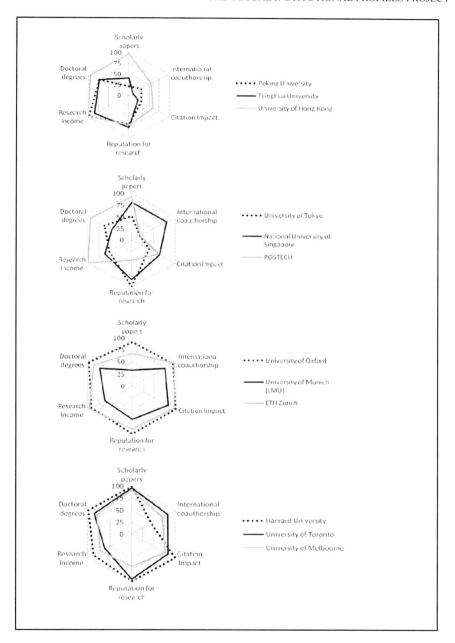

Figure 8. Selected indicators of performance for leading universities globally, presented as a Thomson Reuters Research Footprint®

Research Footprint® visualization enables instantaneous comparisons. For example, one can easily see that the Chinese and Korean systems are investing heavily in their best universities and that this is generating significant levels of productivity as measured by the output of doctoral degrees. However, the quality-related indicators such as the rate of international co-authorship and citation impact are lagging. One should note, however, that both of these indicators will also have local components, such as language, that should be taken into account.

The reputation for research, as would be expected, is relatively high for all the universities. This reflects their status as world-class institutions. The exception is Pohang University of Science and Technology in South Korea which although highly regarded internationally, is a small institution compared to the other universities.

Those universities that are considered among the top 20 in the world such as Harvard University (US), the University of Oxford (UK), the University of Toronto (Canada) and ETH Zurich (Switzerland) perform excellently on all indicators.

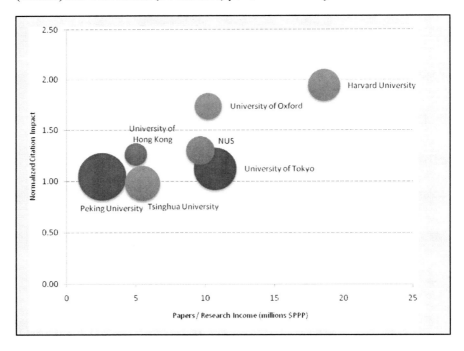

Figure 9. Bubble diagram showing the research productivity against citation impact. The size of the bubble corresponds to the number of staff

Figure 9 shows the productivity of the institution, as measured by the number of articles per million dollars of research income, on the x-axis and an indicator of impact, the normalized citation impact, on the y-axis. The size of the bubble represents the size of the institution as measured by the number of academic staff.

One can see that institutions such as the University of Oxford and Harvard University are both productive and produce high impact articles.

Conversely, the Chinese universities are at the other end of the scale. Previous studies (Adams et al., 2000) by Thomson Reuters have shown that it takes a number of years for large-scale investment to produce high performance. Immediately after an increase in funding, as has been observed in China in recent years, there is not enough capacity of suitably qualified and experienced academics to make effective use of the resources they have. It takes a number of years for personnel to develop to a sufficient level through doctoral education, post-doctoral and beyond.

Chinese investment, such as the 985 Project and the 211 Project, in the last decade has started down that path and further improvements in the coming years can be expected as the capacity of the facilities and faculty catch up to the recent increases in the funding.

CONCLUSIONS

Thomson Reuters has, in a short period of time, generated a very robust data source, with multiple indicators for all kinds of evaluation. There have been many challenges faced with the implementation of the project. Most notably are the challenges of encouraging the universities to participate and to submit subject level breakdowns. As the third cycle of the project begins a great deal has been learnt and engagement by the academic community is strong. Participating levels are high and the depth and breadth of data submitted by participating institutions continues to increase.

The Global Institutional Profiles present a multi-dimensional array of indicators of performance that require the user to commit an investment of time to understand. By providing interpretation and context to profiles it makes it as easy as possible to understand the data but profiles will never replace the simplicity and instant identification of a rankings position.

The Global Institutional Profiles are helping to drive a new understanding of institutional performance across international boundaries and subject silos. Institutions are constantly challenged to demonstrate their value to their local economy and society and, as discussed in this paper, direct measures of performance are difficult if not impossible. One must rely on a suite of indicators to describe the performance from multiple aspects.

As the community gains better understanding of the relationship between indicators and performance the suite of indicators used in the Global Institutional Profiles project is anticipated to grow and develop so that we can capture a complete picture of institutional performance and the value that universities provide.

NOTES

[1] Durham University in the United Kingdom is a small research-intensive university with a long history of excellence and a broad portfolio of disciplines. The University of Manchester, also in the UK is a multidisciplinary university with a long history for research excellence and is generally considered to be the largest university in the UK. The University of Tokyo in Japan is a very large multidisciplinary, research-intensive university whereas Pohang University of Science and Technology in South Korea is a very small research intensive university with a focus on the physical sciences, engineering and technology.

[2] The London School of Economics and Political Science (LSE) is a UK based university with a sole focus on the social sciences. Imperial College London is a UK based university with a focus on science, technology and medicine. Yale University is a US based university with a strong tradition in the Arts and Humanities. Tsinghua University in China covers many disciplines but has a strong focus on Engineering and Technology. The University of Tokyo in Japan is a large multidisciplinary university.

REFERENCES

Adams, J., Baker, K., & Smith, D. N. (2010). Global opinion survey – New outlooks on institutional profiles. *Thomson Reuters White Papers*. Retrieved April 10, 2012, from http://science.thomsonreuters.com/m/pdfs/Global_Opinion_Survey.pdf

Adams, J., Cook, N., Law, G., Marshall, S., Mount, D., Smith, D., et al. (2000). *The Role of Selectivity and the Characteristics of Excellence*.

Baty, P. (2011, September 8). Rankings methodology fine-tuned for 2011-12. *Times Higher Education*. Retrieved April 12, 2012, from http://www.timeshighereducation.co.uk/story.asp?storycode=417368

Boulton, G., & Lucas, C. (2008). What are universities for? *League of European Research Universities: Report*. Retrieved April 12, 2012, from http://www.leru.org/files/general/%E2%80%A2What%20are%20universities%20for%20(September%202008).pdf

King's College, London. (2012). *London 2012 Unveils Anti-Doping Laboratory*. Retrieved April 12, 2012, from http://www.kcl.ac.uk/newsevents/news/newsrecords/2012/01Jan/London-2012-unveil-Anti-Doping-Laboratory.aspx

Pratt, S. (2010). *Academic Reputation Survey: Report of Findings*. Retrieved from April 12, 2012, http://ip-science.thomsonreuters.com/m/pdfs/GIPP_AcamRep_report.pdf.

AFFILIATIONS

Simon M. Pratt
Thomson Reuters

ISIDRO F. AGUILLO AND ENRIQUE ORDUÑA-MALEA

THE RANKING WEB AND THE "WORLD-CLASS" UNIVERSITIES

*New Webometric Indicators Based on G-Factor,
Interlinking, and Web 2.0 Tools*

INTRODUCTION AND OBJECTIVES

The purpose of this paper is to discuss the new developments in the methodology used for building the Ranking Web of Universities, also called the Webometrics Ranking (WebR) . Contrary to other rankings that ignore caveats and shortcomings in order to maintain inter-year stability, the WebR ranking is evolving for improving the reliability of sources, the descriptive power of the quantitative indicators and the justification of unexpected or discrepant results.

The paper intends to show that the WebR ranking offers not only a far larger coverage, including universities in emerging and developing countries, but an evaluation model that takes into account all the academic missions as a whole. The current emphasis on so-called world-class universities, basically research intensive institutions, offers a very narrow overview of the performance and impact of the academic systems of many countries.

The paper's aim is to illustrate that a new generation of web indicators can be used to assess top universities in a very confident way. Multi-dimensional aspects of academic interlinking are explored using G-factor, an indicator that captures the diversity of motivations in the citing behaviour of the academic elite. New scores can be also obtained from open environments, especially through Web 2.0 tools, the 21st century's new scholarly communication channel.

It is expected that findings support the purposes of the WebR ranking, as from a practical point of view universities should move from the "publish or perish" slogan to a more general mantra of "get impact or perish". The objective is to show that there are no better and cheaper actions nowadays for achieving global impact than developing a strong web presence.

THE RANKING WEB

The Cybermetrics Lab is a research group belonging to the largest Spanish public research institution, the Consejo Superior de Investigaciones Científicas (CSIC). Since mid-1990s the team started to work on the quantitative analysis and evaluation of scientific activities and institutions by developing web indicators

Q. Wang, Y. Cheng, & N.C. Liu (eds.), Building World-Class Universities: Different Approaches to a Shared Goal, 197–217.

(Aguillo, 1998). In 2004, following the model of the Academic Ranking of World Universities (ARWU), the group started to publish the WebR (http://www.webometrics.info/).

The Ranking was originally designed to promote web publication and support Open Access initiatives (Aguillo et al., 2008), but soon it showed its capabilities to rank universities, providing a good correlation with data published by other organizations (Aguillo et al., 2010). The main discrepancies were due to bad practices in webdomain naming or incorrect strategies and policies, preventing the web presence from being an actual mirror of the institution. This is in fact one of the important added values of the WebR ranking as it identifies and provides practical information for solving these problems.

Contrary to many criticisms pointing out that only websites are really evaluated, the WebR is using web presence as an overall indicator of the performance and impact of the universities, considering all academic missions (see Figure 1) and being powered by link analysis, a tool that allows the capture of the preferences of billions of internet users in a rich and diverse scenario. Motivations for linking include traditional inter-pares citation for research recognition, references from political, economic, industrial or socio-cultural partners of the university, prestigious mentions in media, public websites or electronic forums, and from usage of quality (useful) information or data published and branded by the universities.

MISSIONS UNIVERSITIES	RESEARCH	TEACHING	COMMUNITY ENGAGEMENT	TECHNOLOGICAL TRANSFER	INTERNATIONALIZATION
WORLD-CLASS	+++	++	+	+++	+++
NATION BUILDING	++	+++	++	+++	++
LOCAL	+	+++	+++	+	+

Figure 1. Main methods to evaluate impact (laterals) of the academic missions, according to a simple classification of universities

One of the main advantages of the WebR ranking is its large coverage, as about 20,000 higher education institutions from all over the world are analysed (Table 1). Only those universities without independent web presences are excluded (probably less than 2,000 in total).

As shown in Table 1, the WebR ranking uncovers an academic digital gap between the Top US universities and their European counterparts, while Asian universities underperform, due to the generally limited internationally oriented contents they publish on the Web.

The WebR ranking composite indicator is based on a model derived from traditional bibliometric analysis, where the most well-known indicator, the impact factor, takes into account both publication activity and the visibility of papers authored by researchers. This ratio 1:1 between number of publications ("activity") and number of citations (the proxy used for describing "visibility" or impact) is preserved in the WebR ranking. In order to make easier the comparison with the other rankings models this is expressed in percentages, so activity amounts for 50% of the total weighting system while visibility accounts for the other 50%.

Table 1. Comparison between the ARWU and Webometrics (WebR) Rankings results (2011). Distribution by region and selected countries

Regions	Top 100		Top 200		Top 500		Top 1000	Total
Countries	ARWU	WebR	ARWU	WebR	ARWU	WebR	WEebR	WebR
Americas	57	75	100	116	184	213	434	6957
US	53	67	89	95	151	172	356	3262
Canada	4	6	8	16	22	24	38	199
Europe	34	16	75	58	204	221	413	5102
UK	10	7	19	10	37	37	67	236
Germany	6	2	14	12	39	47	66	405
Switzerland	4	1	6	3	7	7	10	107
France	3	0	8	1	21	9	53	570
Asia/Pacific	10	9	25	26	108	65	148	6648
Japan	5	2	9	6	23	12	33	716
Australia	4	2	7	6	19	12	28	103
Mainland China and Hong Kong SAR	0	1	2	5	28	14	19	1217
Africa	0	0	0	0	4	1	5	695

Source: ARWU (http://www.arwu.org/); WebR (http://www.webometrics.info/)

As will be shown later in this chapter, visibility measurement is also inspired by the bibliometric experience with successful citation analysis, using in this case external inlinks instead of bibliographic citations, with the important advantage of the larger (by several orders of magnitude) numbers involved. The data is collected from public commercial search engines that are ubiquitous and very simple to use.

For activity evaluation, taken into account are the different missions of the university, so the total number of webpages is only one of the variables considered. File types counted are clearly focused on different targets, not being used only for publication of formal final research papers but also for supporting teaching activities, to improve public communication of science and community engagement and transferring knowledge to the wider economic and industrial sectors. At the end, three variables are combined for this activity index: total number of webpages, number of rich files, such as pdf, doc, ppt and ps formats, and number of papers.

Compared with other rankings, the web presence is a more objective measurement of overall performance than survey-based systems, it is a proxy useful for sensitively discriminating between thousands of universities (not like others that only are useful for a few dozen) and it is having more immediate impact as it is promoting access to academic web content worldwide.

Until very recently the main objectives of this ranking were to cover as many institutions as possible and to promote web publication for supporting Open Access initiatives. But the focus on full coverage means that the elite universities below the 500th rank are not analysed in detail.

The international ranking of universities have been pursued for the so-called world-class universities a group of about 200 to 500 institutions that typically appear in the top positions in rankings. Most of them are close to the US (or neo-Humboldtian) research-intensive university model, as in these rankings the main mission evaluated is precisely research. Moreover, although research output is a relevant indicator, it is usually research impact (citations, prizes) that is the key variable for the final ranking of the universities.

The Cybermetrics Lab now believes that world-class universities presence on the web could play a significant role as a model to be followed by the rest of institutions worldwide, especially in the task of opening knowledge to broader sectors of the human population. In that sense a new indicator pertaining to the elite should be taken into account.

THE G-FACTOR

The G-factor was originally created by P. Hirst in 2006 for generating an International University Ranking (http://www.universitymetrics.com/; discontinued, see Figure 2). It is a web indicator developed for measuring the co-mention of the names of pairs of universities from a list of 300 well-known and prestigious institutions, as the experiment was done using the Google search engine, according to the following syntax example.

"Harvard University" and "the University of Oxford"

The indicator was coined as G-factor, being the sum of all values obtaining for each university in the crossings of the 300*300 matrix (excluding self-mentions and duplicates; the order in the pairs is irrelevant).

Although it is a clever suggestion, the use of mention analysis is problematic as the names of universities are not standardized, and sometimes the same institution uses several variants even in its local language. Also, the motivations for co-mention and the websites where this happens probably are in many situations unrelated to academic activities, undermining the value of the indicator.

Since 2006 (Aguillo et al., 2006) the Cybermetrics Lab explored the possibilities of applying a concept similar to the G-factor. Instead of using mentions, the collection of interlinking data was proposed for a limited group of institutions (about 1,000): that is, a closed source of academic links.

200

www.universitymetrics.com

Home

G-Factor International University Ranking 2006: Top 300

The following table shows the G-Factor international ranking for all 300 universities, along with the 2005 international university ranking by Shanghai Tao Jong University

G-Factor Rank	SJTU 2005 Rank	Institution
1	5	Massachusetts Inst Tech (MIT)
2	1	Harvard Univ
3	4	Univ California - Berkeley
4	3	Stanford Univ
5	8	Princeton Univ
6	15	Univ Pennsylvania
7	17	Univ Washington - Seattle
8	25	Univ Illinois - Urbana Champaign
9	54	Carnegie Mellon Univ
10	43	Rutgers State Univ - New Brunswick
11	2	Univ Cambridge
12	21	Univ Michigan - Ann Arbor
13	16	Univ Wisconsin - Madison
14	12	Cornell Univ
15	73	Univ Arizona
16	6	California Inst Tech
17	27	Swiss Fed Inst Tech - Zurich
18	14	Univ California - Los Angeles
19	32	Univ Minnesota - Twin Cities
20	10	Univ Oxford

Figure 2. Snapshot of the (no-longer public) webpage of the G-factor International University Rankings* as deposited in the Internet Archive Wayback Machine**

Note: * See http://universitymetrics.com/gfactor2006top300.
** See http://wayback.archive.org/web/.

The WebR ranking (Aguillo et al., 2008) has employed link analysis since 2004 to build a visibility indicator, counting external inlinks to university web domains. Although it is not possible to use Google as it counts only links to individual pages, not to the full domains or subdomains, it was decided that the original name for the indicator should be maintained. Currently (till 2012) it can be derived from Yahoo Search! using the following syntax:

Linkdomain:domainuniversityA + Site:domainuniversityB

Figure 3. Example of collection of data for determining the G-factor using the Yahoo search engine with the syntax described in the text

Note: In 2012 Yahoo is going to discontinue this service. The Bing database will be used instead so the method will need to be adapted.

The G-factor was one of the components of the visibility indicator in the January 2011 edition of the WebR ranking. Considering the limitations of the Yahoo API licence and the capabilities and time allowed, that initial G-factor was obtained only for the Top 1000 universities as corresponding to the July 2010 edition of the WebR ranking.

NEW LINK-BASED INDICATORS

In the case of G-factor, the referred pages are obviously webpages owned and controlled by the university and the motivation for linking, although diverse, is related to the contents provided in these academic webdomains.

The largest section of the Webspace is not academic. In many cases the referring pages are very diverse, and links came from third parties only slightly related to universities. An overall indicator based on links of unidentified origin could be useful, as it reflects the impact of the university in other non-academic sectors, the success of the so-called third mission, the prestige in society or the relevance for individual citizens. But there are cases of over-linking due to reasons not related to performance or quality that should be excluded: marketing campaigns, portals with external contents, sponsorships, and extra domains, and bad or unethical practices (link farms).

This paper intends to describe not only the use of G-factor but also other link analysis-derived indicators in order to test their possible use in the WebR ranking. Probably the best way to arrange a classification of link-based indicators is to use the origins of such links, taking into consideration the impact of the Web 2.0 and the new tools available. A preliminary proposal is introduced in Table 2.

Table 2. Classification of indicators derived from hypertextual links in the web

Categories		Indicators
General linking		Total inlinks
		External inlinks
		Internal inlinks
Selective linking	by domain	External inlinks
	by site	External inlinks
	by selected sites (G-factor)	External inlinks
Weighted linking		Domain Authority
		Domain MozRank
		Page Rank
		Others

Direct crawling probably offers a more complete alternative to collect these data (Thelwall & Stuart, 2006), but unfortunately to harvest a large section of the Webspace requires computer and human resources beyond our capabilities. Instead we are using commercial search engines, with powerful crawlers and huge databases for extracting the required information (but see current situation in Thelwall & Sud, 2011).

METHODOLOGY

The main goal of this paper is to test the usefulness of these indicators specially for measuring the impact of the World-class Universities on the Web. The specific objectives are to:
- Describe by means of web indicators a sample of universities (linked group) which covers equally all of the inhabited continents in the world.
- Test the influence of world-class universities in WebR ranking (linking group) in the linked group, at a regional aggregation level.
- Compare the results provided by the different indicators and suggest recommendations regarding their future adoption in the Web ranking.

Two samples of university webdomains (Table 3 and appendices) were selected: The first group (linked) consist of 60 universities (10 each from the following regions: Africa, North America, South America, Asia, Europe and Oceania). The criteria used are based on the appearance and the position of these universities in the WebR ranking (January 2010 edition), taking into consideration each geographical ranking as provided by the editors. The second group (linking) consists of the first 1,000 universities ranked in the WebR ranking.

The population of linked domains (60) were used to test the new set of link indicators, collecting data during December 2010 from the general and specialised search engines as described in Tables 4 and 5.

Table 3. Region, countries and items from linked and linking group of universities

Region	Linked domains		Linking domains	
	Countries	Universities	Countries	Universities
Africa	2	10	1	5
Asia	5	10	13	157
Europe	5	10	28	407
North America	1	10	2	336
Oceania	2	10	3	36
South America	3	10	11	59
Total	18	60	58	1000

Table 4. Link-based indicators according to the source used for compiling them: Open Site Explorer (OSE) Yahoo Site Explorer (YSE) and Yahoo Search! (YS)

Indicators			Search Engine[*]		
			OSE	YSE	YS
General linking		Total inlinks	x	x	x
		External inlinks		x	x
Selective linking	by domain	External inlinks			x (see Table 2)
	by site	External inlinks			x (see Table 2)
	by selected sites (top 1000)	External inlinks			x (see Fig. 3)
Weighted linking		Domain authority	x		
		Domain MozRank	x		

Note: [*] OSE (http://www.opensiteexplorer.org), YSE (http://siteexplorer.search.yahoo.com), and YS (http://search.yahoo.com)

Internal inlinks are not explicitly recovered, but could be approximately calculated by subtracting external inlinks from total inlinks. As regards weighted linking, only Domain Authority (http://apiwiki.seomoz.org/w/page/20902104/Domain%20Authority) and Domain MozRank (see http://www.seomoz.org/learn-seo/mozrank) are considered.

The public figures for Pagerank (PR) are excluded due to its lack of discrimination (its logarithmic scale of 1 to 10 means that most universities even with far different link performances will share the same PR).

The specific domains and sites considered, and commands used with Yahoo! are shown in Table 5 (Academia, Facebook and LinkedIn are social networks, Twitter is a messaging tool and the other three are added value services: the cooperative bookmarking site Delicious, the open encyclopaedia Wikipedia and the video portal YouTube).

In domain linking, there are cases where the Top Level Domain (TLD) of the universities is the same as one of the domains considered, such as the US universities or the American University in Cairo (.edu). The command used for excluding self-links is:

Linkdomain:domainA.edu +Site:.edu – Site:domainA.edu

Additionally, Delicious is added as a selective site by using the command "site:domain" in the query box. Data extracted from Open Site Explorer (Page Authority and Domain Authority) do not need any query command.

Table 5. Examples of the strategies used for obtaining the domain and site linking commands in Yahoo! Search

Indicator	Query
Linkage – domain inlink	linkdomain:domain.tld site:.gov
	linkdomain:domain.tld site:.edu
	linkdomain:domain.tld site:.org
	linkdomain:domain.tld site:.com
Linkage – site linking	linkdomain:domain.tld site:academia.edu
	linkdomain:domain.tld site:facebook.com
	linkdomain:domain.tld site:linkedin.com
	linkdomain:domain.tld site:twitter.com
	linkdomain:domain.tld site:delicious.com
	linkdomain:domain.tld site:wikipedia.org
	linkdomain:domain.tld site:youtube.com

RESULTS

Data were obtained for the interlinks between the two populations described. As already observed elsewhere (Aguillo et al., 2008) the role of US universities in the organization of academic Webspace is very relevant, with local universities also important for national or regional self-organization, as between the Australian or British top institutions (Table 6). Moreover, this data shows some asymmetries among geographical areas. For example, South America receives 4% (8392 links) of their inlinks from Europe, and Europe receives 1.20% (19,210 links) from South America. Despite some methodological differences, this situation has been previously detected (Orduña-Malea, 2011).

Table 6. Interlinking by region

Links to	Links from						
	Africa	Asia	Oceania	Europe	South America	North America	Total
Africa	4.77%	0.28%	0.76%	1.70%	0.08%	92.41%	53023
Asia	0.15%	31.05%	2.65%	8.92%	0.16%	57.07%	1660981
Oceania	0.22%	10.46%	42.69%	27.98%	0.18%	18.46%	291537
Europe	0.66%	2.66%	4.15%	38.47%	1.20%	52.86%	1600813
South America	0.26%	0.91%	2.41%	4.00%	43.65%	48.77%	209798
North America	0.90%	2.99%	4.09%	13.17%	0.64%	78.21%	2306792
Total	37604	660033	334732	1158633	128672	3803270	6122944

As there are even more US universities in the group of world-class universities, the rest of the world's countries should clearly increase the volume of international quality contents to attract more external links in order to avoid enlarging the academic digital gap.

Selective Linking by Selected Sites (G-Factor)

When considering individual universities, the list is also headed by US institutions, attracting most of the links, but the other countries included also perform reasonably well (Table 7).

Again major discrepancies between G-factor and Web Ranking affects mainly non-US universities. They attract large numbers of academic inlinks but their web contents appear not to attract the interests of non-academic websites.

Table 7. Ranking of the top 20 universities according to G-factor

Universities	Domain	G-Factor	Rank Web
Massachusetts Institute of Technology	mit.edu	1430548	1
University of Southampton	soton.ac.uk	437809	32
University of Wisconsin Madison	wisc.edu	399413	6
University of California Berkeley	berkeley.edu	387958	4
Stanford University	stanford.edu	377188	3
Harvard University	harvard.edu	329789	2
National Taiwan University	ntu.edu.tw	321523	12
University of Michigan	umich.edu	217986	7
University of Minnesota	umn.edu	217632	8
Cornell University	cornell.edu	187463	5
University of Cambridge	cam.ac.uk	176134	19
University of Washington	washington.edu	162196	9
Swiss Federal Institute of Technology Zürich	ethz.ch	125897	43
University of Oxford	ox.ac.uk	118458	41
University of Melbourne	unimelb.edu.au	107526	86
Johns Hopkins University	jhu.edu	93097	49
University of Tokyo	u-tokyo.ac.jp	77576	16
University College London	ucl.ac.uk	76201	31
University of Edinburgh	ed.ac.uk	65427	67
National University of Singapore	nus.edu.sg	61120	92

Table 8. General and domain linking correlation

Indicators	External	Total	GOV	EDU	COM	ORG
External inlink	x	0.96	0.91	0.82	0.96	0.92
Total inlink	0.96	x	0.86	0.73	0.92	0.87

Selective Linking by Domain

We used the other link indicators for a deeper analysis. The raw data is provided in the appendices, which provided the basis for performing Spearman correlations. The domain linking results (Table 8) show that the domain .com provides the higher value while the domain .edu, the standard for US universities, shows the lower one.

Although the world-class universities are linking strongly to US universities, these results confirm that non-academic links are more important. Figure 4 addresses this evidence by tailoring the number of external link-ins depending on the Top Level Domain where hyperlinks originate, for the top 30 universities by total external links. These data show the predominance of .com links in the top universities, which correlates with results obtained in Table 8.

As a corollary, the local or non-research oriented universities may not be providing a lot of links, being at the Webspace periphery of the elite nucleus.

Selective Linking by Site (Platforms)

Table 9 provides interesting evidence about the relevance of certain sources of links, especially those related to Web 2.0. The role of these tools for increasing the visibility and impact of university websites is substantiated. The added-value services (Wikipedia, Delicious and YouTube) clearly outperform the social networks (Facebook, LinkedIn).

Figure 5 show the performance of each social platform considered regarding the number of inlinks. As for domain linking, we can observe that the platforms that generate more hyperlinks to universities (Delicious and Wikipedia) are the platforms with more correlation with total external links, as showed in Table 9.

Table 9. General and Selective linking correlation

Indicators	Academia	Delicious	Facebook	LinkedIn	Twitter	Wikipedia	YouTube
External inlink	0.68	0.87	0.64	0.72	0.78	0.89	0.88
Total inlink	0.61	0.83	0.55	0.67	0.75	0.84	0.85

Otherwise, drop values are detected in specific universities and platforms (for example, National Taiwan University and National Chiao Tung University in Academia; Universidade de Brasília and Keio University in Facebook; or Cairo University both on Academia and Twitter). This phenomenon might be understood as a function of the promotion of these universities in the corresponding platforms.

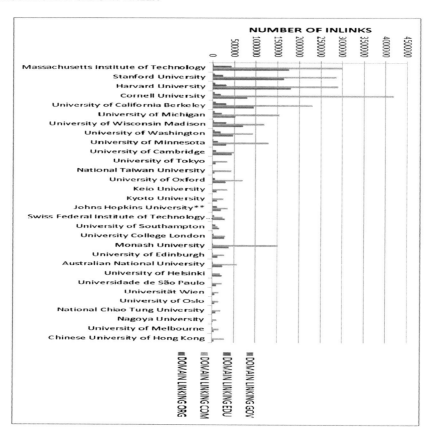

*Figure 4. Number of external links for the top 30 universities with more total
external links, depending on the top-level domain (TLD) of origin
(.gov, .edu, .com and .org)*

Weighted Linking (Domain Authority and Domain MozRank)

Sometimes it is assumed that many inlinks to universities are institutional ones,
driven by the prestige related to the academic nature of the organization
(directories of universities, for example) and not to the actual content of the
websites.

Although links to the main pages of universities are common, it can be
expected that deeper linking (department or personal pages) is responsible for most
of the "citing" behaviour. In this sense, the use of weighted indicators such as
Domain Authority (DomA) and Domain MozRank (DMzR) can provide some
insights about the linking performance of internal sites within general homepages,

regarding also the nature and importance of the linking sites on the web, in a similar way as PageRank (PR) does.

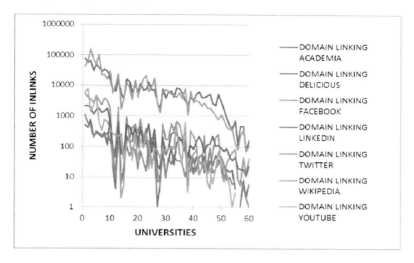

Figure 5. Number of links received for each 60 linked universities depending on the platform of origin

The results from Table 10 indicate that the role of the internal links is limited and when external links are considered (total linking correlation is less good than external linking), which is consistent with the fact that not only are institutional links relevant but also those related to contents nested in directories or different servers to the main institutional one.

Table 10. General and weighed linking correlation

Indicators	DomA	DMzR
External inlink	0.87	0.72
Total inlink	0.78	0.62

Moreover, the correlation between these two indicators is strong (Figure 6), and also can be used to compare the prestige of academic websites. In this case (taking into account that the scale of these indicators is from 0 to 10), no website has fewer than 5 points either in DMzR nor DomA. Otherwise, only one university surpasses 8 points (Keio University, DMrR: 8.04).

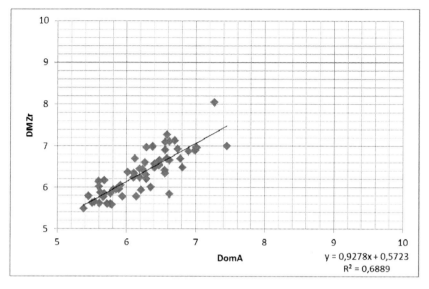

Figure 6. Linear regression between DomA and DMzR

CONCLUSIONS

Academia is changing very fast and rankings should catch up to these changes. Traditional research indicators (bibliometrics) are not taking into account the impact of digital technologies in the university, the new ways of internal and external communication of scholars, researchers and students and the relevance of the Open Access products and services being developed and offered worldwide.

Web publication is especially suited for measuring personal the commitment of both individuals and institutions and it is clearly correlated with investment in resources, excellence in teaching and/or research and the success of community engagement policies. Best practice and plausible medium and long-term strategies should seek to reflect the role of the web.

But to achieve these aims, further webometric developments are needed, including improved indicators for identifying highly linked webdomains and websites, variables with discriminant capabilities for measuring multimedia environments, management systems and the degree of appropriation of Web 2.0 related technologies.

In some cases the success of Open Access initiatives can explain rankings (University of Southampton, National Taiwan University), while in others learning-supporting materials (such as OpenCourseWare from Massachusetts Institute of Technology) explain better the top position. Overall, prestige driven links are also to be considered.

Feasibility issues pertain but a solution can be proposed. If the focus is on world-class universities, not only is data collection easier but the indicators shown are meaningful enough so that the ranks obtained can be more accurate and reliable. It is because selective linking avoids external links from dubious sites, reducing the noise and giving more importance to the academic websites. G-factor is an important factor for future developments.

Empirical results provide some suggestions for improving rankings. The proposed changes in methodology are oriented to obtain better accuracy in the ranking processes but also to guide further actions by universities in the way they share the knowledge they generate.

Link visibility is the most important indicator in the Webometrics model (50% of the total weight of the composite indicator). Total number of external inlinks has been the preferred set of statistics till now, but in order to reflect explicitly academic impact, the G-factor obtained from interlinking between world-class universities has been tested and supported by evidence. Additionally inlinks from other sources has been tested with positive results, as they not only represent the new academic Web 2.0 environments but also correlate well with global visibility.

REFERENCES

Aguillo, I. F. (1998, December 8–10). STM Information on the web and the development of new Internet R&D databases and indicators. In D. I. Raitt (Ed.), *Online Information 98: 22nd International Online Information Meeting: Proceedings* (pp. 239–243). London.

Aguillo, I. F., Granadino, B., Ortega, J. L., & Prieto, J. A. (2006). Scientific research activity and communication measured with cybermetric indicators. Journal of the American Society of Information Science & Technology, 57(10), 1296–1302.

Aguillo, I. F., Ortega, J. L., & Fernández, M. (2008). Webometric ranking of World Universities: Introduction, methodology, and future developments. *Higher Education in Europe, 33*(2/3), 234–244.

Aguillo, I. F., Bar-Ilan, J., Levene, M., & Ortega, J. L. (2010). Comparing university rankings. *Scientometrics, 85*(1), 243–256.

Orduña-Malea, E. (2011). Asimetría en la conexión académica online entre Sudamérica y Europa a través de un análisis de enlaces (2011). In *XV Congreso de la FIEALC.* Valencia (Spain).

Thelwall, M., & Stuart, D. (2006). Web crawling ethics revisited: Cost, privacy and denial of service. *Journal of the American Society for Information Science and Technology, 57*(13), 1771–1779.

Thelwall, M., & Sud, P. (2011). A comparison of methods for collecting web citation data for academic organizations. *Journal of the American Society for Information Science and Technology, 62*(8), 1488–1497.

AFFILIATIONS

Isidro F. Aguillo
The Cybermetrics Lab
Spanish National Research Council (CSIC), Spain

Enrique Orduña-Malea
Institute of Design and Manufacturing (IDF)
Polytechnic University of Valencia (UPV), Valencia, Spain

APPENDICES: *Weighted linking (Domain Authority and Domain MozRank)*

UNIVERSITIES	URL	GENERAL LINKING		DOMAIN LINKING					WEIGHTED LINKING	
		EXTERNAL INLINK	TOTAL INLINK	GOV	EDU	EDU (Ext)	COM	ORG	DomA	DMzR
University of Cambridge	cam.ac.uk	1328439	163090	3690	81700		500000	446000	6.56	7.10
University of Oxford	ox.ac.uk	1168145	1882232	2380	57300		698000	306000	6.59	7.28
Swiss Federal Institute of Technology ETH Zürich	ethz.ch	693353	1161025	2960	45600		241000	299000	6.59	6.70
Norwegian University of Science and Technology	ntnu.no	318157	535945	143	12600		126000	35500	6.28	6.31
University of Edinburgh	ed.ac.uk	560159	872048	1030	20700		277000	119000	6.56	6.91
University of Oslo	uio.no	478144	821696	633	8110		156000	61100	6.23	6.44
University College London	ucl.ac.uk	637384	987767	10100	27500		304000	276000	6.81	6.49
University of Helsinki	helsinki.fi	532167	877824	506	11700		188000	235000	6.62	5.84
Universität Wien	univie.ac.at	511231	728483	480	10100		157000	57500	6.62	6.66
University of Southampton	soton.ac.uk	685975	921052	4390	66800		126000	168000	6.48	6.66
University of Tokyo	u-tokyo.ac.jp	1251464	2905309	1120	9280		349000	79000	6.56	6.35
Kyoto University	kyoto-u.ac.jp	832699	1693072	744	8630		253000	108000	6.35	6.01
National Taiwan University	ntu.edu.tw	1195956	2985357	430	4530		425000	50200	5.94	5.78
University of Hong Kong	hku.hk	362727	735439	1940	9040		198000	54200	6.29	6.21
Chinese University of Hong Kong	cuhk.edu.hk	374119	786294	1870	5920		297000	44100	6.21	5.94
Hebrew University of Jerusalem	huji.ac.il	248510	374966	347	19500		121000	503000	6.11	6.35

APPENDICES: *Continued*

Keio University	keio.ac.jp	895855	1421548	113	2910	348000	96500	7.27	8.04
National University of Singapore	nus.edu.sg	324565	558956	416	47600	195000	75900	6.41	6.48
National Chiao Tung University	nctu.edu.tw	422529	957058	106	1520	207000	81700	5.61	5.62
Nagoya University	nagoya-u.ac.jp	383689	699458	495	4060	118000	20900	6.14	5.78
Australian National University	anu.edu.au	536551	841060	915	25600	577000	240000	6.47	6.56
Monash University	monash.edu.au	578472	802914	300	23000	1520000	382000	6.38	6.99
University of Sydney	usyd.edu.au	300339	546989	422	15900	177000	42100	6.41	6.57
University of New South Wales	unsw.edu.au	315157	560155	430	14100	178000	53100	6.19	6.45
University of Melbourne	unimelb.edu.au	380648	668028	4270	15400	159000	48000	6.29	6.97
University of Queensland	uq.edu.au	271172	492772	556	8720	136000	117000	6.55	6.42
University of Adelaide	adelaide.edu.au	203680	251159	368	8140	128000	38800	6.27	6.61
University of Auckland	auckland.ac.nz	198581	289587	199	8590	119000	51600	6.02	6.37
Queensland University of Technology	qut.edu.au	107875	157925	65	4110	39700	13800	6.12	6.70
University of Western Australia	uwa.edu.au	170261	276912	226	11500	80600	27900	6.12	6.26
University of Cape Town	uct.ac.za	123561	227610	140	7940	50200	18900	6.1	6.24
University of Pretoria	up.ac.za	4191	5714	3	1250	1990	1300	5.5	5.63
Stellenbosch University	sun.ac.za	49779	87397	69	1210	23200	7220	5.85	5.95
University of the Witwatersrand	wits.ac.za	647	7828	12	271	4920	1710	5.79	5.58
Rhodes University	ru.ac.za	36912	54745	32	1040	20300	6220	5.68	5.85
University of Kwazulu Natal	ukzn.ac.za	27922	46620	22	1620	14800	7420	5.77	5.85
University of the Western Cape	uwc.ac.za	17923	42244	41	813	10900	6930	5.54	5.65
University of South Africa	unisa.ac.za	12291	15834	12	583	10200	2200	5.72	5.60

APPENDICES: *Continued*

University	Domain									
Cairo University	cu.edu.eg	21215	25528	12	286		14400	4800	5.38	5.49
American University in Cairo	aucegypt.edu	24012	33368	20	33300	12400	18600	4930	5.68	6.17
Harvard University	harvard.edu	5404266	7100048	61500	2020000	317000	2900000	1800000	6.62	7.11
Massachusetts Institute of Technology	mit.edu	7979362	12140652	23800	5330000	427000	3010000	1760000	6.78	6.70
Stanford University	stanford.edu	5476147	7363772	43900	2310000	244000	2860000	1640000	7.45	7.01
University of California Berkeley	berkeley.edu	4229933	5923457	74000	2200000	317000	2310000	954000	6.9	6.88
Cornell University	cornell.edu	4793957	6725718	44700	2050000	189000	4200000	794000	6.7	7.14
University of Washington	washington.edu	1879823	2858599	47300	1600000	188000	931000	461000	6.99	6.90
University of Minnesota	umn.edu	1760192	2818007	19000	1430000	125000	1300000	328000	6.47	6.54
Johns Hopkins University**	jhu.edu	710823	973179	3050	509000	118000	364000	202000	6.58	6.70
University of Michigan	umich.edu	2603440	388005	40300	1840000	217000	1540000	517000	7.01	6.97
University of Wisconsin Madison	wisc.edu	2366262	3851948	31200	1950000	325000	1200000	696000	6.74	6.94
Universidade de São Paulo	usp.br	532113	1229228	351	5690		230000	104000	6.19	6.24
Universidade Estadual de Campinas	unicamp.br	193366	626002	129	2210		99300	29600	5.89	5.96
Universidad de Chile	uchile.cl	200807	343984	104	2770		140000	16700	5.91	6.05
Universidade Federal de Santa Catarina	ufsc.br	137157	334801	53	978		95100	19600	5.45	5.79
Universidade Federal do Rio Grande do Sul	ufrgs.br	149629	279505	83	3450		80200	15100	5.77	5.60
Universidade Federal do Rio de Janeiro	ufrj.br	182552	357167	72	4450		97600	18700	5.6	6.02
Universidade de Buenos Aires	uba.ar	131607	253817	86	1760		101000	19400	5.66	5.77
Universidade Federal de Minas Gerais	ufmg.br	97004	207139	24	1280		54000	9330	5.59	6.15
Universidade Estadual Paulista	unesp.br	79896	195334	64	532		34400	38300	5.62	5.87
Universade de Brasília	unb.br	220896	303623	47	738		93500	30300	5.81	5.95

APPENDICES: *Continued*

UNIVERSITIES	URL	SELECTIVE LINKING						
		ACADEMIA	DELICIOUS	FACEBOOK	LINKEDIN	TWITTER	WIKIPEDIA	YOUTUBE
University of Cambridge	cam.ac.uk	1100	16198	1850	717	151	29800	357
University of Oxford	ox.ac.uk	1820	16301	1700	593	149	24200	211
Swiss Federal Institute of Technology ETH Zürich	ethz.ch	144	12861	175	440	50	8240	192
Norwegian University of Science and Technology	ntnu.no	25	4105	325	294	50	4650	85
University of Edinburgh	ed.ac.uk	476	11459	782	344	69	8940	182
University of Oslo	uio.no	114	7163	373	345	58	17000	83
University College London	ucl.ac.uk	536	10269	490	348	78	14000	246
University of Helsinki	helsinki.fi	146	7416	378	239	16	20800	253
Universität Wien	univie.ac.at	194	6946	152	65	25	9200	20
University of Southampton	soton.ac.uk	149	5787	415	244	88	3290	34
University of Tokyo	u-tokyo.ac.jp	23	7233	28	104	99	5490	272
Kyoto University	kyoto-u.ac.jp	21	3597	5	53	38	3700	34
National Taiwan University	ntu.edu.tw	4	6255	91	45	9	10200	228
University of Hong Kong	hku.hk	31	5999	172	83	41	6560	86
Chinese University of Hong Kong	cuhk.edu.hk	11	3771	166	53	9	7250	65
Hebrew University of Jerusalem	huji.ac.il	67	3010	144	124	10	7600	614
Keio University	keio.ac.jp	6	4962	2	57	112	1680	255
National University of Singapore	nus.edu.sg	98	6628	563	258	26	5000	83
National Chiao Tung University	nctu.edu.tw	1	2604	19	25	7	2390	75
Nagoya University	nagoya-u.ac.jp	5	1678	5	18	7	1270	42

APPENDICES: *Continued*

University	Domain							
Australian National University	anu.edu.au	103	6712	183	134	32	16600	86
Monash University	monash.edu.au	96	5802	269	162	18	3970	31
University of Sydney	usyd.edu.au	200	7720	526	162	34	5620	61
University of New South Wales	unsw.edu.au	124	8234	673	256	36	4160	528
University of Melbourne	unimelb.edu.au	84	7641	560	204	75	5820	87
University of Queensland	uq.edu.au	137	5638	215	171	29	3620	30
University of Adelaide	adelaide.edu.au	51	4017	334	111	15	6640	28
University of Auckland	auckland.ac.nz	46	5035	134	138	15	3180	77
Queensland University of Technology	qut.edu.au	34	5113	250	110	27	786	68
University of Western Australia	uwa.edu.au	47	3979	228	66	14	2640	27
University of Cape Town	uct.ac.za	52	2135	203	104	19	1010	19
University of Pretoria	up.ac.za	2	72	13	11	2	71	0
Stellenbosch University	sun.ac.za	18	909	28	88	8	443	14
University of the Witwatersrand	wits.ac.za	6	159	41	24	1	109	1
Rhodes University	ru.ac.za	15	478	46	49	10	357	5
University of Kwazulu Natal	ukzn.ac.za	17	385	64	35	6	368	1
University of the Western Cape	uwc.ac.za	1	456	5	18	8	213	3
University of South Africa	unisa.ac.za	8	461	46	18	5	351	0
Cairo University	cu.edu.eg	0	111	8	20	0	79	0
American University in Cairo	aucegypt.edu	4	718	82	45	6	124	3
Harvard University	harvard.edu	756	63799	3520	1840	474	159000	1390
Massachusetts Institute of Technology	mit.edu	517	77795	5410	2090	1100	40800	5740
Stanford University	stanford.edu	410	56758	3970	2080	574	69200	7410

APPENDICES: *Continued*

University	Domain							
University of California Berkeley	berkeley.edu	269	48383	4570	1530	316	49500	4700
Cornell University	cornell.edu	204	29485	2660	1140	191	68100	2290
University of Washington	washington.edu	294	34017	3800	1400	209	21700	750
University of Minnesota	umn.edu	110	28912	3140	1750	282	15900	636
Johns Hopkins University**	jhu.edu	210	15989	900	505	100	12600	125
University of Michigan	umich.edu	247	37574	3260	1790	271	101000	676
University of Wisconsin Madison	wisc.edu	200	28494	2270	1290	239	22000	336
Universidade de São Paulo	usp.br	45	12437	18	546	155	6220	119
Universidade Estadual de Campinas	unicamp.br	33	6200	12	212	45	2890	29
Universidad de Chile	uchile.cl	13	3231	222	81	41	2740	58
Universidade Federal de Santa Catarina	ufsc.br	33	5100	4	122	91	1770	19
Universidade Federal do Rio Grande do Sul	ufrgs.br	14	4506	7	116	23	1790	12
Universidade Federal do Rio de Janeiro	ufrj.br	26	3957	20	140	54	2070	27
Universidade de Buenos Aires	uba.ar	24	2597	66	220	14	1460	6
Universidade Federal de Minas Gerais	ufmg.br	27	2884	16	90	47	1090	27
Universidade Estadual Paulista	unesp.br	8	1601	7	71	25	728	18
Universidade de Brasília	unb.br	17	2336	3	44	26	1070	11

ABOUT THE AUTHORS

Isidro F. Aguillo is the Head of the Cybermetrics Lab at the Center of Social and Human Sciences (CCHS) of the Spanish National Research Council (CSIC). His academic background includes a BS degree in Zoology (Universidad Complutense de Madrid, 1985) and a MS degree in Information Science (Universidad Carlos III de Madrid, 1992). He is the founder of the electronic journal "Cybermetrics" (since 1997), and the editor of the Webometrics Rankings, including the Rankings Web of Universities (since 2004), Research Centres (since 2006), Hospitals, Repositories and Business Schools (since 2008). He has published more than 60 papers in international journals on such research topics as evaluation of the scientific activity, electronic journals, open access initiatives and specially webometrics and web indicators. He was appointed as a member of the CSIC delegation (1998–99) to the Spanish Office of Science and Technology (SOST) in Brussels. In 2002 he was invited as Metcalfe Visitor Fellow to the University of New South Wales (Sydney, Australia). His teaching activity comprises more than 400 workshops, seminars and conferences in more than 80 Universities and professional societies worldwide. In 2009 he was awarded Doctor Honoris Causa by the University of Indonesia.

Ying Cheng is an associate professor and the Executive Director of the Center for World-Class Universities at Graduate School of Education, Shanghai Jiao Tong University (SJTU). He entered SJTU in 1996. There he obtained his Bachelor degree in Polymer Science and Engineering (2000) and his doctoral degree in S&T and Education Management (2007). From 2007 to 2008, Dr Cheng went to Paris as a postdoctoral fellow attached to Ecole des Hautes Etudes en Sciences Sociales (EHESS) but conducted his studies at the Observatoire des Sciences et des Techniques (OST). He has worked full time at Office of Planning and Graduate School of Education (formerly Institute of Higher Education) of SJTU since 2000. His current research interests include the benchmarking, evaluation and ranking of universities, and the use, analysis and design of scientometric indicators and methods for supporting decision-making. He is responsible for the annual update and new development of the Academic Ranking of World Universities.

Chung-Lin Chiang (Johnson) serves as a project assistant in Faculty Development and Instructional Resources Center in Fu Jen Catholic University. He majored in statistics and graduated from Graduate Institute of Applied Statistics in Fu Jen Catholic University. He specializes in educational statistics. From 2007 to 2010, he participated in many higher educational projects such as research ranking projects for universities. He is interested in higher educational research. In the future, he will keep improving himself in the domain.

Julia Dmitrieva is the Head of the International Research and Technology, the Department of the Research Office at the Saint-Petersburg State University. She is responsible for international research cooperation with foreign partner universities and development of different international research and analytics projects. Before then, Julia served at the University as the Head of the Information and Analytics Department in the International Office. Her main research interests are research and education evaluation of higher education and international rankings. In 2007 she graduated from Saint-Petersburg State University with a MA degree in International Relations. In 2012 she received her PhD in Politics from the School of International Relations at Saint-Petersburg State University.

Lauritz B. Holm-Nielsen has been Rector of Aarhus University since 2005. He is Vice-Chairman of Universities Denmark and Board Member and Vice President of the European University Association (EUA). Furthermore, Lauritz B. Holm-Nielsen has been a member of the Danish Prime Minister's Growth Forum, a member of several OECD expert review teams on higher education, Chairman of the Nordic University Association, a member of the Africa Commission, Board Member of the Danish National Research Foundation, Rector of the Danish Research Academy, Vice-Chairman of the Danish Research Commission, Chairman of the Danish Natural Science Research Council and the Danish Council for Development Research. Lauritz B. Holm-Nielsen has a degree in botany from Aarhus University (1971) and was Dean of the Faculty of Science at Aarhus University (1976–79) before he became professor at Pontificia Universidad Católica, Quito, Ecuador (1979–81). Lauritz B. Holm-Nielsen has spent 18 years working abroad, 12 of these at the World Bank in Washington D.C. (1993–2005).

Yung-Chi Hou (Angela), Professor of higher education, serves as the Director of Faculty Development and Instructional Resources Center of Fu Jen Catholic University as well as the Dean of the Office of Research and Development of Higher Education Evaluation and Accreditation Council of Taiwan (HEEACT). She specializes in higher education quality management, internationalization of higher education, faculty development, quality assurance of cross border higher education. She has been conducting several national QA and ranking research projects for universities and the government over the past decade, including "Mutual Recognition and its Impact on Asian Higher Education", "Internationalization of Quality Assurance in higher Education", "College Navigator in Taiwan". She is the APQN Board Member and consultant now. Up to present, she has published more 100 Chinese and English papers, articles, books and reports in the areas of higher education evaluation and rankings in local and international referred journals. She is also the associate-editor of "Evaluation in Higher Education" published by HEEACT and IREG.

Martin Ince is the Chair of the Advisory Board for the Quacquarelli Symonds (QS) World University Rankings. He is a science and education journalist based in London, and advises universities in Europe and Asia on media issues, reputation and ranking. He is the author of nine books including the Rough Guide to the Earth (2007). He has been communications director of two UK government research councils.

Jisun Jung is a Post-doctoral Fellow in the Faculty of Education at the University of Hong Kong. She received a PhD from Seoul National University, Korea, in 2011. She is involved with the international comparative research project "The Changing Academic Profession". Her current research focuses on research productivity of academics and university ranking systems.

Nian Cai Liu took his undergraduate studies in chemistry at Lanzhou University of China. He obtained his master's and PhD degrees in polymer science and engineering from Queen's University at Kingston, Canada. Professor Liu worked as an associate and full professor at the School of Chemistry and Chemical Engineering of Shanghai Jiao Tong University from 1993 to 1998. He moved to the field of higher education research in 1999. He is now the Dean of Graduate School of Education and the Director of Center for World-Class Universities, Shanghai Jiao Tong University. His current research interests include world-class universities, science policy, and strategic planning of universities. He has published extensively in both Chinese and English journals. The Academic Ranking of World Universities, an online publication of his group, has attracted attentions from all over the world. He is on the advisory boards of Scientometrics and Research Evaluation.

Simon Marginson is Professor of Higher Education in the Centre for the Study of Higher Education, Melbourne Graduate School of Education, the University of Melbourne, Australia, where he has worked since 2006. Previously he was Professor of Education and Director of the Monash Centre for Research in International Education at Monash University. He is a Fellow of the Academy of Social Sciences, Australia and the Society for Research in Higher Education in the UK. His work is focused on globalization and higher education, comparative and international education and national and global higher education policy. One of the Coordinating Editors of the world journal Higher Education, he is a member of 15 international journal boards including Higher Education Policy, Journal of Higher Education, Educational Researcher and Journal of Studies in International Education. He has prepared several papers for OECD. Books include Markets in Education (1997), The Enterprise University (with Mark Considine, 2000), International Student Security (with Chris Nyland, Erlenawati Sawir and Helen Forbes-Mewett, 2010), Higher Education in the Asia-Pacific (with Sarjit Kaur and Erlenawati Sawir, 2011) and Ideas for Intercultural Education (with Erlenawati Sawir, 2011). Four of his books have been published in China.

Freya Mearns joined Griffith University (Brisbane, Australia) in 2009 as a Policy Officer – Research Excellence in the University's Office for Research. Griffith's research policy team works to enhance the University's research quality culture by measuring and monitoring research performance, and developing strategies for creating environments conducive to research excellence. Freya was responsible for the project management of the University's submission to the national Excellence in Research for Australia (research assessment) initiative both in 2010 and 2012. Freya was previously employed in the journal publishing industry (2006–2009) in the editorial department of the Royal Society of Chemistry (Cambridge, England). She obtained her PhD in Analytical Chemistry from the University of New South Wales (Sydney, Australia) in 2006.

Olga Moskaleva graduated from Biology and Soil Faculty of Leningrad State University and worked at the Department of Plant Physiology and Biochemistry in 1980, and achieved the degree of PhD in Biology in 1990. Olga Moskaleva has worked in the Research Office of St. Petersburg State University since 1995 and has served as the Head of the Research Office since 2007.Her research interest is scientometrics. Olga has participated in four conferences, including "Science on-line: Digital Resources for Science and Education", and has presented plenary lectures in different conferences and seminars on the use of modern analytical instruments in research evaluation, organized by Elsevier and Thomson Reuters.

Enrique Orduña-Malea is a specialist in sound and image, Technical Telecommunications engineer. He obtains a MA in Documentation and a master's degree in Multichannel contents in the Web. He works currently as a fellowship researcher at Polytechnic University of Valencia (UPV), in the research division of technology and information (CALSI I+D), at Institute of Design and Manufacturing (IDF), where develops his dissertation thesis in the field of cybermetrics and university rankings. He also works as an external teacher at Audiovisual Communication, Documentation, and History of Art Department (DCADHA) at UPV, in the area of contents' management and dissemination on the Web, and is the responsible of some journals' websites, such as ThinkEPI yearbook. He has published several works related with the design, implementation, and analysis of quantitative information on the Web. He has also participated on consultancy actions in international projects, both in the environment of open information systems, and scientific production and bibliometrics.

Simon Pratt is the product manager for Institutional Research at Thomson Reuters. He oversees the development and implementation of the Institutional Profiles initiative which aims to capture a comprehensive picture of academic institutions around the globe. Mr Pratt is directly responsible with all the major components of the project including the academic reputation survey, data collection, validation and analysis. Mr Pratt has more than 14 years of business management and specialised technical experience in the scientific information industry spanning Europe, North America and Asia. Prior to his current position, he was Manager, Sales Training at Thomson Reuters where he was responsible for planning and implementing training programmes for a global sales team. Mr Pratt has also held the portfolio of Strategic Business Manager where he was responsible for business strategy and product positioning. A proficient Japanese speaker, Mr Pratt was previously Senior Manager, Business Operations at Thomson Reuters, Tokyo, where he was in charge of the domestic business operations, marketing and technical support departments. Mr Pratt graduated with a Bachelor of Science Honours in Chemistry from the University of East Anglia and holds a Masters of

Arts in electronic communication and publishing from University College London. He is a regular speaker at conferences on bibliometrics and university and research evaluation across the world and contributes to articles and books on the evaluation of higher education and research.

Gerard A. Postiglione is Professor and Head, Division of Policy, Administration and Social Sciences at the Faculty of Education, and Director of the Wah Ching Center of Research on Education in China of the University of Hong Kong. His scholarship focuses on reform and development in China and East Asia, especially in education and society. He has published over 100 journal articles and book chapters, and 10 books. He is editor of the journal, Chinese Education and Society, and four book series. His books include: Asian Higher Education, East Asia at School, Education and Social Change in China, China's National Minority Education, and Crossing Borders in East Asian Higher Education. He was a researcher/consultant/trainer for projects of the Academy of Educational Development, Asian Development Bank, Department for International Development, Institute of International Education, International Development Research Center, United Nations Development Programme, World Bank, and other international development agencies. He has advised many NGOs and international foundations, including the Carnegie Foundation for the Advancement of Teaching on the academic profession in Hong Kong, and as senior consultant at the Ford Foundation/Beijing for one year to establish a grants framework for China on educational reform and cultural vitality.

Seeram Ramakrishna, FREng, FNAE, FAAAS, is the author of book 'The Changing Face of Innovation' and co-founder of GC for the Study of Higher Education, Research, Innovation and Entrepreneurship (gc-sherie.org). He is an advisor and sought after speaker worldwide on higher education, scientific research, and innovation trends. He participates in discussions organized by various think tanks, media, governments, World Bank, OECD, and ASEAN. He is trained as a materials engineer at the University of Cambridge, and received general management training from the Harvard University. He authored ~500 peer reviewed scholarly papers and five books. Various international scientific databases place him among the top one per cent of materials scientists worldwide. Products based on his inventions are sold in more than fifty countries. He is an elected international fellow of major professional societies in Singapore, ASEAN, India, UK and US. He is a professor at the National University of Singapore and held several senior leadership positions which include University Vice-President of research strategy, Dean of Engineering, and Founding Director of Bioengineering department and Nanoscience and Nanotechnology Institute; and Vice-President of International Federation of Engineering Education Societies (ifees.org), and Founding Chair of Global Engineering Deans Council (gedec.org).

Sadiq M. Sait obtained a Bachelor's degree in Electronics from Bangalore University in 1981, and master's and PhD degrees in Electrical Engineering from

King Fahd University of Petroleum & Minerals (KFUPM), Dhahran, Saudi Arabia in 1983 and 1987 respectively. He was awarded a research/teaching assistantship by the Department of Electrical Engineering during 1981–1986. Since 1987 he has been working at the Department of Computer Engineering where he is now a Professor, teaching graduate and undergraduate courses in the areas related to Digital Design Automation, VLSI System Design and Computer Architecture. In 1981 Sait received the best Electronic Engineer award from the Institute of Electrical Engineers, Bangalore. In 1990, 1994 and 1999 he was awarded the "Distinguished Researcher Award" by KFUPM. In 1988, 1989, 1990, 1995 and 2000 he was nominated by the Computer Engineering Department for the "Best Teacher Award" which he received in 1995, and 2000. Sait has authored over 100 research papers in international journals and conferences. He has also contributed two chapters to a book entitled "Progress in VLSI Design". He served on the editorial board of International Journal of Computer Aided Design between 1988–1990, and was invited to serve as a guest editor for their special issue on Hardware Description Languages. He is currently the Computer Science Editor of Arabian Journal for Science and Engineering. Sait has also served as a referee for several leading journals. He is the member of the reviewers board of the Computer-Aided Design Journal, UK. He has given invited lectures in the University of Erlangen-Nurenberg, and at IBM Research Center, Rushlikon. His current areas of interest are in Digital Design Automation, VLSI System Design, High Level Synthesis, and Iterative Algorithms.

Tony Sheil is the Deputy Director, Research Policy at Griffith University and is a regular contributor to Australian university research policy debate on a range of issues such as assessment of research performance and world university rankings. He is currently a member of the Australian Government's Higher Education Research Data Advisory Committee while in 2008-2009 he served on the Australian Research Council's Indicators Development Group for the Excellence in Research for Australia (research assessment) initiative. He is also a member of the QS World University Rankings Advisory Committee – a group that draws members from more than 15 nations. His career in university management spans more than 20 years working for three universities (Griffith, the University of Manchester and the former University of Manchester Institute of Science and Technology). Prior to taking up his current position at Griffith University, Tony served as Foundation Executive Officer, Innovative Research Universities (a consortium of seven Australian universities) from 2004–2007. Sheil has delivered papers on the implications of world university rankings for national and institutional research strategy at conferences and workshops in Australia, China, Iceland, the Netherlands, United Kingdom and Malaysia.

Marilet Sienaert completed a master's degree in French Literature and a PhD degree in South African Literary Studies. She worked at the universities of Pretoria, Natal (Durban) and Durban-Westville as lecturer, and in later years, as professor in Language and Literature Studies (1979–1999). Her own academic research and ongoing involvement in research committee work led to a growing interest in Higher Education research management and a career change in 2000, when she was appointed to her current position of Director, Research Office, at the University of Cape Town. In response to changes in the South African political and socio-economic landscape, the responsibilities of this office have evolved enormously over the past ten years. Her remit now includes strategic research planning and policy development; benchmarking and reporting; quality assurance of research management systems; the development and implementation of a framework of academic support based on staff development programmes for researchers at different levels in their research careers; and oversight of research programmes' grantsmanship. In this capacity, Dr Sienaert is a member of all research-related committees within the University and works closely with colleagues from Research Councils, funding agencies, other research-intensive universities and a broad range of government departments.

Nikolay Skvortsov is Professor and Doctor of Science (Sociology) at the Faculty of Sociology in Saint-Petersburg State University. In 2008 Professor Skvortsov was appointed as Vice-Rector for Research in Saint-Petersburg State University. His research interests and publications cover such topics as ethnic studies, cultural and social anthropology. He is a member of the International Sociological Association. Professor Skvortsov is the President of Scientific Council on Sociology at the Federal Agency for Education of the Russian Federation, President of the Sociology Society of M. Kovalevsky, Vice-President of the Russian Sociological Association. He is a member of the editorial boards of the leading Russian journals in the field of Sociology and President of the Dissertation Committee for the Doctorates in Saint-Petersburg State University. In the period 2000–2010 he was the Dean of the Faculty of Sociology; from 2003 Professor Skvortsov has been Co-Director of the Center for German and European Studies in Saint-Petersburg State University. Prior to this position he has been Head of Department of Comparative Sociology at the faculty of Sociology and before – he had been Head of the Department of Cultural Anthropology at the faculty of Sociology, Director of the Center for the Humanities Research in Saint-Petersburg State University. In 2004 Professor Skvortsov was awarded the "Honorary employee of the higher professional education in the Russian Federation" by the Ministry for Education of the Russian Federation. He holds Candidate of Science (1983) in Philosophy from Saint-Petersburg State University and Doctor of Science (1998) in Sociology from Saint-Petersburg State University

Danie Visser is Professor of Private Law and Deputy Vice-Chancellor (with primary responsibility for research) at the University of Cape Town. He was educated in South Africa and the Netherlands, obtaining doctorates in law from Pretoria University in 1980 (under JMT Labuschagne) and the University of Leyden in 1985 (under Robert Feenstra). He is a former Dean of the Faculty of Law at the University of Cape Town (1996-1998) and a sometime holder of the Huber C Hurst Eminent Visiting Scholar Chair at the University of Florida (Spring

Term 2001). He has taught Comparative Law, Comparative Legal History, the Law of Delict, and Unjust Enrichment at the University of Cape Town and he has taught Comparative Law in the Juris Doctor programme at the University of Melbourne, Australia as a Visiting Professor. He is a former Chair of the South African Chapter of the International Academy of Comparative Law; and a former President of the Southern African Society of Legal Historians. He has also been Chair of the Specialist Committee of the National Research Foundation's Rating Panel for Law.

Qi Wang is an assistant professor at the Graduate School of Education (GSE), Shanghai Jiao Tong University (SJTU). She completed her MA and PhD studies in the Department of Education, University of Bath, UK, from September 2002 to November 2008. She joined SJTU in May 2009 and works in the Centre for World-Class Universities. Her research interests include building world-class universities, employability building and skill training, and educational sociology.

Marijk van der Wende is the founding Dean of Amsterdam University College. She is a professor in higher education at VU University Amsterdam and an honorary professor at CHEPS, the University of Twente. She chairs the Undergraduate Committee of VU University Amsterdam and previously chaired its Honours Committee and its Internationalization Board. She is the Vice President of the Governing Board of the Programme on Institutional Management in Higher Education (IMHE) of the OECD, Member of the International Advisory Board of the Centre for World-Class Universities at Shanghai Jiao Tong University, Member of the Higher Education Authority Ireland, Member of the Scientific Board of the Dutch Military Academy, and member of various national and international editorial boards. She previously held positions at CHEPS, the University of Twente (1998–2008), the University of Amsterdam (1998-2000), the Academic Cooperation Association (ACA) in Brussels (1994-1998), Nuffic (1992–1998), and was a visiting scholar at the Centre for Studies in Higher Education, at the University of California at Berkeley (US). Van der Wende holds BA degree in teaching and pedagogy, and MA and PhD degrees in educational sciences, from the University of Amsterdam and the University of Utrecht respectively.

GLOBAL PERSPECTIVES ON HIGHER EDUCATION

Volume 1
WOMEN'S UNIVERSITIES AND COLLEGES
An International Handbook
Francesca B. Purcell, Robin Matross Helms, and Laura Rumbley (Eds.)
ISBN 978-90-77874-58-5 hardback
ISBN 978-90-77874-02-8 paperback

Volume 2
PRIVATE HIGHER EDUCATION
A Global Revolution
Philip G. Altbach and D. C. Levy (Eds.)
ISBN 978-90-77874-59-2 hardback
ISBN 978-90-77874-08-0 paperback

Volume 3
FINANCING HIGHER EDUCATION
Cost-Sharing in International perspective
D. Bruce Johnstone
ISBN 978-90-8790-016-8 hardback
ISBN 978-90-8790-015-1 paperback

Volume 4
UNIVERSITY COLLABORATION FOR INNOVATION
Lessons from the Cambridge-MIT Institute
David Good, Suzanne Greenwald, Roy Cox, and Megan Goldman (Eds.)
ISBN 978-90-8790-040-3 hardback
ISBN 978-90-8790-039-7 paperback

Volume 5
HIGHER EDUCATION
A Worldwide Inventory of Centers and Programs
Philip G. Altbach, Leslie A. Bozeman, Natia Janashia, and Laura E. Rumbley
ISBN 978-90-8790-052-6 hardback
ISBN 978-90-8790-049-6 paperback

Volume 6
FUTURE OF THE AMERICAN PUBLIC RESEARCH UNIVERSITY
R. L. Geiger, C. L. Colbeck, R. L. Williams, and C. K. Anderson (Eds.)
ISBN 978-90-8790-048-9 hardback
ISBN 978-90-8790-047-2 paperback

Gregory S. Poole and Ya-chen Chen (Eds.)
ISBN 978-94-6091-127-9 hardback
ISBN 978-94-6091-126-2 paperback

Volume 20
ACCESS AND EQUITY: COMPARATIVE PERSPECTIVES
Heather Eggins (Ed.)
ISBN 978-94-6091-185-9 hardback
ISBN 978-94-6091-184-2 paperback

Volume 21
UNDERSTANDING INEQUALITIES IN AND BY HIGHER EDUCATION
Gaële Goastellec (Ed.)
ISBN 978-94-6091-307-5 hardback
ISBN 978-94-6091-306-8 paperback

Volume 22
TRENDS IN GLOBAL HIGHER EDUCATION: TRACKING AN ACADEMIC
REVOLUTION
Philip G. Altbach, Liz Reisberg and Laura E. Rumbley
ISBN 978-94-6091-338-9 hardback
ISBN 978-94-6091-339-6 paperback

Volume 23
PATHS TO A WORLD-CLASS UNIVERSITY: LESSONS FROM PRACTICES
AND EXPERIENCES
Nian Cai Liu, Qi Wang and Ying Cheng
ISBN 978-94-6091-354-9 hardback
ISBN 978-94-6091-353-2 paperback

Volume 24
TERTIARY EDUCATION AT A GLANCE: CHINA
Kai Yu, Andrea Lynn Stith, Li Liu, Huizhong Chen
ISBN 978-94-6091-744-8 hardback
ISBN 978-94-6091-745-5 paperback

Volume 25
BUILDING WORLD-CLASS UNIVERSITIES: DIFFERENT APPROACHES
TO A SHARED GOAL
Qi Wang, Ying Cheng, Nian Cai Liu
ISBN 978-94-6209-033-0 hardback
ISBN 978-94-6209-032-3 paperback

CPSIA information can be obtained at www.ICGtesting.com
Printed in the USA
BVOW041423030613

322293BV00004B/63/P